S0-ADZ-651

g

GEOMETRY

Math Preparation Guide

This comprehensive guide illustrates every geometric principle, formula, and problem type tested on the GMAT. Understand and master the intricacies of shapes, planes, lines, angles, and objects.

Geometry GMAT Preparation Guide, 2007 Edition

10-digit International Standard Book Number: 0-9790175-4-8
13-digit International Standard Book Number: 978-0-9790175-4-4

Copyright © 2007 MG Prep, Inc.

ALL RIGHTS RESERVED. No part of this work may be reproduced or used in any form or by any means—graphic, electronic, or mechanical, including photocopying, recording, taping, Web distribution—without the prior written permission of the publisher, MG Prep Inc.

Note: *GMAT, Graduate Management Admission Test, Graduate Management Admission Council,* and *GMAC* are all registered trademarks of the Graduate Management Admission Council which neither sponsors nor is affiliated in any way with this product.

8 GUIDE INSTRUCTIONAL SERIES

Math GMAT Preparation Guides

Number Properties (ISBN: 978-0-9790175-0-6)

Fractions, Decimals, & Percents (ISBN: 978-0-9790175-1-3)

Equations, Inequalities, & VIC's (ISBN: 978-0-9790175-2-0)

Word Translations (ISBN: 978-0-9790175-3-7)

Geometry (ISBN: 978-0-9790175-4-4)

Verbal GMAT Preparation Guides

Critical Reasoning (ISBN: 978-0-9790175-5-1)

Reading Comprehension (ISBN: 978-0-9790175-6-8)

Sentence Correction (ISBN: 978-0-9790175-7-5)

HOW OUR GMAT PREP BOOKS ARE DIFFERENT

One of our core beliefs at Manhattan GMAT is that a curriculum should be more than just a guidebook of tricks and tips. Scoring well on the GMAT requires a curriculum that builds true content knowledge and understanding. Skim through this guide and this is what you will see:

You will *not* find page after page of guessing techniques.

Instead, you will find a highly organized and structured guide that actually teaches you the content you need to know to do well on the GMAT.

You *will* find many more pages-per-topic than in all-in-one tomes.

Each chapter covers one specific topic area in-depth, explaining key concepts, detailing in-depth strategies, and building specific skills through Manhattan GMAT's *In-Action* problem sets (with comprehensive explanations). Why are there 8 guides? Each of the 8 books (5 Math, 3 Verbal) covers a major content area in extensive depth, allowing you to delve into each topic in great detail. In addition, you may purchase only those guides that pertain to those areas in which you need to improve.

This guide is challenging - it asks you to do more, not less.

It starts with the fundamental skills, but does not end there; it also includes the *most advanced content* that many other prep books ignore. As the average GMAT score required to gain admission to top business schools continues to rise, this guide, together with the 6 computer adaptive online practice exams and bonus question bank included with your purchase, provides test-takers with the depth and volume of advanced material essential for achieving the highest scores, given the GMAT's computer adaptive format.

This guide is ambitious - developing mastery is its goal.

Developed by Manhattan GMAT's staff of REAL teachers (all of whom have 99th percentile official GMAT scores), our ambitious curriculum seeks to provide test-takers of all levels with an in-depth and carefully tailored approach that enables our students to achieve mastery. If you are looking to learn more than just the "process of elimination" and if you want to develop skills, strategies, and a confident approach to any problem that you may see on the GMAT, then our sophisticated preparation guides are the tools to get you there.

HOW TO ACCESS YOUR ONLINE RESOURCES

Please read this entire page of information, all the way down to the bottom of the page! This page describes WHAT online resources are included with the purchase of this book and HOW to access these resources.

[**If you are a registered Manhattan GMAT student** and have received this book as part of your course materials, you have AUTOMATIC access to ALL of our online resources. This includes all simulated practice exams, question banks, and online updates to this book. To access these resources, follow the instructions in the Welcome Guide provided to you at the start of your program. Do NOT follow the instructions below.]

If you have purchased this book, your purchase includes 1 YEAR OF ONLINE ACCESS to the following:

> **6 Computer Adaptive Online Practice Exams**
>
> **Bonus Online Question Bank for GEOMETRY**
>
> **Online Updates to the Content in this Book**

The 6 full-length computer adaptive practice exams included with the purchase of this book are delivered online using Manhattan GMAT's proprietary computer adaptive online test engine. The exams adapt to your ability level by drawing from a bank of more than 1200 unique questions of varying difficulty levels written by Manhattan GMAT's expert instructors, all of whom have scored in the 99th percentile on the Official GMAT. At the end of each exam you will receive a score, an analysis of your results, and the opportunity to review detailed explanations for each question. You may choose to take the exams timed or untimed.

The Bonus Online Question Bank for Geometry consists of 25 extra practice questions (with detailed explanations) that test the variety of Geometry concepts and skills covered in this book. These questions provide you with extra practice *beyond* the problem sets contained in this book. You may use our online timer to practice your pacing by setting time limits for each question in the bank.

The content presented in this book is updated periodically to ensure that it reflects the GMAT's most current trends. You may view all updates, including any known errors or changes, upon registering for online access.

Important Note: The 6 computer adaptive online exams included with the purchase of this book are the SAME exams that you receive upon purchasing ANY book in Manhattan GMAT's 8 Book Preparation Series. On the other hand, the Bonus Online Question Bank for GEOMETRY is a unique resource that you receive ONLY with the purchase of this specific title.

To access the online resources listed above, you will need this book in front of you and you will need to register your information online. This book includes access to the above resources for ONE PERSON ONLY.

To register and start using your online resources, please go online to the following URL:

http://www.manhattangmat.com/access.cfm   (Double check that you have typed this in accurately!)

Your one-year of online access begins on the day that you register at the above URL. You only need to register your product ONCE at the above URL. To use your online resources any time AFTER you have completed the registration process, please login to the following URL:

http://www.manhattangmat.com/practicecenter.cfm

ManhattanGMAT*Prep
the new standard

TABLE OF CONTENTS

g

g

Chapter 1
of
GEOMETRY

POLYGONS

In This Chapter . . .

POLYGONS

A polygon is defined as a closed shape formed by line segments. The polygons tested on the GMAT include:

> Three-sided shapes: Triangles.
> Four-sided shapes: Quadrilaterals.
> Other polygons with *n* sides (where *n* is five or more).

This section will focus on polygons of four or more sides. In particular, the GMAT emphasizes quadrilaterals—or four-sided polygons—including trapezoids, parallelograms, and special parallelograms, such as rhombuses, rectangles, and squares.

Polygons are two-dimensional shapes; they lie in a plane. The GMAT tests your ability to work with different measurements associated with polygons. The measurements you must be adept with are: (1) interior angles, (2) perimeter, and (3) area.

The GMAT also tests your knowledge of three-dimensional shapes formed from polygons, particularly rectangular solids and cubes. The measurements you must be adept with are (1) surface area and (2) volume.

A polygon is a closed shape formed by line segments.

Quadrilaterals: An Overview

The most common non-triangle polygon tested on the GMAT is the quadrilateral (any four-sided polygon). Almost all GMAT polygon problems involve the special types of quadrilaterals shown below.

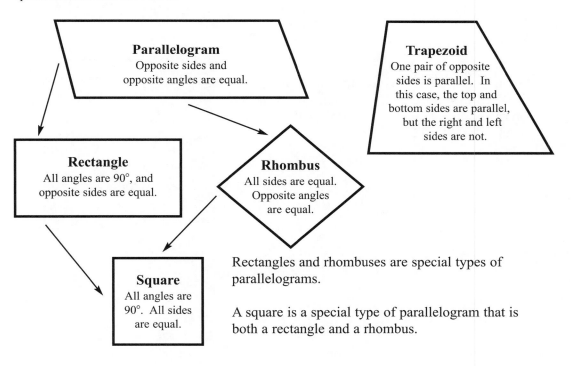

Parallelogram
Opposite sides and opposite angles are equal.

Trapezoid
One pair of opposite sides is parallel. In this case, the top and bottom sides are parallel, but the right and left sides are not.

Rectangle
All angles are 90°, and opposite sides are equal.

Rhombus
All sides are equal. Opposite angles are equal.

Square
All angles are 90°. All sides are equal.

Rectangles and rhombuses are special types of parallelograms.

A square is a special type of parallelogram that is both a rectangle and a rhombus.

Polygons and Interior Angles

The sum of the interior angles of a given polygon depends only on the number of sides of the polygon. The following chart displays the relationship between the type of polygon and the sum of its interior angles:

Notice that the sum of the interior angles of a polygon follows a regular pattern that is dependent on *n*, the number of sides of the polygon. Specifically, the sum of the angles of a polygon is always 2 less than *n* (the number of sides) times 180°.

Polygon	# of sides	Sum of Interior Angles
Triangle	3	180°
Quadrilateral	4	360°
Pentagon	5	540°
Hexagon	6	720°

> Another way to find the sum of the interior angles in a polygon is to divide the polygon into triangles. The interior angles of each triangle sum to 180°.

This can be expressed with the following formula:

$$(n - 2)180 = \text{Sum of Interior Angles of a Polygon}$$

As this is a four-sided polygon, the sum of its interior angles is $(4 - 2)180 = 2(180) = 360°$. Alternately, note that a quadrilateral can be cut into two triangles; thus, the sum of the angles $= 2(180) = 360°$.

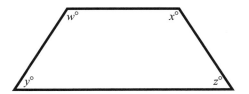

As this is a six-sided polygon, the sum of its interior angles is $(6 - 2)180 = 4(180) = 720°$. Alternately, note that a hexagon can be cut into four triangles; thus, the sum of the angles $= 4(180) = 720°$.

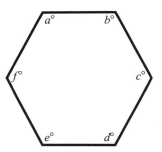

Polygons and Perimeter

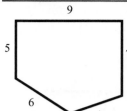

The perimeter refers to the distance around a polygon, or the sum of the lengths of all the sides. The amount of fencing needed to surround a yard would be equivalent to the perimeter of that yard (the sum of all the sides).

The perimeter of the pentagon to the left is:
$$9 + 7 + 4 + 6 + 5 = \textbf{31}.$$

Polygons and Area

The area refers to the space inside a polygon. Area is delineated in square units, such as cm^2 (square centimeters) or m^2 (square meters) or ft^2 (square feet). The amount of space that a garden occupies is the area of that garden.

On the GMAT, there are two polygon area formulas you MUST know:

1) Area of a TRIANGLE: $\dfrac{\textbf{Base} \times \textbf{Height}}{\textbf{2}}$

The base refers to the bottom side of the triangle. The height refers to a line that is perpendicular (at a 90° angle) to the base.

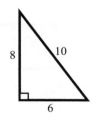

In this triangle, the base is 6 and the height (perpendicular to the base) is 8. The area = $(6 \times 8) \div 2 = 48 \div 2 = 24$.

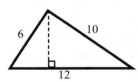

In this triangle, the base is 12, but the height is not shown. Neither of the other two sides of the triangle is perpendicular to the base. In order to find the area of this triangle, we would first need to determine the height, which is represented by the dotted line.

2) Area of a RECTANGLE: **Length × Width**

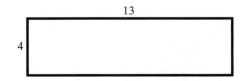

The length of this rectangle is 13, and the width is 4. Therefore, the area = $13 \times 4 = 52$.

You must memorize the formulas for the area of a triangle and for the area of the quadrilaterals shown in this section.

The GMAT will occasionally ask you to find the area of a polygon more complex than a simple triangle or rectangle. The following formulas can be used to find the areas of other types of quadrilaterals:

3) Area of a TRAPEZOID $= \dfrac{(\textbf{Base}_1 + \textbf{Base}_2) \times \textbf{Height}}{2}$

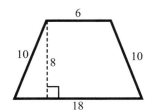

Note that the height refers to the line perpendicular to the two bases. In the trapezoid to the right, base$_1$ = 18, base$_2$ = 6, and the height = 8. The area = 8 × (18 + 6) ÷ 2 = 96. Another way to think about this is to take the *average* of the two bases and multiply it by the height.

Notice that most of these formulas involve finding a base and a line perpendicular to that base (a height).

4) Area of any PARALLELOGRAM = **Base × Height**

Note that the height refers to the line perpendicular to the base. In the parallelogram to the right, the base = 5 and the height = 8. The area is 5 × 8 = 40.

5) Area of a RHOMBUS = $\dfrac{\textbf{Diagonal}_1 \times \textbf{Diagonal}_2}{2}$

Note that the diagonals of a rhombus are perpendicular. The area of this rhombus is $\dfrac{6 \times 8}{2} = \dfrac{48}{2} = 24$.

Although these formulas are very useful to memorize for the GMAT, you may notice that all of the above shapes can actually be cut up into some combination of rectangles and right triangles. Therefore, if you forget the area formula for a particular shape, simply cut the shape into rectangles and right triangles, and find the areas of these individual pieces. For example:

3 Dimensions: Surface Area

The GMAT tests two particular three-dimensional shapes formed from polygons: the rectangular solid and the cube. Note that a cube is just a special type of rectangular solid.

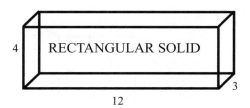

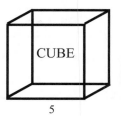

The surface area of a three-dimensional shape is the amount of space on the surface of that particular object. For example, the amount of paint that it would take to fully cover a rectangular box could be determined by finding the surface area of that box. As with simple area, surface area is delineated using square units such as inches^2 (square inches) or ft^2 (square feet).

> **Surface Area = the SUM of the areas of ALL the faces**

Both a rectangular solid and a cube have **six faces**.

To determine the surface area of a rectangular solid, you must find the area of each face. Notice, however, that in a rectangular solid, the front and back faces have the same area, the top and bottom faces have the same area, and the two side faces have the same area. In the solid above, the area of the front face is equal to $12 \times 4 = 48$. Thus, the back face also has an area of 48. The area of the bottom face is equal to $12 \times 3 = 36$. Thus, the top face also has an area of 36. Finally, each side face has an area of $3 \times 4 = 12$. Therefore, the surface area, or the sum of the areas of all six faces = $48(2) + 36(2) + 12(2) = 192$.

To determine the surface area of a cube, you only need the length of one side. We can see from the cube above that a cube is made of six square surfaces. First, find the area of one face: $5 \times 5 = 25$. Then, multiply by six to account for all the faces: $6 \times 25 = 150$.

You don't need to memorize a formula for surface area. Simply find the sum of all the faces.

3 Dimensions: Volume

The volume of a three-dimensional shape is the amount of "stuff" it can hold. For example, the amount of liquid that a rectangular milk carton holds can be determined by finding the volume of the carton. Volume is delineated using cubic units such as inches³ (cubic inches) or ft³ (cubic feet).

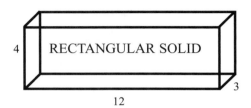

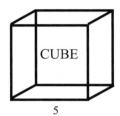

Another way to think about this formula is that the volume is equal to the area of the base multiplied by the height.

$$\boxed{\textbf{Volume = length} \times \textbf{width} \times \textbf{height}}$$

By looking at the rectangular solid above, we can see that the length is 12, the width is 3, and the height is 4. Therefore, the volume is $12 \times 3 \times 4 = 144$.

In a cube, all three of the dimensions—length, width, and height—are identical. Therefore, knowing the measurement of just one side of the cube is sufficient for finding the volume. In the cube above, the volume is $5 \times 5 \times 5 = 125$.

Beware of the GMAT volume trick:

> **How many books, each with a volume of 100 in³, can be packed into a crate with a volume of 5,000 in³?**

It is tempting to answer: 50 books (since $50 \times 100 = 5,000$). However, this is incorrect, because we don't know the exact dimensions of each book! One book might be $5 \times 5 \times 4$, while another book might be $20 \times 5 \times 1$. Even though both have a volume of 100 in³, they have different rectangular shapes. Without knowing the exact shapes of all the books, there is no way to tell if they would all fit into the crate. Remember, when fitting 3-dimensional objects into other 3-dimensional objects, knowing the respective volumes is not enough; we must know the specific dimensions (length, width, and height) of each object to determine if it can fit.

Problem Set (Note: Figures are not drawn to scale.)

1. Frank the Fencemaker needs to fence in a rectangular yard. He fences in the entire yard, except for one 40-foot side of the yard. The yard has an area of 280 square feet. How many feet of fence does Frank use?

2. A pentagon has three sides with length x, and two sides with the length $3x$. If x is $\frac{2}{3}$ of an inch, what is the perimeter of the pentagon?

3. ABCD is a quadrilateral, with AB parallel to CD (see figure). E is a point between C and D such that AE represents the height of ABCD, and E is the midpoint of CD. If AB is 4 inches long, AE is 5 inches long, and the area of triangle AED is 12.5 square inches, what is the area of ABCD?

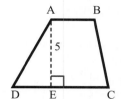

4. A rectangular tank needs to be coated with insulation. The tank has dimensions of 4 feet, 5 feet, and 2.5 feet. Each square foot of insulation costs $20. How much will it cost to cover the tank with insulation?

5. Triangle ABC (see figure) has a base of $2y$, a height of y, and an area of 49. What is y?

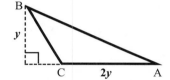

6. 40 percent of Andrea's living room floor is covered by a Mexican carpet that is 4 feet by 9 feet. What is the area of her living room floor?

7. If the perimeter of a rectangular flower bed is 30 feet, and its area is 44 square feet, what is the length of each of its shorter sides?

8. There is a rectangular parking lot with a length of $2x$ and a width of x. What is the ratio of the perimeter of the parking lot to the area of the parking lot, in terms of x?

9. A rectangular solid has a square base, with each side of the base measuring 4 meters. If the volume of the solid is 112 cubic meters, what is the surface area of the solid?

10. ABCD is a parallelogram (see figure). The ratio of DE to EC is 1:3. AE has a length of 3. If quadrilateral ABCE has an area of 21, what is the area of ABCD?

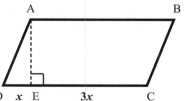

11. A swimming pool has a length of 30 meters, a width of 10 meters, and an average depth of 2 meters. If a hose can fill the pool at a rate of .5 cubic meters per minute, how many hours will it take the hose to fill the pool?

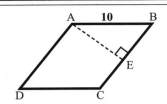

12. ABCD is a rhombus (see figure). ABE is a right triangle. AB is 10 meters. CE and EB are in the ratio of 2 to 3. What is the area of trapezoid AECD?

13. A Rubix cube has an edge of 5 inches. What is the ratio of the cube's surface area to its volume?

14. If the length of an edge of Cube A is one third the length of an edge of Cube B, what is the ratio of the volume of Cube A to Cube B?

15. ABCD is a square picture frame (see figure). EFGH is a square inscribed within ABCD as a space for a picture. The area of EFGH (for the picture) is equal to the area of the picture frame (the area of ABCD minus the area of EFGH). If AB = 6, what is the length of EF?

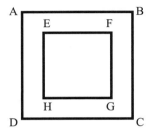

1. **54 feet:** We know that one side of the yard is 40 feet long; let's call this the length. We also know that the area of the yard is 280 square feet. In order to determine the perimeter, we must know the width of the yard.

$$A = l \times w$$
$$280 = 40w$$
$$w = 280 \div 40 = 7 \text{ feet}$$

Frank fences in the two 7-foot sides and one of the 40-foot sides. $40 + 2(7) = 54$.

2. **6 inches:** The perimeter of a pentagon is the sum of its five sides: $x + x + x + 3x + 3x = 9x$. If x is 2/3 of an inch, the perimeter is 9(2/3), or 6 inches.

3. **35 in²:** If E is the midpoint of C, then CE = DE = x. We can determine the length of x by using what we know about the area of triangle AED.

$$A = \frac{b \times h}{2} \qquad 12.5 = \frac{5x}{2}$$

$$25 = 5x$$
$$x = 5$$

Therefore, the length of CD is $2x$, or 10.

To find the area of the trapezoid, use the formula: $A = \dfrac{b_1 + b_2}{2} \times h$

$$= \frac{4 + 10}{2} \times 5$$

$$= 35 \text{ in}^2$$

4. **$1,700:** To find the surface area of a rectangular solid, sum the individual areas of all six faces:

Top and Bottom: $5 \times 4 = 20 \quad \rightarrow \quad 2 \times 20 = 40$
Side 1: $5 \times 2.5 = 12.5 \quad \rightarrow \quad 2 \times 12.5 = 25$
Side 2: $4 \times 2.5 = 10 \quad \rightarrow \quad 2 \times 10 = 20$

$$40 + 25 + 20 = 85 \text{ ft}^2$$

To cover the entire tank, it will cost $85 \times \$20 = \$1,700$.

5. **7:** The area of a triangle is equal to half the base times the height. Therefore,

$$\frac{2y(y)}{2} = 49$$

$$y^2 = 49$$
$$y = 7$$

6. **90 ft²:** The area of the Mexican carpet is equal to $l \times w$, or 36 ft². Set up a percent table or a proportion to find the area of the whole living room floor:

$$\frac{40}{100} = \frac{36}{x} \qquad \text{Cross-multiply to solve.}$$

$$40x = 3600$$
$$x = 90 \text{ ft}^2$$

7. **4:** Set up equations to represent the area and perimeter of the flower bed:

$$A = l \times w \qquad\qquad P = 2(l + w)$$

Then, substitute the known values for the variables A and P:

$$44 = l \times w \qquad\qquad 30 = 2(l + w)$$

Solve the two equations with the substitution method:

$$l = \frac{44}{w}$$

$$30 = 2(\frac{44}{w} + w)$$

Multiply the entire equation by $\frac{w}{2}$.

$$15w = 44 + w^2$$
$$w^2 - 15w + 44 = 0$$
$$(w - 11)(w - 4) = 0$$
$$w = \{4, 11\}$$

Solving the quadratic equation yields two solutions: 4 and 11. Since we are looking only for the length of the shorter side, the answer is 4.

8. $\dfrac{3}{x}$: If the length of the parking lot is $2x$ and the width is x, we can set up a fraction to represent the ratio of perimeter to area as follows:

$$\frac{\text{perimeter}}{\text{area}} = \frac{2(2x + x)}{(2x)(x)} = \frac{6x}{2x^2} = \frac{3}{x}$$

9. **144 m²:** The volume of a rectangular solid equals (length) × (width) × (height). If we know that the length and width are both 4 meters long, we can substitute values into the formulas as shown:

$$112 = 4 \times 4 \times h$$
$$h = 7$$

To find the surface area of a rectangular solid, sum the individual areas of all six faces:

Top and Bottom:	$4 \times 4 = 16$	$\rightarrow$	$2 \times 16 = 32$
Sides:	$4 \times 7 = 28$	$\rightarrow$	$4 \times 28 = 112$

$$32 + 112 = 144 \text{ m}^2$$

10. **24:** First, break quadrilateral ABCE into 2 pieces: a 3 by $3x$ rectangle, and a right triangle with a base of x and a height of 3. The area of quadrilateral ABCE, therefore, is:

$$(3 \times 3x) + \frac{3 \times x}{2} = 9x + 1.5x = 10.5x$$

If ABCE has an area of 21, then $21 = 10.5x$, and $x = 2$. Quadrilateral ABCD is a parallelogram; its area is equal to (base) × (height), or $4x \times 3$. Substitute the known value of 2 for x and simplify:

$$A = 4(2) \times 3 = 24$$

11. **20 hours:** The volume of the pool is (length) × (width) × (height), or $30 \times 10 \times 2 = 600$ cubic meters. Use a standard work equation, $RT = D$, where D represents the total work of 600 m³.

$$.5t = 600$$
$$t = 1200 \text{ minutes}$$

Convert this to hours by dividing by 60: $1200 \div 60 = 20$ hours.

12. **56 m²:** To find the area of a trapezoid, we need the lengths of both parallel bases and the height. If ABCD is a rhombus, then AD = AB = 10. This gives us the length of the first base, AD. We also know that CB = 10 and $\dfrac{CE}{EB} = \dfrac{2}{3}$. Use the unknown multiplier concept to find the length of the second base, CE:

$$2x + 3x = 10$$
$$5x = 10$$
$$x = 2$$

Thus, CE = 2x = 2(2) = 4.

Now all that remains is the height of the trapezoid, AE. If you recognize that AE forms the long leg of a right triangle (ABE), you can use the Pythagorean Theorem to find the length of AE:

$$6^2 + b^2 = 10^2$$
$$b = 8$$

The area of the trapezoid is: $\dfrac{b_1 + b_2}{2} \times h = \dfrac{10 + 4}{2} \times 8 = 56$ m².

13. $\dfrac{6}{5}$**:** To find the surface area of a cube, find the area of 1 face, and multiply that by 6: $6(5^2) = 150$. To find the volume of a cube, cube its edge length: $5^3 = 125$.

The ratio of the cube's surface area to its volume, therefore, is $\dfrac{150}{125}$, or $\dfrac{6}{5}$.

14. **1 to 27:** First, let's call the length of one side of Cube A, x. Thus, the length of one side of Cube B is $3x$. The volume of Cube A is x^3. The volume of Cube B is $(3x)^3$, or $27x^3$.

Therefore, the ratio of the volume of Cube A to Cube B is $\dfrac{x^3}{27x^3}$, or 1 to 27.

15. **3√2:** The area of the frame and the area of the picture sum to the total area of the image, which is 6^2, or 36. Therefore, the area of the frame and the picture are each equal to half of 36, or 18. Since EFGH is a square, the length of EF is $\sqrt{18}$, or $3\sqrt{2}$.

g

Chapter 2
of
GEOMETRY

TRIANGLES &
DIAGONALS

In This Chapter . . .

- The Angles of a Triangle
- The Sides of a Triangle
- The Pythagorean Theorem
- Common Right Triangles
- Isosceles Triangles and the 45 - 45 - 90 Triangle
- Equilateral Triangles and the 30 - 60 - 90 Triangle
- Diagonals of Other Polygons
- Similar Triangles

TRIANGLES & DIAGONALS

The most popular polygon on the GMAT is the triangle.

Right triangles (those with a 90° angle) require particular attention, because they have special properties that are useful for solving many GMAT geometry problems.

The most important property of a right triangle is the unique relationship of the three sides. Given the lengths of any two of the sides of a right triangle, one can determine the length of the third side using the Pythagorean Theorem. There are even two special types of right triangles—the 30-60-90 triangle and the 45-45-90 triangle—for which you only need the length of ONE side to determine the lengths of the triangle's other two sides (without using trigonometry, which is not required knowledge on the GMAT).

Finally, right triangles are essential for solving problems involving other polygons. Cutting more complex polygons into right triangles is the MOST IMPORTANT TOOL for solving GMAT geometry problems.

The sum of the interior angles of a triangle is 180°.

The Angles of a Triangle

The angles in any given triangle have two key properties:

(1) The sum of the three angles of a triangle equals 180°.

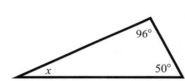
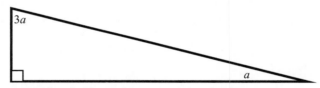

What is x? Since the sum of the three angles must be 180°, we can solve for x as follows:
$180 - 96 - 50 = x = 34°$.

What is a? Since the sum of the three angles must be 180°, we can solve for x as follows:
$90 + 3a + a = 180 \rightarrow a = 22.5°$.

(2) Angles correspond to their opposite sides. This means that the largest angle is opposite the longest side, while the smallest angle is opposite the shortest side. Additionally, if two sides are equal, their opposite angles are also equal.

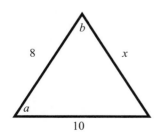

If angle a = angle b, what is the length of side x? As the opposite side of angle b has a length of 10, the opposite side of angle a must have the same length; therefore, $x = 10$.

The Sides of a Triangle

Consider the following "impossible" triangle and what it reveals about the relationship between the three sides of any triangle:

The triangle to the right could never be drawn with the given measurements. Why? Consider that the shortest distance between any two points is a straight line. According to the triangle shown, the direct straight line distance between point C and point B is 14; however, the indirect path from point C to B (the path that goes from C to A to B) is 10 + 3, or 13, which is shorter than the direct path! This is clearly impossible.

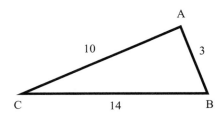

The above example leads to the following rule about the sides of any triangle:

> **The sum of any two sides of a triangle must be GREATER than the third side.**

Therefore, the maximum integer distance for side BC in the triangle above is 12. If the length of side BC is not restricted to integers, then this length has to be less than 13.

Note that the length cannot be as small as we wish, either. It must be <u>greater</u> than the difference between the lengths of the other two sides. In this case, side BC must be longer than 10 − 3 = 7. This is a consequence of the same idea.

Consider the following triangle and the proof that the given measurements are possible:

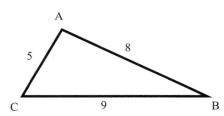

Test each combination of sides to prove that the measurements of this triangle are possible.

$$5 + 8 > 9$$
$$5 + 9 > 8$$
$$8 + 9 > 5$$

Note that the sum of two sides cannot be equal to the third side; the sum of two sides must always be GREATER than the third side.

The Pythagorean Theorem

A right triangle is a triangle with one right angle (90°). Every right triangle is composed of two legs and a hypotenuse. The hypotenuse is the side opposite the right angle and is often assigned the letter c. The two legs which form the right angle are often called a and b (it does not matter which leg is a and which leg is b).

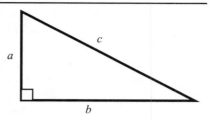

Given the lengths of two sides of a right triangle, how can you determine the length of the third side? Use the Pythagorean Theorem, which states that the sum of the square of the two legs of a right triangle $(a^2 + b^2)$ is equal to the square of the hypotenuse of that triangle (c^2).

$$\text{Pythagorean Theorem: } a^2 + b^2 = c^2$$

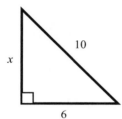

What is x?
$$a^2 + b^2 = c^2$$
$$x^2 + 6^2 = 10^2$$
$$x^2 + 36 = 100$$
$$x^2 = 64$$
$$x = 8$$

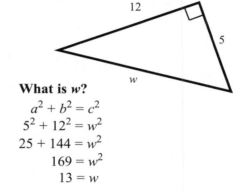

What is w?
$$a^2 + b^2 = c^2$$
$$5^2 + 12^2 = w^2$$
$$25 + 144 = w^2$$
$$169 = w^2$$
$$13 = w$$

Whenever you see a right triangle on the GMAT, look for a way to use the Pythagorean Theorem.

Common Right Triangles

Certain right triangles appear over and over on the GMAT. It pays to memorize these common combinations in order to save time on the exam. Instead of using the Pythagorean Theorem to solve for the lengths of the sides of these common right triangles, you should know the following Pythagorean triples from memory:

Common Combinations	Key Multiples
3 - 4 - 5 The most popular of all right triangles $3^2 + 4^2 = 5^2$ $(9 + 16 = 25)$	6 - 8 - 10 9 - 12 - 15 12 - 16 - 20
5 - 12 - 13 Also quite popular on the GMAT $5^2 + 12^2 = 13^2$ $(25 + 144 = 169)$	10 - 24 - 26
8 - 15 - 17 This one appears less frequently $8^2 + 15^2 = 17^2$ $(64 + 225 = 289)$	

Isosceles Triangles and the 45 - 45 - 90 Triangle

An isosceles triangle is one in which two sides (and their corresponding angles) are equal. The most important isosceles triangle on the GMAT is the isosceles right triangle.

An isosceles right triangle has one 90° angle (opposite the hypotenuse) and two 45° angles (opposite the two equal legs). This triangle is called the 45 - 45 - 90 triangle.

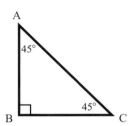

The lengths of the legs of every 45 - 45 - 90 triangle have a specific ratio, which you must memorize:

45°	→ 45°	→ 90°
leg	leg	hypotenuse
1:	1:	$\sqrt{2}$

Given that side AB is 5, what are the lengths of sides BC and AC?

Since AB is 5, we use the ratio $1:1:\sqrt{2}$ for sides AB: BC: AC to determine that the multiplier is 5. We then find that the sides of the triangle have lengths 5: 5: $5\sqrt{2}$ (so side BC = 5 and side AC = $5\sqrt{2}$).

Given that side AC is $\sqrt{18}$, what are the lengths of sides AB and BC?

Since AC is $\sqrt{18}$, we use the ratio $1:1:\sqrt{2}$ for sides AB: BC: AC to determine that the multiplier is $\sqrt{18} \div \sqrt{2} = \sqrt{9} = 3$. We then find that the sides of the triangle have lengths 3: 3: $3\sqrt{2}$ (so sides AB and BC are both equal to 3).

Why is the 45 - 45 - 90 triangle so important? Notice that this triangle is exactly half of a square! That is, two 45 - 45 - 90 triangles put together make up a square! Thus, if you are given the diagonal of a square, you can use the 45 - 45 - 90 ratio to find the length of a side of the square.

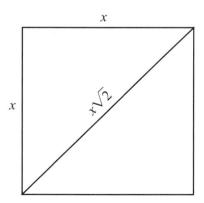

Equilateral Triangles and the 30 - 60 - 90 Triangle

An equilateral triangle is one in which all three sides (and all three angles) are equal. Each angle of an equilateral triangle is 60° (because all 3 angles must sum to 180°). A close relative of the equilateral triangle is the 30 - 60 - 90 triangle. Notice that two of these triangles, when put together, form an equilateral triangle:

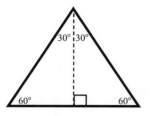

EQUILATERAL TRIANGLE

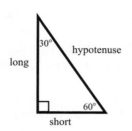

30 - 60 - 90 TRIANGLE

The lengths of the legs of every 30 - 60 - 90 triangle have the following ratio, which you must memorize:

30°	→	60°	→	90°
short leg		long leg		hypotenuse
1:		$\sqrt{3}$:		2

Remember, $\sqrt{3}$ corresponds to the long leg of the triangle, and 2 corresponds to the hypotenuse, which is actually the longest side. $\sqrt{3} < 2$

Given that the short leg of a 30 - 60 - 90 triangle has a length of 6, what are the lengths of the long leg and the hypotenuse?

The short leg, opposite the 30 degree angle, is 6, so we use the ratio 1:$\sqrt{3}$: 2 to determine that the multiplier is 6. We then find that the sides of the triangle have lengths 6: 6$\sqrt{3}$: 12 (so the long leg measures 6$\sqrt{3}$ and the hypotenuse measures 12).

Given that an equilateral triangle has a side length of 10, what is its height?

Looking at the equilateral triangle above, we can see that the side of an equilateral triangle is the same as the hypotenuse of a 30 - 60 - 90 triangle. Additionally, the height of an equilateral triangle is the same as the long leg of a 30 - 60 - 90 triangle. Since we are told that the hypotenuse is 10, we use the ratio 1:$\sqrt{3}$: 2 to determine that the multiplier is 5. We then find that the sides of the 30 - 60 - 90 triangle have lengths 5: 5$\sqrt{3}$: 10 (so the long leg = 5$\sqrt{3}$, which is the height of the equilateral triangle).

Diagonals of Other Polygons

Right triangles are useful for more than just triangles. They are also helpful for finding the diagonals of other polygons, specifically squares, cubes, rectangles, and rectangular solids.

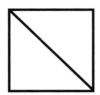

The diagonal of a square can be found using the formula:
$d = s\sqrt{2}$, where s is a side of the square.

The diagonal of a cube can be found using the formula:
$d = s\sqrt{3}$, where s is an edge of the cube.

Recall that the diagonal of a square is the hypotenuse of a 45 - 45 - 90 triangle.

Given a square with side 5, what is the diagonal of the square?

Using the formula, $d = s\sqrt{2}$, we find that the diagonal of the square is $5\sqrt{2}$.

What is the measure of an edge of a cube with a diagonal of $\sqrt{60}$?

Again, using the formula, $d = s\sqrt{3}$, we solve as follows:

$$\sqrt{60} = s\sqrt{3} \rightarrow s = \frac{\sqrt{60}}{\sqrt{3}} = \sqrt{20}$$

Thus, the edge of the cube is $\sqrt{20}$.

To find the diagonal of a rectangle, you must know the length and the width, OR one dimension and the proportion of one to the other.

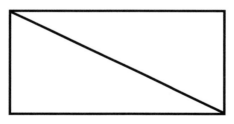

If the rectangle to the left has a length of 12 and a width of 5, what is the diagonal?

Using the Pythagorean Theorem, we solve:
$$5^2 + 12^2 = c^2 \rightarrow 25 + 144 = c^2 \rightarrow c = 13$$

The diagonal is 13.

If the rectangle above has a width of 6, and the ratio of the width to the length is 3:4, what is the diagonal?

Using the ratio, we find that the length is 8. Then, we can use the Pythagorean Theorem, or recognize that this is a 6-8-10 triangle, so the diagonal is 10.

What is the length of the diagonal of this rectangular solid?

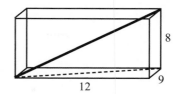

To find the diagonal of a rectangular solid, use the Pythagorean Theorem TWICE.

First, find the diagonal of the bottom face: $9^2 + 12^2 = c^2$ yields $c = 15$ (this is a multiple of a 3-4-5 triangle), so the bottom (dashed) diagonal is 15. Then, we can consider this bottom diagonal of length 15 as the base leg of another right triangle with a height of 8. Now we use the Pythagorean Theorem a second time: $8^2 + 15^2 = c^2$ yields $c = 17$, so the long diagonal is 17.

Similar Triangles

One final tool that you can use for GMAT triangle problems is the similar triangle strategy. Often, looking for similar triangles can help you solve complex problems.

If two right triangles have one other angle in common, they are similar triangles.

Triangles are defined as similar if all their corresponding angles are equal and their corresponding sides are in proportion.

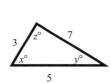 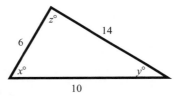

Once you find that triangles have 2 equal angles, you know they are similar. (If 2 angles are congruent, then the third angle must be congruent, since the sum of the angles in any triangle is 180°.)

What is the length of side EF?

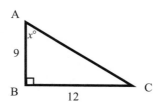 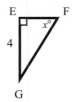

We know that the above two triangles are similar, because they have 2 angles in common (x and the right angle). Since they are similar triangles, their corresponding sides must be in proportion.

Side BC corresponds to side EG (since they both are opposite angle x). Since they are in the ratio of 12:4, we can determine that the large triangle is three times bigger than the smaller one, or in the ratio of 3:1. Using this ratio, we can determine that, since side AB corresponds to side EF, and AB is 9, side EF must be 3.

*Manhattan*GMAT*Prep

Problem Set   (Note: Figures are not drawn to scale.)

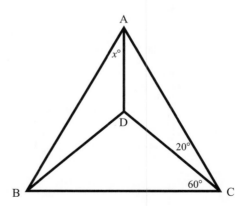

1.   A square is bisected into two equal triangles (see figure). If BD is $16\sqrt{2}$ inches, what is the area of the square?

2.   Beginning in Town A, Biker Bob rides his bike 10 miles west, 3 miles north, 5 miles east, and then 9 miles north, to Town B. How far apart are Town A and Town B?

3.   Now in Town B, Biker Bob goes due west, and then straight north to Town C. Town B and Town C are 26 miles apart. If Biker Bob went 10 miles west, how many miles north did he go?

4.   Triangle A has a base of x and a height of $2x$. Triangle B is similar to Triangle A, and has a base of $2x$. What is the ratio of the area of Triangle A to Triangle B?

5.   What is the measure of angle x in the figure to the right?

6.   The longest side of an isosceles right triangle measures $20\sqrt{2}$. What is the area of the triangle?

7.   Two similar triangles have areas in the ratio of 9:1. What is the ratio of these triangles' perimeters?

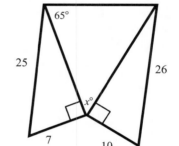

8.   The size of a square computer screen is measured by the length of its diagonal. How much bigger is the visible area of a square 24-inch screen than the area of a square 20-inch screen?

9.   A square field has an area of 400 square meters. Posts are set at all corners of the field. What is the longest distance between any two posts?

10. In Triangle ABC, AD = DB = DC (see figure). Given that angle DCB is 60° and angle ACD is 20°, what is angle x?

11. Two sides of a triangle are 4 and 10. If the third side is an integer x, how many possible values are there for x?

12. Jack makes himself a clay box in the shape of a cube, the edges of which are 4 inches long. What's the longest object he could fit inside the box (i.e., what is the diagonal of the cube)?

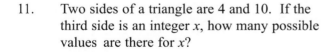

13. What is the area of an equilateral triangle whose sides measure 8 cm long?

14. Alexandra wants to pack away her posters without bending them. She rolls up the posters to put in a rectangular box that is 120 inches long, 90 inches wide, and 80 inches high. What is the longest a poster can be for Alexandra to pack it away without bending it (i.e., what is the diagonal of the rectangular box)?

15. The points of a six-pointed star consist of six identical equilateral triangles, with each side 4 cm (see figure). What is the area of the entire star, including the center?

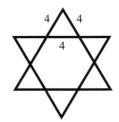

1. **256 square units:** The diagonal of a square is $s\sqrt{2}$; therefore, the side length of square ABCD is 16. The area of the square is s^2, or $16^2 = 256$.

2. **13 miles:** If you draw a rough sketch of the path Biker Bob takes, as shown to the right, you can see that the direct distance from A to B forms the hypotenuse of a right triangle. The short leg (horizontal) is $10 - 5 = 5$ miles, and the long leg (vertical) is $9 + 3 = 12$ miles. Therefore, you can use the Pythagorean Theorem to find the direct distance from A to B:

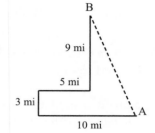

$$5^2 + 12^2 = c^2$$
$$25 + 144 = c^2$$
$$c^2 = 169$$ You might recognize the common right triangle:
$$c = 13$$ 5 - 12 - 13.

3. **24 miles:** If you draw a rough sketch of the path Biker Bob takes, as shown to the right, you can see that the direct distance from B to C forms the hypotenuse of a right triangle.

$$10^2 + b^2 = 26^2$$
$$100 + b^2 = 676$$ To find the square root of 576, you may find
$$b^2 = 576$$ it helpful to prime factor it first:
$$b = 24$$ $$576 = 2^6 \times 3^2$$
                          Therefore, $\sqrt{576} = 2^3 \times 3 = 24$.

You might recognize this as a multiple of the common 5 - 12 - 13 triangle.

4. **1 to 4:** Since we know that Triangle B is similar to Triangle A, we can set up a proportion to represent the relationship between the sides of both triangles:

$$\frac{\text{base}}{\text{height}} = \frac{x}{2x} = \frac{2x}{?}$$

By proportional reasoning, the height of Triangle B must be $4x$. Calculate the area of each triangle with the formula:

Triangle A: $A = \dfrac{b \times h}{2} = \dfrac{(x)(2x)}{2} = x^2$

Triangle B: $A = \dfrac{b \times h}{2} = \dfrac{(2x)(4x)}{2} = 4x^2$

The ratio of the area of Triangle A to Triangle B is 1 to 4.

5. **50°:** Use the Pythagorean Theorem to establish the missing lengths of the two right triangles on the right and left sides of the figure:

$$7^2 + b^2 = 25^2 \qquad\qquad 10^2 + b^2 = 26^2$$
$$49 + b^2 = 625 \qquad\qquad 100 + b^2 = 676$$
$$b^2 = 576 \qquad\qquad\qquad b^2 = 576$$
$$b = 24 \qquad\qquad\qquad\quad b = 24$$

The inner triangle is isosceles. Therefore, both angles opposite the equal sides measure 65°. Since there are 180° in a right triangle, $x = 180 - 2(65) = 50°$.

6. **200:** An isosceles right triangle is a 45 - 45 - 90 triangle, with sides in the ratio of $1:1:\sqrt{2}$. If the longest side, the hypotenuse, measures $20\sqrt{2}$, the two other sides each measure 20. Therefore, the area of the triangle is:

$$A = \frac{b \times h}{2} = \frac{20 \times 20}{2} = 200$$

7. **3 to 1:** If two triangles have areas in the ratio of 9 to 1, their linear measurements have a ratio of $\sqrt{9}$ to $\sqrt{1}$, or 3 to 1. You can derive this rule algebraically with the following reasoning:

Imagine two similar triangles: a smaller one with base b and height h, and a larger one with base bx and height hx. The ratio of the areas of the larger triangle to the smaller one, therefore, would be:

$$\frac{.5(bx \times hx)}{.5(b \times h)} = \frac{.5bhx^2}{.5bh} = \frac{x^2}{1}$$

If we know that $x^2 = 9$, then $x = 3$. The ratio of the linear measurements (perimeter) is 3 to 1.

Alternately, solve this problem by picking real numbers. To do this, create two triangles whose areas have a 9:1 ratio.

First, draw the smaller triangle with an area of 6. Since the area of a triangle is half the product of the base and the height, the base and the height must multiply to 12. If possible, use a common right triangle: $3 \times 4 = 12$.

$$A_{small} = \frac{bh}{2} = \frac{3 \times 4}{2} = 6$$

Now draw the larger triangle. Since the smaller triangle has an area of 6, we need to draw a larger triangle with an area 9 times larger. $6 \times 9 = 54$. Since the area of a triangle is half the product of the base and height, the base and height must multiply to 108. If possible, use a common right triangle: $9 \times 12 = 108$.

$$A_{large} = \frac{bh}{2} = \frac{9 \times 12}{2} = 54$$

Then, find the ratio of the perimeters: $\dfrac{9 + 12 + 15}{3 + 4 + 5} = \dfrac{36}{12} = 3$.

8. **88 in²:** If the diagonal of the larger screen is 24 inches, and we know that $d = s\sqrt{2}$, then $s = \dfrac{24}{\sqrt{2}}$. By the same reasoning, the side length of the smaller screen is $\dfrac{20}{\sqrt{2}}$. The areas of the two screens are:

Large screen: $A = \dfrac{24}{\sqrt{2}} \times \dfrac{24}{\sqrt{2}} = 288$

Small screen: $A = \dfrac{20}{\sqrt{2}} \times \dfrac{20}{\sqrt{2}} = 200$

The visible area of the larger screen is 88 square inches bigger than the visible area of the smaller screen.

9: **20√2:** The longest distance between any two posts is the diagonal of the field. If the area of the field is 400 square meters, then each side must measure 20 meters. Diagonal = $d = s\sqrt{2}$, so $d = 20\sqrt{2}$.

10. **10:** If AD = DB = DC, then the three triangular regions in this figure are all isosceles triangles. Therefore, we can fill in some of the missing angle measurements as shown to the right. Since we know that there are 180° in the large triangle ABC, we can write the following equation:

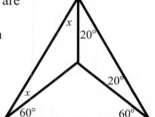

$$x + x + 20 + 20 + 60 + 60 = 180$$
$$2x + 160 = 180$$
$$x = 10$$

11. **7:** If two sides of a triangle are 4 and 10, the third side must be greater than $10 - 4$ and smaller than $10 + 4$. Therefore, the possible values for x are {7, 8, 9, 10, 11, 12, and 13}. You can draw a sketch to convince yourself of this:

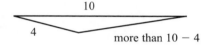
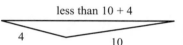

12. **4√3:** The diagonal of a cube is $s\sqrt{3}$. Therefore, the longest object Jack could fit inside the box would be $4\sqrt{3}$ inches long.

13. **16√3:** Draw in the height of the triangle (see figure). If triangle ABC is an equilateral triangle, and ABD is a right triangle, then ABD is a 30 - 60 - 90 triangle. Therefore, its sides are in the ratio of $1:\sqrt{3}:2$. If the hypotenuse is 8, the short leg is 4, and the long leg is $4\sqrt{3}$. This is the height of triangle ABC. Find the area of triangle ABC with the formula for area of a triangle:

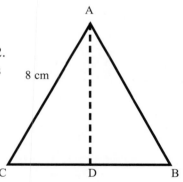

$$A = \frac{b \times h}{2} = \frac{8 \times 4\sqrt{3}}{2} = 16\sqrt{3}$$

14. **170 inches:** Find the diagonal of this rectangular solid by applying the Pythagorean Theorem twice. First, find the diagonal across the bottom of the box:

$$120^2 + 90^2 = c^2$$
$$14,400 + 8100 = c^2$$
$$c^2 = 22,500$$
$$c = 150$$

You might recognize this as a multiple of the common 3 - 4 - 5 right triangle.

Then, find the diagonal of the rectangular box:

$$80^2 + 150^2 = c^2$$
$$6400 + 22,500 = c^2$$
$$c^2 = 28,900$$
$$c = 170$$

You might recognize this as a multiple of the common 8 - 15 - 17 right triangle.

15. $48\sqrt{3}$ **cm^2:** We can think of this star as a large equilateral triangle with sides 12 cm long, and three additional smaller equilateral triangles with sides 4 inches long. Using the same 30 - 60 - 90 logic we applied in problem #13, we can see that the height of the larger equilateral triangle is $6\sqrt{3}$, and the height of the smaller equilateral triangle is $2\sqrt{3}$. Therefore, the areas of the triangles are as follows:

Large triangle: $A = \dfrac{b \times h}{2} = \dfrac{12 \times 6\sqrt{3}}{2} = 36\sqrt{3}$

Small triangles: $A = \dfrac{b \times h}{2} = \dfrac{4 \times 2\sqrt{3}}{2} = 4\sqrt{3}$

The total area of three smaller triangles and one large triangle is:
$$36\sqrt{3} + 3(4\sqrt{3}) = 48\sqrt{3} \text{ cm}^2.$$

g

Chapter 3
_of_
GEOMETRY

CIRCLES & CYLINDERS

In This Chapter . . .

- Circumference of a Circle
- Circumference and Arc Length
- Perimeter of a Sector
- Area of a Circle
- Area of a Sector
- Inscribed vs. Central Angles
- Inscribed Triangles
- Cylinders and Surface Area
- Cylinders and Volume

CIRCLES & CYLINDERS

A circle is defined as the set of points in a plane that are equidistant from a fixed center point. A circle contains 360°.

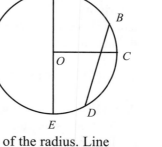

Any line segment that connects the center point to a point on the circle is termed a radius of the circle. Segment *OC* is a radius of the circle shown to the right.

Any line segment that connects two points on a circle is called a chord. Any chord that passes through the center of the circle is called a diameter. Notice that the diameter is two times the length of the radius. Line segment *BD* is a chord of the circle shown to the right. Line segment *AE* is a diameter of the circle.

The GMAT tests your ability to find (1) the circumference and (2) the area of whole and partial circles. In addition, you must know how to work with cylinders, which are three-dimensional shapes made, in part, of circles. The GMAT tests your ability to find (3) the surface area and (4) the volume of cylinders.

If you know the circumference, the radius, the diameter, or the area of a circle, you can use one to find any of the other measurements.

Circumference of a Circle

The distance around a circle is termed the circumference. This is equivalent to the perimeter of a polygon. The only information you need to find the circumference of a circle is the radius of that circle. The formula for the circumference of any circle is:

$$C = 2\pi r$$

where *C* is the circumference, *r* is the radius, and π is a number that is approximately 3.14.

For the purposes of the GMAT, π should be approximated as 3. In fact, most problems require no approximation, as the GMAT includes π as part of the answer choices. For example, a typical answer choice for a circumference problem would be 8π, instead of 24.

What is the distance around a circle that has a diameter of 10?

To solve this, first determine the radius, which is half of the diameter, or 5. Then plug this into the circumference formula $C = 2\pi r = 2\pi(5) = 10\pi$. This is generally a sufficient answer. You do not need to multiply 10 by π.

Circumference and Arc Length

Often, the GMAT will ask you to solve for a portion of the distance on a circle, instead of the entire circumference. This portion is termed an arc. Arc length can be found by determining what fraction the arc is of the entire circumference. This can be done by looking at the central angle that defines the arc.

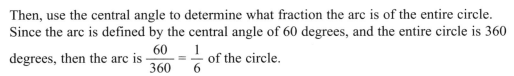

What is the length of arc AXB?

Arc AXB is the arc from A to B, passing through the point X. To find its length, first find the circumference of the circle. The radius is given as 12. To find the circumference, use the formula $C = 2\pi r = 2\pi(12) = 24\pi$.

There are a total of 360° in a circle.

Then, use the central angle to determine what fraction the arc is of the entire circle. Since the arc is defined by the central angle of 60 degrees, and the entire circle is 360 degrees, then the arc is $\dfrac{60}{360} = \dfrac{1}{6}$ of the circle.

Therefore, the measure of arc AXB $= \left(\dfrac{1}{6}\right)(24\pi) = 4\pi$.

Perimeter of a Sector

The boundaries of a sector of a circle are formed by the arc and two radii. Therefore, if you know the length of the radius and the central (or inscribed) angle, you can find the perimeter of the sector.

What is the perimeter of sector ABC?

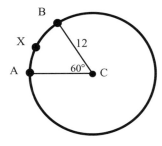

In the previous example, we found the length of arc AXB to be 4π. Therefore, the perimeter of the sector is:

$$4\pi + 12 + 12 = 24 + 4\pi.$$

Area of a Circle

The space inside a circle is termed the area of the circle. This is just like the area of a polygon. Just as with circumference, the only information you need to find the area of a circle is the radius of that circle. The formula for the area of any circle is:

$$A = \pi r^2$$

where A is the area, r is the radius, and π is a number that is approximately 3.14.

What is the area of a circle with a circumference of 16π?

In order to find the area of a circle, all we must know is its radius. If the circumference of the circle is 16π (and $C = 2\pi r$), then the radius must be 8. Plug this into the area formula:

$$A = \pi r^2 = \pi(8^2) = 64\pi.$$

Area of a Sector

Often, the GMAT will ask you to solve for the area of a portion of a circle, instead of the area of the entire circle. A portion of a circle is termed a sector. Sector area can be found by determining what fraction it is of the entire area. This can be done by looking at the central angle which defines the sector.

What is the area of sector ACB (the striped region) below?

First, find the area of the entire circle:
$$A = \pi r^2 = \pi(3^2) = 9\pi.$$

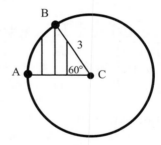

Then, use the central angle to determine what fraction the sector is of the entire circle. Since the sector is defined by the central angle of 60°, and the entire circle is 360°, the sector is a sixth of the area of the circle.

Therefore, the area of sector ACB is $\left(\dfrac{1}{6}\right)(9\pi) = 1.5\pi.$

Central or inscribed angles can help you determine arc length and sector area.

Inscribed vs. Central Angles

Thus far, in dealing with arcs and sectors, we have referred to the concept of a central angle. A central angle is defined as an angle whose vertex lies at the center point of a circle. As we have seen, a central angle defines both an arc and a sector of a circle.

Another type of angle is termed an inscribed angle. An inscribed angle has its vertex on the circle itself. The following diagrams illustrate the difference between a central angle and an inscribed angle.

If you are given the measure of an inscribed angle, find the measure of the corresponding central angle to solve the problem.

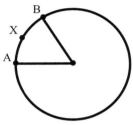

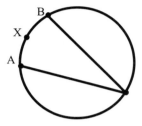

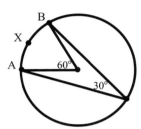

CENTRAL ANGLE   INSCRIBED ANGLE

Notice that, in the circle at the far right, there is a central angle and an inscribed angle, both of which intercept arc *AXB*. It is the central angle that defines the arc; that is, the arc is 60° (or one sixth of the complete 360° circle). An inscribed angle is equal to half of the arc it intercepts (in this case, the inscribed angle is 30°, which is half of 60°).

Inscribed Triangles

Related to this idea of an inscribed angle is that of an inscribed triangle. A triangle is said to be inscribed in a circle if all of the vertices of the triangle are points on the circle. The important rule to remember is: **if a triangle is inscribed in a circle, such that one of its sides is a diameter of the circle, then the triangle MUST be a right triangle.** Conversely, any right triangle inscribed in a circle must have one of its sides as the diameter of the circle (thereby splitting the circle in half).

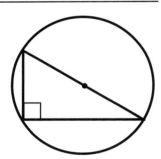

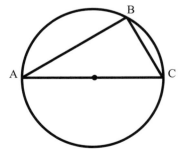

In the inscribed triangle to the left, triangle ABC must be a right triangle, since AC is a diameter of the circle.

Cylinders and Surface Area

Two circles and a rectangle combine to form a three-dimensional shape called a right circular cylinder (referred to from now on simply as a cylinder). The top and bottom of the cylinder are circles, while the middle of the cylinder is formed from a rolled-up rectangle, as shown in the diagram below:

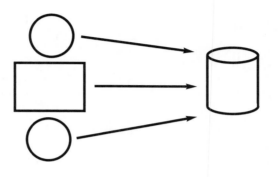

In order to determine the surface area of a cylinder, sum the areas of the 3 surfaces: The area of each circle is πr^2, while the area of the rectangle is length × width. Looking at the figures on the left, we can see that the length of the rectangle is equal to the circumference of the circle ($2\pi r$), and the width of the rectangle is equal to the height of the cylinder (h). Therefore, the area of the rectangle is $2\pi r$ × h. To find the total surface area of a cylinder, sum the surface area of the circular top and bottom, as well as the rectangle that wraps around the outside.

> Think of the formula for the volume of a cylinder as the area of the circular base multiplied by the height, just like the formula for the volume of a rectangular solid.

$$SA = 2 \text{ circles} + \text{rectangle} = 2(\pi r^2) + 2\pi rh$$

The only information you need to find the surface area of a cylinder is (1) the radius of the cylinder and (2) the height of the cylinder.

Cylinders and Volume

The volume of a cylinder measures how much "stuff" it can hold inside. In order to find the volume of a cylinder, use the following formula:

$$V = \pi r^2 h$$

where V is the volume, r is the radius of the cylinder, and h is the height of the cylinder.

As with finding surface area, determining the volume of a cylinder requires two pieces of information: (1) the radius of the cylinder and (2) the height of the cylinder.

The diagram below shows that two cylinders can have the same volume but different shapes (and therefore each fits differently inside a larger object).

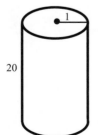

$$V = \pi r^2 h$$
$$= \pi (1)^2 20$$
$$= 20\pi$$

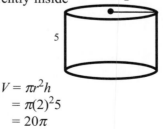

$$V = \pi r^2 h$$
$$= \pi (2)^2 5$$
$$= 20\pi$$

Problem Set (Note: Figures are not drawn to scale.)

1. Triangle ABC is inscribed in a circle, such that AC is a diameter of the circle (see figure). If AB is 8 and BC is 15, what is the circumference of the circle?

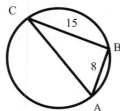

2. A cylinder has a surface area of 360π, and is 3 units tall. What is the diameter of the cylinder's circular base?

3. Randy can run π meters every 20 seconds. If the circular track has a radius of 75 meters, how long does it take Randy to run twice around the track?

4. Randy then moves on to the Jumbo Track, which has a radius of 200 meters (as compared to the first track, with a radius of 75 meters). Ordinarily, Randy runs 8 laps on the normal track. How many laps on the Jumbo Track would Randy have to run in order to have the same workout?

5. A circular lawn with a radius of 5 meters is surrounded by a circular walkway that is 4 meters wide (see figure). What is the area of the walkway?

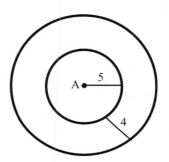

6. A cylindrical water tank has a diameter of 14 meters and a height of 20 meters. A water truck can fill π cubic meters of the tank every minute. How long will it take the water truck to fill the water tank from empty to half-full?

7. Red Giant cola comes in two sizes, Giant and Super-Giant. Each comes in a cylindrical container, and the Giant size sells for $1.20. If the Super-Giant container has twice the height and its circular base has twice the radius of the Giant size, and the price per ml of Red Giant cola is the same, how much does the Super-Giant container cost?

8. BE and CD are both diameters of Circle A (see figure). If the area of Circle A is 180 units^2, what is the area of sector ABC + sector ADE?

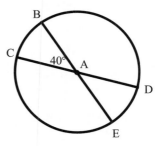

9. Jane has to paint a cylindrical column that is 14 feet high and that has a circular base with a radius of 3 feet. If one bucket of paint will cover 10π square feet, how many buckets does Jane need to buy in order to paint the column, including the top and bottom?

10. A rectangular box has the dimensions 12 inches $\times$ 10 inches $\times$ 8 inches. What is the largest possible volume of a right cylinder that is placed inside the box?

11. A circular flower bed takes up half the area of a square lawn. If an edge of the lawn is 200 feet long, what is the radius of the flower bed? (Express the answer in terms of π.)

12. If angle ABC is 40 degrees (see figure), and the area of the circle is 81π, how long is arc AXC?

13. A Hydrogenator water gun has a cylindrical water tank, which is 30 centimeters long. Jack fills his Hydrogenator at a hose that will fill up π cubic centimeters of his water tank every second. If it takes him 8 minutes to fill the tank with water, what is the diameter of the circular base of the gun's water tank?

14. Triangle ABC is inscribed in a circle, such that AC is a diameter of the circle and angle BAC is 45° (see figure). If the area of triangle ABC is 72 square units, how much larger is the area of the circle than the area of triangle ABC?

15. Triangle ABC is inscribed in a circle, such that AC is a diameter of the circle and angle BAC is 45°. (Refer to the same figure as for problem #14.) If the area of triangle ABC is 84.5 square units, what is the length of arc BC?

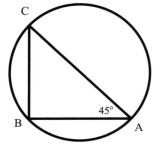

1. **17π:** If AC is a diameter of the circle, then inscribed triangle ABC is a right triangle, with AC as the hypotenuse. Therefore, we can apply the Pythagorean Theorem to find the length of AC.

$8^2 + 15^2 = c^2$

$64 + 225 = c^2$ The circumference of the circle is $2\pi r$, or 17π.

$c^2 = 289$

$c = 17$ You might recognize the common 8 -15 - 17 right triangle.

2. **24:** The surface area of a cylinder is the area of the circular top and bottom, plus the area of its wrapped-around rectangular third face. We can express this in formula form as:

$SA = 2(\pi r^2) + 2\pi rh$

Substitute the known values into this formula to find the radius of the circular base:

$360\pi = 2(\pi r^2) + 2\pi r(3)$

$360\pi = 2\pi r^2 + 6\pi r$

$r^2 + 3r - 180 = 0$

$(r + 15)(r - 12) = 0$

$r + 15 = 0$ OR $r - 12 = 0$

$r = \{-15, 12\}$

Use only the positive value of r: 12. If $r = 12$, the diameter of the cylinder's circular base is 24.

3. **1 hour and 40 minutes:** The distance around the track is the circumference of the circle:

$C = 2\pi r$

$= 150\pi$

Running twice around the circle would equal a distance of 300π meters. If Randy can run π meters every 20 seconds, he runs 3π meters every minute. Therefore, it will take him 100 minutes (or 1 hour and 40 minutes) to run around the circular track twice.

4. **3 laps:** 8 laps on the normal track is a distance of 1200π meters. (Recall from problem #3 that the circumference of the normal track is 150π meters.) If the Jumbo Track has a radius of 200 meters, its circumference is 400π meters. It will take 3 laps around this track to travel 1200π meters.

5. **$56\pi m^2$:** The area of the walkway is the area of the entire image (walkway + lawn) minus the area of the lawn. To find the area of each circle, use the formula:

Large circle: $A = \pi r^2 = \pi(9)^2 = 81\pi$

Small circle: $A = \pi r^2 = \pi(5)^2 = 25\pi$ $81\pi - 25\pi = 56\pi m^2$

6. **8 hours and 10 minutes:** First find the volume of the cylindrical tank:

$V = \pi r^2 \times h$

$= \pi(7)^2 \times 20$

$= 980\pi$

If the water truck can fill π cubic meters of the tank every minute, it will take 980 minutes to fill the tank completely; therefore, it will take $980 \div 2 = 490$ minutes to fill the tank halfway. This is equal to 8 hours and 10 minutes.

7. **$9.60:** Let h = the height of the giant size $\rightarrow 2h$ = the height of the super-giant size.

Let r = the radius of the giant size → $2r$ = the radius of the super-giant size.

The volume of the giant can = $\pi r^2 h$.
The volume of the super-giant can = $\pi(2r)^2 \times 2h = 8(\pi r^2 \times h) = 8\pi r^2 h$.
The super-giant can holds 8 times as much cola. If the price per ml is the same, and the Giant can sells for $1.20, the Super-Giant can sells for 8($1.20) = $9.60.

8. **40 units^2:** The two central angles, CAB and DAE, describe a total of 80°. Simplify the fraction to find out what fraction of the circle this represents:

$$\frac{80}{360} = \frac{2}{9} \qquad \frac{2}{9} \text{ of 180 units}^2 \text{ is 40 units}^2.$$

9. **11 buckets:** The surface area of a cylinder is the area of the circular top and bottom, plus the area of its wrapped-around rectangular third face.

Top & Bottom: $A = \pi r^2 = 9\pi$
Rectangle: $A = 2\pi r \times h = 84\pi$

The total surface area, then, is $9\pi + 9\pi + 84\pi = 102\pi$ ft^2. If one bucket of paint will cover 10π ft^2, then Jane will need 10.2 buckets to paint the entire column. Since paint stores do not sell fractional buckets, she will need to purchase 11 buckets.

10. **200π:** The radius of the cylinder must be equal to half of the smaller of the 2 dimensions that form the box's bottom. The height, then, can be equal to the remaining dimension of the box. There is no general way to tell which way the cylinder will have the largest dimension; you must simply try all possibilities:
$V = \pi r^2 \times h$

Case 1: $r = 5, h = 8$ Case 2: $r = 4, h = 10$ Case 3: $r = 4, h = 12$
$V = 25\pi \times 8 = 200\pi$ $V = 16\pi \times 10 = 160\pi$ $V = 16\pi \times 12 = 192\pi$

Case 1 yields the largest volume. (Case 2 can be seen to be inferior right away, because it makes no use of the largest dimension of the box.)

11. $\sqrt{\dfrac{20{,}000}{\pi}}$: The area of the lawn is $(200)^2 = 40{,}000$ ft^2.

Therefore, the area of the flower bed is $40{,}000 \div 2 = 20{,}000$ ft^2.

$A = \pi r^2 = 20{,}000$ The radius of the flower bed is equal to $\sqrt{\dfrac{20{,}000}{\pi}}$.

12. **4π:** If the area of the circle is 81π, then the radius of the circle is 9 ($A = \pi r^2$). Therefore, the total circumference of the circle is 18π ($C = 2\pi r$). Angle ABC, an inscribed angle of 40°, corresponds to a central angle of 80°. Thus, arc AXC is equal to $80/360 = 2/9$ of the total circumference:
$2/9(18\pi) = 4\pi$.

13. **8 cm:** In 8 minutes, or 480 seconds, 480 πcm^3 of water flows into the tank. Therefore, the volume of the tank is 480π. We are given a height of 30, so we can solve for the radius.

$$V = \pi r^2 \times h$$
$$480\pi = 30\pi r^2$$
$$r^2 = 16$$
$$r = 4$$

Therefore, the diameter of the tank's base is 8 cm.

14. **$72\pi - 72$:** If AC is a diameter of the circle, then angle ABC is a right angle. Therefore, triangle ABC is a 45 - 45 - 90 triangle, and the base and height are equal. Assign the variable x to represent both the base and height:

$$A = \frac{bh}{2} \qquad\qquad \frac{x^2}{2} = 72$$
$$x^2 = 144$$
$$x = 12$$

The base and height of the triangle are equal to 12, and so the area of the triangle is $\dfrac{12 \times 12}{2} = 72$.

The hypotenuse of the triangle, which is also the diameter of the circle, is equal to $12\sqrt{2}$. Therefore, the radius is equal to $6\sqrt{2}$ and the area of the circle, πr^2, $= 72\pi$. The area of the circle is $72\pi - 72$ square units larger than the area of triangle ABC.

15. $\dfrac{13\sqrt{2}\pi}{4}$: We know that the area of triangle ABC is 84.5 square units, so we can use the same logic as in the previous problem to establish the base and height of the triangle:

$$A = \frac{bh}{2} \qquad\qquad \frac{x^2}{2} = 84.5$$
$$x^2 = 169$$
$$x = 13$$

The base and height of the triangle are equal to 13. Therefore, the hypotenuse, which is also the diameter of the circle, is equal to $13\sqrt{2}$, and the circumference ($C = \pi d$) is equal to $13\sqrt{2}\pi$. Angle A, an inscribed angle, corresponds to a central angle of 90°. Thus, arc BC = 90/360 = 1/4 of the total circumference:

$$\frac{1}{4} \text{ of } 13\sqrt{2}\pi \text{ is } \frac{13\sqrt{2}\pi}{4}.$$

g

Chapter 4
of
GEOMETRY

LINES & ANGLES

In This Chapter . . .

- Intersecting Lines
- Exterior Angles of a Triangle
- Parallel Lines Cut by a Transversal

LINES & ANGLES

A straight line is 180°. Think of a line as half of a circle.

Parallel lines are lines in a plane that never intersect. No matter how far you extend the lines, they never meet. Two parallel lines are shown below:

Perpendicular lines are lines that intersect at a 90° angle. Two perpendicular lines are shown below:

There are 180° in a straight line.

There are two major line-angle relationships that you must know for the GMAT:
  (1) The angles formed by any intersecting lines.
  (2) The angles formed by parallel lines cut by a transversal.

Intersecting Lines

Intersecting lines have three important properties.

First, the interior angles formed by intersecting lines form a circle, so the sum of these angles is 360°. In the diagram shown, $a + b + c + d = 360$.

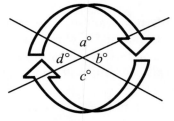

Second, interior angles that combine to form a line sum to 180°. These are termed supplementary angles. Thus, in the diagram shown, $a + b = 180$, because angles a and b form a line together. Other supplementary angles are: $b + c = 180$, $c + d = 180$, and $d + a = 180$.

Third, angles formed by the same two lines are equal. These are called vertical angles. Thus, in the diagram above, $a = c$, because both of these angles are formed from the same two lines. Additionally, $b = d$ for the same reason.

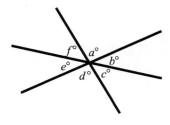

Note that all of the above rules apply to more than two lines that intersect at a point, as shown to the left. In the diagram to the left, $a + b + c + d + e + f = 360$, because these angles combine to form a circle. In addition, $a + b + c = 180$, because these three angles combine to form a line. Finally, $a = d$, $b = e$, and $c = f$, because these are pairs of vertical angles.

Exterior Angles of a Triangle

An exterior angle of a triangle is equal in measure to the sum of the two non-adjacent interior angles of the triangle.

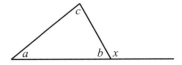

$a + b + c = 180$ (sum of angles in a triangle).
$b + x = 180$ (supplementary angles).
Therefore, $x = a + c$.

Sometimes parallel lines cut by a transversal appear when a rectangle, a parallelogram, a rhombus, or a trapezoid is cut in half by a diagonal.

Parallel Lines Cut By a Transversal

The GMAT makes frequent use of diagrams that include parallel lines cut by a transversal, as shown here.

Notice that there are 8 angles formed by this construction, but there are only TWO different angle measures (a and b). All the acute angles formed when parallel lines are cut by a transversal are congruent. Likewise, all the obtuse angles formed are congruent. Any acute angle is supplementary to any obtuse angle. Thus, any a summed with any b will yield 180.

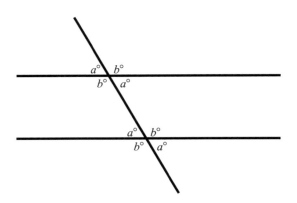

Whenever you see a transversal problem on the GMAT, immediately fill in all the a (acute) and b (obtuse) angles, just as in the diagram above. You will then be able to see all the angles that are equal, and all the combinations of angles that sum to 180°. This generally will lead you towards the solution to the problem.

Sometimes the GMAT disguises the parallel lines and the transversal so that they are not readily apparent, as in the diagram pictured to the right.

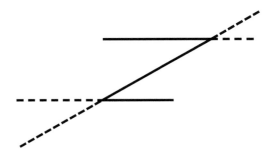

In these "disguised" cases, it is a good idea to extend the lines so that you can easily see the parallel lines and the transversal. Just remember always to be on the lookout for parallel lines; when you see them, start extending lines and labeling the acute and obtuse angles.

Problem Set

Problems 1 through 4 refer to the diagram below, where line AB is parallel to line CD.

1.   If $x - y = 10$, what is x?

2.   If the ratio of x to y is 3:2, what is y?

3.   If $x + (x + y) = 320$, what is x?

4.   If $\dfrac{x}{x-y} = 2$, what is x?

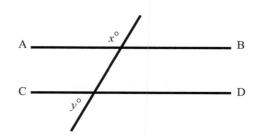

Problems 5 through 8 refer to the diagram below.

5.   If a is 95, what is $b + d - e$?

6.   If $c + f = 70$, and d is 80, what is b?

7.   If $a + b$ are complementary angles (they sum to 90°), name three other pairs of complementary angles.

8.   If e is 45, what is the sum of all the other angles?

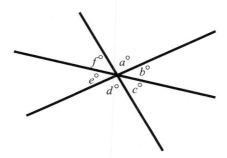

Problems 9 through 12 refer to the diagram below, where line XY is parallel to line QU.

9.   If $a + e = 150$, find f.

10.   If $a = y$, $g = 3y + 20$, and $f = 2x$, find x.

11.   If $g = 11y$, $a = 4x - y$, and $d = 5y + 2x - 20$, find h.

12.   If $b = 4x$, $e = x + 2y$, and $d = 3y + 8$, find h.

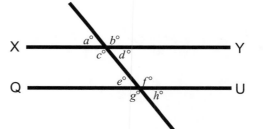

Problems 13 through 15 refer to the diagram to the right.

13.   If $c + g = 140$, find k.

14.   If $g = 90$, what is $a + k$?

15.   If $f + k = 150$, find b.

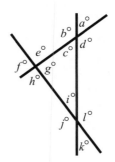

*Manhattan*GMAT*Prep
the new standard

1. **95:** We know that $x + y = 180$, since any acute angle formed by a transversal that cuts across two parallel lines is supplementary to any obtuse angle. Use the information given to set up a system of two equations with two variables:

$$x + y = 180$$
$$\underline{x - y = 10}$$
$$2x = 190$$
$$x = 95$$

2. **72:** Set up a ratio, using the unknown multiplier, a.

$$\frac{x}{y} = \frac{3a}{2a}$$

$$180 = x + y = 3a + 2a = 5a$$
$$180 = 5a$$
$$a = 36$$
$$y = 2a = 2(36) = 72$$

3. **140:** Use the fact that $x + y = 180$ to set up a system of two equations with two variables:

$$x + y = 180 \quad \rightarrow \quad -x - y = -180$$
$$\underline{+ \quad 2x + y = 320}$$
$$x = 140$$

4. **120:** Use the fact that $x + y = 180$ to set up a system of two equations with two variables:

$$\frac{x}{x - y} = 2 \quad \rightarrow \quad x - 2y = 0$$
$$\underline{- \quad x + y = 180}$$
$$-3y = -180$$
$$y = 60 \quad \rightarrow \quad \text{Therefore, } x = 120.$$

5. **95:** Because a and d are vertical angles, they have the same measure: $a = d = 95°$. Likewise, since b and e are vertical angles, they have the same measure: $b = e$. Therefore, $b + d - e = d = 95°$.

6. **65:** Because c and f are vertical angles, they have the same measure: $c + f = 70$, so $c = f = 35$. Notice that b, c, and d form a straight line: $b + c + d = 180$. Substitute the known values of c and d into this equation:

$$b + 35 + 80 = 180$$
$$b + 115 = 180$$
$$b = 65$$

7. **b and d, a and e, & d and e:** If a is complementary to b, then d (which is equal to a, since they are vertical angles), is also complementary to b. Likewise, if a is complementary to b, then a is also complementary to e (which is equal to b, since they are vertical angles). Finally, d and e must be complementary, since $d = a$ and $e = b$.

8. **315:** If $e = 45°$, then the sum of all the other angles is $360 - 45 = 315$.

9. **105:** We are told that $a + e = 150$. Since they are both acute angles formed by a transversal cutting across two parallel lines, they are also congruent. Therefore, $a = e = 75$. Any acute angle in this diagram is supplementary to any obtuse angle, so $75 + f = 180$, and $f = 105$.

10. **70:** We know that angles a and g are supplementary; their measures sum to 180. Therefore:

$$y + 3y + 20 = 180$$
$$4y = 160$$
$$y = 40$$

Angle f is congruent to angle g, so its measure is also $3y + 20$. The measure of angle $f = g = 3(40) + 20 = 140$. If $f = 2x$, then $140 = 2x \rightarrow x = 70$.

11. **70:** We are given the measure of one acute angle (a) and one obtuse angle (g). Since any acute angle in this diagram is supplementary to any obtuse angle, $11y + 4x - y = 180$, or $4x + 10y = 180$. Since angle d is congruent to angle a, we know that $5y + 2x - 20 = 4x - y$, or $2x - 6y = -20$. We can set up a system of two equations with two variables:

$$2x - 6y = -20 \qquad \rightarrow \qquad \begin{array}{r} -4x + 12y = 40 \\ \underline{4x + 10y = 180} \\ 22y = 220 \\ y = 10; x = 20 \end{array}$$

Since h is one of the acute angles, h has the same measure as a: $4x - y = 4(20) - 10 = 70$.

12. **68:** Because b and d are supplementary, $4x + 3y + 8 = 180$, or $4x + 3y = 172$. Since d and e are congruent, $3y + 8 = x + 2y$, or $x - y = 8$. We can set up a system of two equations with two variables:

$$x - y = 8 \qquad \rightarrow \qquad \begin{array}{r} 4x + 3y = 172 \\ \underline{3x - 3y = 24} \\ 7x = 196 \\ x = 28; y = 20 \end{array}$$

Since h is congruent to d, $h = 3y + 8$, or $3(20) + 8 = 68$.

13. **40:** If $c + g = 140$, then $i = 40$, because there are 180° in a triangle. Since k is vertical to i, k is also $= 40$. Alternately, if $c + g = 140$, then $j = 140$, since j is an exterior angle of the triangle and is therefore equal to the sum of the two remote interior angles. Since k is supplementary to j, $k = 180 - 140 = 40$.

14. **90:** If $g = 90$, then the other two angles in the triangle, c and i, sum to 90. Since a and k are vertical angles to c and i, they sum to 90 as well.

15. **150:** Angles f and k are vertical to angles g and i. These two angles, then, must also sum to 150. Angle b, an exterior angle of the triangle, must be equal to the sum of the two remote interior angles g and i. Therefore, $b = 150$.

Chapter 5
of
GEOMETRY

COORDINATE
PLANE

In This Chapter . . .

- The Slope of a Line
- The 4 Types of Slopes
- The Intercepts of a Line
- Slope-Intercept Equation
- Horizontal and Vertical Lines
- Step by Step: From 2 Points to a Line
- The Distance Between 2 Points
- Positive and Negative Quadrants
- Perpendicular Bisectors

THE COORDINATE PLANE

The coordinate plane is formed by a horizontal axis (the "*x*" axis) and a vertical axis (the "*y*" axis), as shown here.

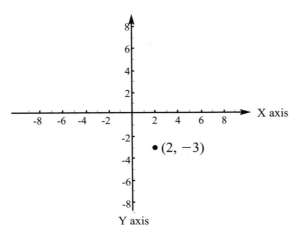

The purpose of the coordinate plane is to help us identify points. Points are identified by using an ordered pair, such as the one to the left (2, −3). The first member of the ordered pair (2) is the *x*-coordinate, and corresponds to the point's location on the horizontal axis. The second member of the ordered pair is the *y*-coordinate, and corresponds to the point's location on the vertical axis. A line in the plane is formed by the connection of two or more points. The GMAT tests your ability to use ordered pairs and lines in the coordinate plane.

The slope of a line is equal to

$$\frac{rise}{run} = \frac{y_1 - y_2}{x_1 - x_2}$$

The Slope of a Line

The slope of a line is defined as "rise over run"—that is, the amount the line <u>rises</u> vertically over the amount the line <u>runs</u> horizontally.

The slope of a line can be determined by taking any two points on the line and (1) determining the "rise," or difference between their *y*-coordinates and (2) determining the "run," or difference between their *x*-coordinates.

The slope is simply $\frac{rise}{run}$.

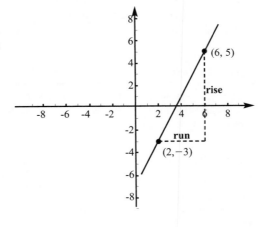

For example, in the diagram at the right, the line rises vertically from −3 to 5. This distance can be found by subtracting the *y*-coordinates: 5 − (−3) = 8. Thus, the line rises 8 units.

The line runs horizontally from 2 to 6. This distance can be found by subtracting the *x*-coordinates: 6 − 2 = 4. Thus, the line runs 4 units.

Therefore, the slope of the line is: $\frac{rise}{run} = \frac{8}{4} = 2$.

The 4 Types of Slopes

There are four types of slopes that a line can have:

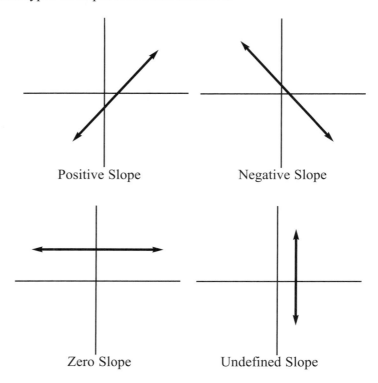

Positive Slope   Negative Slope

Zero Slope   Undefined Slope

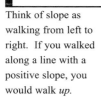

Think of slope as walking from left to right. If you walked along a line with a positive slope, you would walk *up*.

A positive slope rises upward from left to right. A negative slope falls downward from left to right. A zero slope is a horizontal line. An undefined slope is a vertical line, also called "no slope."

The Intercepts of a Line

A point where a line hits a coordinate axis is called an intercept. There are two types of intercepts: the *y*-intercept, where the line hits the *y*-axis, and the *x*-intercept, where the line hits the *x*-axis.

The *y*-intercept is expressed using the ordered pair $(0, y)$, where *y* is the point where the line hits the *y*-axis. In the diagram to the right, 6 is the *y*-intercept, expressed by the ordered pair (0,6).

The *x*-intercept is expressed using the ordered pair $(x, 0)$, where *x* is the point where the line hits the *x*-axis. In the diagram to the right, the *x*-intercept is −4, and is expressed by the ordered pair (−4, 0).

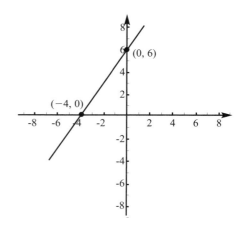

Slope-Intercept Equation: $y = mx + b$

All lines can be written as equations in the form $y = mx + b$, where m represents the slope of the line and b represents the y-intercept of the line. Some examples:

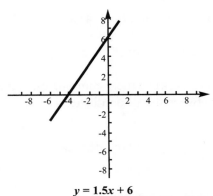

$y = 1.5x + 6$
The slope of the line is 1.5 (positive).
The y-intercept of the line is 6.

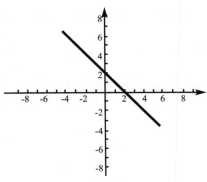

$y = -1x + 2$
The slope of the line is -1 (negative).
The y-intercept of the line is 2.

Vertical lines take the form $x =$ a number. Horizontal lines take the form $y =$ a number.

Note that not all line equations are written in the form $y = mx + b$. In such cases, rewrite the equation so that it is expressed in the slope-intercept form. For example:

What is the slope-intercept form for a line with the equation $6x + 3y = 18$?

Rewrite the equation by solving for y as follows:

$6x + 3y = 18$
$\quad 3y = 18 - 6x$ (Subtract $6x$ from both sides)
$\quad\; y = 6 - 2x$ (Divide both sides by 3)
$\quad\; y = -2x + 6$ (Rewrite in $y = mx + b$ form)

Horizontal and Vertical Lines

Horizontal and vertical lines are not expressed in the $y = mx + b$ form. Instead, they are expressed as simple, one-variable equations.

Horizontal lines are expressed in the form:
$\quad y =$ some number, such as $y = 3$ or $y = 5$.
Vertical lines are expressed in the form:
$\quad x =$ some number, such as $x = 4$ or $x = 7$.

All the points on a vertical line have the same x-coordinate, which is why its equation is defined only by x. Likewise, all the points on a horizontal line have the same y-coordinate, which is why its equation is defined only by y.

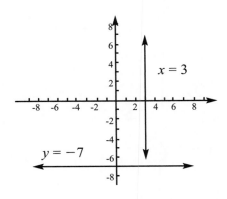

$x = 3$

$y = -7$

Step by Step: From 2 Points to a Line

If you are given any two points on a line, you should be able to write an equation for that line in the form $y = mx + b$. Here is the step-by-step method:

Find the equation of the line containing the points (3, 4) and (5, −2).

FIRST: Find the slope of the line by calculating the rise over the run.

The rise is determined by finding the difference between the y-coordinates, while the run is determined by finding the difference between the x-coordinates.

To find the equation of a line, you should start by finding its slope.

$$\frac{\text{rise}}{\text{run}} = \frac{y_1 - y_2}{x_1 - x_2} = \frac{-2 - 4}{5 - 3} = \frac{-6}{2} = -3$$ The slope of the line is negative three.

SECOND: Plug the slope in for m in the slope-intercept equation.

$$y = -3x + b$$

THIRD: Solve for b, the y-intercept, by plugging one of the ordered pairs into the equation.

Plugging the point (3, 4) into the equation (3 for x and 4 for y) yields the following:

$$4 = -3(3) + b$$
$$4 = -9 + b$$ The y-intercept of the line is 13.
$$b = 13$$

FOURTH: Write the equation in the form $y = mx + b$.

$$y = -3x + 13$$ This is the equation of the line.

Note that sometimes the GMAT will only give you one point on the line, along with the y-intercept. This is the same thing as giving you two points on the line, because the y-intercept is a point! A y-intercept of 4 is the same as the ordered pair (0, 4).

The Distance Between 2 Points

The distance between any two points in the coordinate plane can be calculated by using the Pythagorean Theorem. For example:

What is the distance between the points (1, 3) and (7, −5)?

(1) Draw a right triangle connecting the points.

(2) Find the two legs of the triangle by calculating the rise and the run.

The *y*-coordinate changes from 3 to −5, a difference of 8 (the vertical leg).

The *x*-coordinate changes from 1 to 7, a difference of 6 (the horizontal leg).

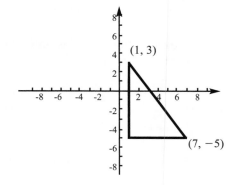

Draw a right triangle to find the distance between two points.

(3) Use the Pythagorean Theorem to calculate the length of the diagonal, which is the distance between the points.

$$6^2 + 8^2 = c^2$$
$$36 + 64 = c^2$$
$$100 = c^2$$
$$c = 10$$

The distance between the 2 points is 10 units.

Positive and Negative Quadrants

There are four quadrants in the coordinate plane, as shown in the diagram below.

Quadrant I contains only those points with a **positive** *x*-coordinate & a **positive** *y*-coordinate.

Quadrant II contains only those points with a **negative** *x*-coordinate & a **positive** *y*-coordinate.

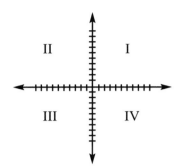

Quadrant III contains only those points with a **negative** *x*-coordinate & a **negative** *y*-coordinate.

Quadrant IV contains only those points with a **positive** *x*-coordinate & a **negative** *y*-coordinate.

You do not need to memorize the numbers of the quadrants. The numbers will always be provided for you.

The GMAT sometimes asks you to determine which quadrants a given line passes through. For example:

Which quadrants does the line 2*x* + *y* = 5 pass through?

(1) First, rewrite the line in the form $y = mx + b$.

$$2x + y = 5$$
$$y = 5 - 2x$$
$$y = -2x + 5$$

(2) Then, find two points on your line by setting *x* and *y* equal to zero. These are the *x*- and *y*- intercepts.

$x = 0$	$y = 0$
$y = -2x + 5$	$0 = -2x + 5$
$y = -2(0) + 5$	$2x = 5$
$y = 5$	$x = 2.5$

The points (0, 5) and (2.5, 0) are both on the line.

(3) Finally, sketch the line, using the points you have identified.

If you plot (0, 5) and (2.5, 0) on the coordinate plane, you can connect them to see the position of the line.

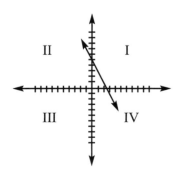

The line passes through quadrants I, II, and IV.

Perpendicular Bisectors

The perpendicular bisector of a line segment forms a 90° angle with the segment and divides the segment exactly in half. Questions about perpendicular bisectors are rare on the GMAT, but they do appear occasionally.

> **If the coordinates of A are (2, 2) and the coordinates of B are (0,−2), what is the equation of the perpendicular bisector of segment AB?**

The key to solving perpendicular bisector problems is remembering this property: the perpendicular bisector has the negative inverse slope of the line segment it bisects.

(1) Find the slope of segment AB.

$$\text{slope} = \frac{\text{rise}}{\text{run}} = \frac{y_1 - y_2}{x_1 - x_2} = \frac{2 - (-2)}{2 - 0} = \frac{4}{2} = 2$$

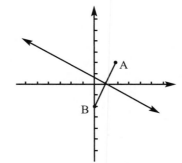

The slope of AB is 2.

Perpendicular lines have negative inverse slopes.

(2) Find the slope of the perpendicular bisector of AB.

Since perpendicular lines have negative inverse slopes, flip the fraction and change the sign.

The slope of the perpendicular bisector of AB is $-\frac{1}{2}$.

Now we know that the equation of the perpendicular bisector has the following form:

$$y = -\frac{1}{2}x + b$$

However, we still need to find the value of b (the y-intercept). To do this, we will need to find one point on the perpendicular bisector, and plug the coordinates of this point into the equation above.

(3) Find the midpoint of *AB*.

The perpendicular bisector passes through the midpoint of *AB*. Thus, if we find the midpoint of *AB*, we will have found a point on the perpendicular bisector. Organize a chart such as the one shown below to find the coordinates of the midpoint. Simply write the *x*- and *y*-coordinates of *A* and *B*. The coordinates of the midpoint will be the numbers right in between each pair of *x*- and *y*-coordinates. In other words, the *x*-coordinate of the midpoint is the <u>average</u> of the *x*-coordinates of *A* and *B*; likewise, the *y*-coordinate of the midpoint is the average of the *y*-coordinates of *A* and *B*.

	x	*y*
A	2	2
Midpoint	**1**	**0**
B	0	−2

> To find the midpoint of a line segment, find the midpoints of the *x*- and *y*- coordinates separately.

(4) Put the information together.

To find the value of *b* (the *y*-intercept), substitute the coordinates of the midpoint for *x* and *y*.

$$0 = -\frac{1}{2}(1) + b$$

$$b = \frac{1}{2}$$

The perpendicular bisector of segment *AB* has the equation: $y = -\frac{1}{2}x + \frac{1}{2}$.

Problem Set

1.   A line has the equation $y = 3x + 7$. At which point will this line intersect the y-axis?

2.   A line has the equation $x = \dfrac{y}{80} - 20$. At which point will this line intersect the x-axis?

3   A line has the equation $x = -2y + z$. If $(3, 2)$ is a point on the line, what is z?

4.   What are the equations for the four lines that form the
        boundaries of the shaded area in the figure shown?

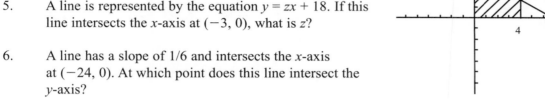

5.   A line is represented by the equation $y = zx + 18$. If this
        line intersects the x-axis at $(-3, 0)$, what is z?

6.   A line has a slope of $1/6$ and intersects the x-axis
        at $(-24, 0)$. At which point does this line intersect the
        y-axis?

7.   A line has a slope of $3/4$ and intersects the point $(-12, -39)$. At which point does this
        line intersect the x-axis?

8.   The line represented by the equation $y = x$ is the perpendicular bisector of line segment
        AB. If A has the coordinates $(-3, 3)$, what are the coordinates of B?

9.   The line represented by the equation $y = -2x + 6$ is the perpendicular bisector of the
        line segment AB. If A has the coordinates $(7, 2)$, what are the coordinates for B?

10.   What are the coordinates for the point on Line AB (see figure)
        that is three times as far from A as from B, and that is in
        between points A and B?

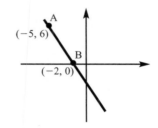

11.   Which quadrants, if any, do not contain any points on the line
        represented by $x - y = 18$?

12.   Which quadrants, if any, do not contain any points on the line represented by $x = 10y$?

13.   Which quadrants, if any, contain points on the line $y = \dfrac{x}{1000} + 1{,}000{,}000$?

14.   Which quadrants, if any, contain points on the line represented by $x + 18 = 2y$?

15. What is the equation of the line shown to the right?

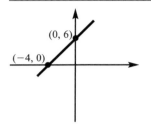

1. **(0, 7):** A line intersects the y-axis at the y-intercept. Since this equation is written in slope-intercept form, the y-intercept is easy to identify: 7. Thus, the line intersects the y-axis at the point (0, 7).

2. **(−20, 0)** : A line intersects the x-axis at the x-intercept, or when the y-coordinate is equal to zero. Substitute zero for y and solve for x:
$$x = 0 - 20$$
$$x = -20$$

3. **7:** Substitute the coordinates (3, 2) for x and y and solve for z.
$$3 = -2(2) + z$$
$$3 = -4 + z$$
$$z = 7$$

4. $x = 0$, $x = 4$, $y = 0$, **and** $y = -\dfrac{1}{2}x + 4$**:**

The shaded area is bounded by 2 vertical lines: $x = 0$ AND $x = 4$. Notice that all the points on each line share the same x-coordinate. The shaded area is bounded by 1 horizontal line, the x-axis. The equation for the x-axis is $y = 0$. Finally, the shaded area is bounded by a slanted line. To find the equation of this line, first calculate the slope, using two points on the line: (0, 4) and (4, 2).

$$\text{slope} = \frac{\text{rise}}{\text{run}} = \frac{4-2}{0-4} = \frac{2}{-4} = -\frac{1}{2}$$

We can read the y-intercept from the graph; it is the point at which the line crosses the y-axis, or 4.

Therefore, the equation of this line is $y = -\dfrac{1}{2}x + 4$.

5. **6:** Substitute the coordinates (3, 2) for x and y and solve for z.
$$0 = z(-3) + 18$$
$$3z = 18$$
$$z = 6$$

6. **(0, 4):** Use the information given to find the equation of the line:

$$y = \frac{1}{6}x + b$$

$$0 = \frac{1}{6}(-24) + b$$

$$0 = -4 + b$$
$$b = 4$$

The variable b represents the y-intercept. Therefore, the line intersects the y-axis at (0, 4).

7. **(40, 0):** Use the information given to find the equation of the line:

$$y = \frac{3}{4}x + b$$

$$-39 = \frac{3}{4}(-12) + b$$

$$-39 = -9 + b$$
$$b = -30$$

The line intersects the x-axis when $y = 0$. Set y equal to zero and solve for x:

$$0 = \frac{3}{4}x - 30$$

$$\frac{3}{4}x = 30$$

$$x = 40$$

The line intersects the x-axis at $(0, 40)$.

8. **(3, −3):** Perpendicular lines have negative inverse slopes. Therefore, if $y = x$ is perpendicular to segment AB, we know that the slope of the perpendicular bisector is 1, and therefore the slope of segment AB is -1. The line containing segment AB takes the form of $y = -x + b$. To find the value of b, substitute the coordinates of A, $(-3, 3)$, into the equation:

$$3 = -(-3) + b$$
$$b = 0$$

The line containing segment AB is $y = -x$.

Find the point at which the perpendicular bisector intersects AB by setting the two equations, $y = x$ and $y = -x$, equal to each other:

$$x = -x$$
$$x = 0;\ y = 0$$

The two lines intersect at $(0, 0)$, which is the midpoint of AB.

Use a chart to find the coordinates of B.

	x	y
A	−3	3
Midpoint	0	0
B	**3**	**−3**

*Manhattan*GMAT°Prep
the new standard

9. **(−1, −2):** If $y = -2x + 6$ is the perpendicular bisector of segment AB, then the line containing segment AB must have a slope of .5 (the negative inverse of −2). We can represent this line with the equation $y = .5x + b$. Substitute the coordinates (7, 2) into the equation to find the value of b.

$$2 = .5(7) + b.$$
$$b = -1.5$$

The line containing AB is $y = .5x − 1.5$.

Find the point at which the perpendicular bisector intersects AB by setting the two equations, $y = -2x + 6$ and $y = .5x − 1.5$, equal to each other.

$$-2x + 6 = .5x − 1.5$$
$$2.5x = 7.5$$
$$x = 3; y = 0$$

The two lines intersect at (3, 0), which is the midpoint of AB.

	x	y
A	7	2
Midpoint	3	0
B	**−1**	**−2**

Use a chart to find the coordinates of B.

10. **(−2.75, 1.5):** The point in question is 3 times farther from A than it is from B. We can represent this fact by labeling the point $3x$ units from A and x units from B, as shown, giving us a total distance of $4x$ between the two points. If we drop vertical lines from the point and from A to the x-axis, we get 2 similar triangles, the smaller of which is a quarter of the larger. (We can get this relationship from the fact that the larger triangle's hypotenuse is 4 times larger than the hypotenuse of the smaller triangle.)

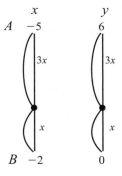

The horizontal distance between points A and B is 3 units (from −2 to −5). Therefore, $4x = 3$, and $x = .75$. The horizontal distance from B to the point is x, or .75 units. The x-coordinate of the point is .75 away from −2, or −2.75.

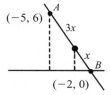

The vertical distance between points A and B is 6 units (from 0 to 6). Therefore, $4x = 6$, and $x = 1.5$. The vertical distance from B to the point is x, or 1.5 units. The y-coordinate of the point is 1.5 away from 0, or 1.5.

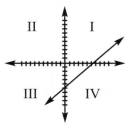

11. **II:** First, rewrite the line in slope-intercept form:

$$y = x − 18$$

Find the intercepts by setting x to zero and y to zero:

$$y = 0 − 18 \qquad\qquad 0 = x − 18$$
$$y = -18 \qquad\qquad x = 18$$

Plot the points: (0, −18), and (18, 0). From the sketch, we can see that the line does not pass through quadrant II.

12. **II and IV:** First, rewrite the line in slope-intercept form:

$$y = \frac{x}{10}$$

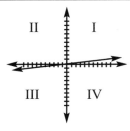

Notice from the equation that the y-intercept of the line is $(0,0)$. This means that the line crosses the y-intercept at the origin, so the x- and y-intercepts are the same. To find another point on the line, substitute any convenient number for x; in this case, 10 would be a convenient, or "smart," number.

$$y = \frac{10}{10} = 1 \qquad \text{The point } (10, 1) \text{ is on the line.}$$

Plot the points: $(0, 0)$ and $(10, 1)$. From the sketch, we can see that the line does not pass through quadrants II and IV.

13. **I, II, and III:** First, rewrite the line in slope-intercept form:

$$y = \frac{x}{1000} + 1{,}000{,}000$$

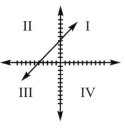

Find the intercepts by setting x to zero and y to zero:

$$0 = \frac{x}{1000} + 1{,}000{,}000 \qquad\qquad y = \frac{0}{1000} + 1{,}000{,}000$$

$$x = -1{,}000{,}000{,}000 \qquad\qquad y = 1{,}000{,}000$$

Plot the points: $(-1{,}000{,}000{,}000, 0)$ and $(0, 1{,}000{,}000)$. From the sketch, we can see that the line passes through quadrants I, II, and III.

14. **I, II, and III:** First, rewrite the line in slope-intercept form:

$$y = \frac{x}{2} + 9$$

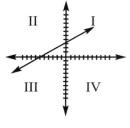

Find the intercepts by setting x to zero and y to zero:

$$0 = \frac{x}{2} + 9 \qquad\qquad y = \frac{0}{2} + 9$$

$$x = -18 \qquad\qquad y = 9$$

Plot the points: $(-18, 0)$ and $(0, 9)$. From the sketch, we can see that the line passes through quadrants I, II, and III.

15. $y = \dfrac{3}{2}x + 6$: First, calculate the slope of the line:

$$\text{slope} = \frac{\text{rise}}{\text{run}} = \frac{6 - 0}{0 - (-4)} = \frac{6}{4} = \frac{3}{2}$$

We can see from the graph that the line crosses the y-axis at $(0,6)$. The equation of the line is:

$$y = \frac{3}{2}x + 6$$

Chapter 6
of
GEOMETRY

STRATEGIES FOR DATA SUFFICIENCY

In This Chapter . . .

- Rephrasing: Access Useful Formulas and Rules
- Sample Rephrasings for Challenging Problems

Rephrasing: Access Useful Formulas and Rules

Geometry data sufficiency problems require you to identify the rules and formulas of geometry. For example, if you are given a problem about a circle, you should immediately access the rules and formulas you know that involve circles:

> Area of a circle $= \pi r^2$
> Circumference of a circle $= 2\pi r$
> A central angle describes an arc that is proportional to a fractional part of 360°.
> An inscribed angle describes an arc that is proportional to a fractional part of 180°.

If *B* is the center of the circle to the right, what is the length of line segment *AC*?

(1) The area of sector *ABCD* is 4π
(2) The circumference of the circle is 8π

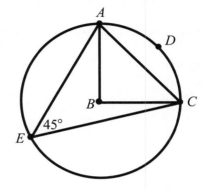

To solve Data Sufficiency problems in Geometry, apply the formulas and rules you have memorized.

A   Statement (1) ALONE is sufficient, but statement (2) alone is not sufficient.
B   Statement (2) ALONE is sufficient, but statement (1) alone is not sufficient.
C   BOTH statements TOGETHER are sufficient, but NEITHER statement ALONE is sufficient.
D   EACH statement ALONE is sufficient.
E   Statements (1) and (2) together are NOT sufficient.

Always start by focusing on the question itself. Do not jump to the statements before first attempting to rephrase the question into something easier.

The diagram shows that $\angle AEC$ (an inscribed angle that intercepts arc *ADC*) is 45°.

Therefore, using the relationship between an inscribed angle and a central angle, we know that $\angle ABC$ (a central angle that also intercepts arc *ADC*) must be 90°.

Thus, triangle *ABC* is a right triangle.

The question asks us to find the length of line segment *AC*, which is the hypotenuse of the right triangle. In order to find the length of hypotenuse *AC*, we must determine the length of the legs of the triangle. Notice that each leg of the triangle (*BA* and *BC*) is a radius of the circle.

Thus, this question can be rephrased: **What is the radius of the circle?**

The 2 circle formulas you should know that include the radius are the formula for area and the formula for circumference.

Statement (1) tells us the area of a sector of the circle. Since the sector described is one quarter of the circle, we will be able to determine the area of the entire circle using a proportion. Given the area of the circle, we can find the radius.

Thus, statement (1) alone is sufficient to answer our rephrased question.

Statement (2) tells us the circumference of the circle. Using the formula for circumference, we can determine the radius of the circle.

Thus, statement (2) alone is sufficient to answer our rephrased question.

The answer to this data sufficiency problem is (D): EACH statement ALONE is sufficient.

Try to determine whether each statement provides enough information to answer your *rephrased* question.

Rephrasing: Challenge Short Set

At the very end of this book, you will find lists of GEOMETRY problems that have appeared on past official GMAT exams. These lists reference problems from *The Official Guide for GMAT Review, 11th Edition* and *The Official Guide for GMAT Quantitative Review* (the questions contained therein are the property of The Graduate Management Admission Council, which is not affiliated in any way with Manhattan GMAT).

As you work through the Data Sufficiency problems listed at the end of this book, be sure to focus on *rephrasing*. If possible, try to *rephrase* each question into its simplest form *before* looking at the two statements. In order to rephrase, focus on figuring out the specific information that is absolutely necessary to answer the question. After rephrasing the question, you should also try to *rephrase* each of the two statements, if possible. Rephrase each statement by simplifying the given information into its most basic form.

In order to help you practice rephrasing, we have taken the most difficult Data Sufficiency problems on *The Official Guide* problem list (these are the problem numbers listed in the "Challenge Short Set" on page 97) and have provided you with our own sample rephrasings for each question and statement. In order to evaluate how effectively you are using the rephrasing strategy, you can compare your rephrased questions and statements to our own rephrasings that appear below. Questions and statements that are significantly rephrased appear in **bold**.

Rephrasings from *The Official Guide For GMAT Review, 11th Edition*

The questions and statements that appear below are only our *rephrasings*. The original questions and statements can be found by referencing the problem numbers below in the Data Sufficiency section of *The Official Guide for GMAT Review, 11th edition* (pages 278-290).

Note: Problem numbers preceded by "D" refer to questions in the Diagnostic Test chapter of *The Official Guide for GMAT Review, 11th edition* (pages 24-25).

D39. *x*-intercept is the point on line where $y = 0$.

   At point (x, 0) on line k, is x positive?

   (1) Slope = distance between any 2 points on line: $-5 = \dfrac{rise}{run} = \dfrac{y_2 - y_1}{x_2 - x_1}$

   Plug in two points on line k: (x, 0) and (-5, r)

   $$-5 = \frac{r - 0}{-5 - x} = \frac{r}{-5 - x}$$

   $$25 + 5x = r$$

   $$x = \frac{r - 25}{5}$$

   x is positive if r is greater than 25

   (2) $r > 0$

D48.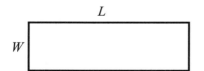

   What is $2L + 2W$?   OR   **What is $L + W$?**

   (1)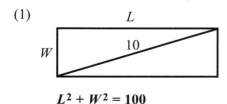

   $L^2 + W^2 = 100$

   (2) $LW = 48$

15.   Recall the signs of coordinates in each quadrant:

QUADRANT	a	b
I	positive	positive
II	negative	positive
III	negative	negative
IV	positive	negative

What are the signs of a and b?

(1) a is negative; b is positive

(2) a is negative; b is positive

38.   **Is the total thickness of the first 10 volumes less than or equal to x?**

(1) $x = 50$ centimeters

(2) 12 volumes are a total of 60 centimeters thick.

41.   **What is the diameter of each can?**

(1) $r = 4$
    $d = 8$

(2) $6d = 48$
    $d = 8$

51.   There are 180° in a triangle: $x + y + z = 180$
                                        $z = 180 - (x + y)$
       What is the value of $x + y$?

(1) $x + y = 139$

(2) $y + z = 108$

113.   **What is the length of one side of triangle D?**

(1) **The length of the height of triangle D is 3.**

(2) **The length of the base of triangle D is $\dfrac{8}{3}$.**

117. **What is the ratio of $\dfrac{KN}{MN}$?**

(1) $KM + MN = 15$

(2) $MN = 1.5(KN)$

$$\frac{KN}{MN} = \frac{1}{1.5}$$

136. $C = 2\pi r$

What is the radius?   OR

Arc lengths are determined by central angles.

Thus, the length of arc $XYZ = \dfrac{90}{360} = \dfrac{1}{4}$ of the circumference.

What is the length of arc XYZ?

(1) Triangle OXZ is a 45 - 45 - 90 triangle with sides in the ratio of $1 : 1 : \sqrt{2}$, and each of the shorter legs is a radius of the circle. Thus, the perimeter is $r + r + \sqrt{2}r$. Using the value for the perimeter given in statement (1), solve for the radius:

$r = 10$

(2) arc $XYZ = 5\pi$

140. The distance of a point to the origin can be determined with the Pythagorean Theorem.

Does $r^2 + s^2 = u^2 + v^2$?

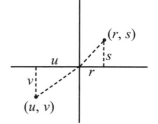

(1) $s = -r + 1$

(2) $v = 1 - s$ AND $u = 1 - r$

(COMBINED)
$v = 1 - (-r + 1)$ AND $u = 1 - r$
$v = r + 2$

Using substitution, we can answer the rephrased question.

*Manhattan*GMAT*Prep
the new standard

152.   The large triangle (*PQR*) is inscribed in a semi-circle, and its hypotenuse (*PR*) is the diameter of the semi-circle. Therefore, triangle *PQR* is a right triangle; its right angle is at point *Q*.

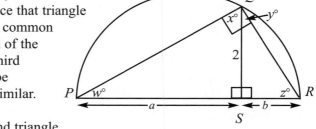

Now we have one large right triangle (*PQR*) and two small right triangles (*PSQ* and *RSQ*). Notice that triangle *PQR* and triangle *PSQ* share two angles in common (angle *w* and a right angle). Since the sum of the angles in any triangle is 180 degrees, the third angle in each of these triangles must also be congruent. Therefore, these triangles are similar.

The same logic applies for triangle *PQR* and triangle *RSQ*. These two triangles are similar as well.

Since the large triangle *PQR* is similar to both of the smaller triangles, *PSQ* and *RSQ*, then these two smaller triangles must also be similar to each other. Therefore, knowing any pair of corresponding sides will give us the proportions of the other pairs of corresponding sides.

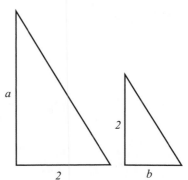

What is *a*?   OR   What is *b*?

(1) *a* = 4

(2) *b* = 1

Rephrasings from *The Official Guide for GMAT Quantitative Review*

The questions and statements that appear below are only our *rephrasings*. The original questions and statements can be found by referencing the problem numbers below in the Data Sufficiency section of *The Official Guide for GMAT Quantitative Review* (pages 149-157).

58. Circumference of a circle $= 2\pi r$

Number of rotations $= \dfrac{100}{2\pi r}$

What is the value of *r*?

(1) diameter $= 0.5$ meter

(2) speed $= 20$ rotations per minute

70. **What is the measure of angle *ABC*?   OR**
What are the measures of *ABX, XBY,* and *YBC*?

(1) $ABX = XBY$ **AND** $XBY = YBC$
   $ABX = XBY = YBC$

(2) $ABX = 40°$

87. TUV is a 45 - 45 - 90 right triangle. RUV is a 30 - 60 - 90 right triangle.
TU = RS

What is the length of the base of each of these triangles?   OR
What is the length of the hypotenuse these triangles share?   OR
(BEST): What is the length of any side in either triangle?
**Note that knowing 1 side allows us to solve for all other sides.

(1) TU = 10 m

(2) RV = 5 m

91. Let $r =$ the radius of the smaller region.
Let $R =$ the radius of the larger region.
What is *R*?

(1) $\pi r^2 + \pi R^2 = 90\pi$
   $r^2 + R^2 = 90$

(2) $R = 3r$

109.   **What is lw?**

(1) $l + w = 6$
   $(l + w)^2 = 36$
   $l^2 + 2lw + w^2 = 36$

(2) $l^2 + w^2 = 20$

(COMBINED)
$$
\begin{array}{r}
l^2 + 2lw + w^2 = 36 \\
-\ l^2 \quad\quad + w^2 = 20 \\
\hline
2lw \quad\quad = 16 \\
lw = 8
\end{array}
$$

117.   Name angles y and z as shown in the figure to the right.

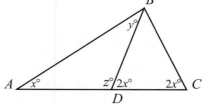

$2x + z = 180$	OR	$z = 180 - 2x$
$x + y + z = 180$	OR	$z = 180 - (x + y)$
Therefore, $2x = x + y$	OR	$x = y$. Thus, $AD = BD$.

We also know that $BD = BC$.
Therefore, $AD = BD = BC$.

What is the length of BC, BD, or AD?

(1) $AD = 6$

(2) $x = 36$

Chapter 7
of
GEOMETRY

OFFICIAL GUIDE
PROBLEM SETS

In This Chapter . . .

- Geometry Problem Solving List from *The Official Guides*
- Geometry Data Sufficiency List from *The Official Guides*

Practicing with REAL GMAT Problems

Now that you have completed your study of GEOMETRY, it is time to test your skills on problems that have actually appeared on real GMAT exams over the past several years.

The problem sets that follow are composed of questions from two books published by the Graduate Management Admission Council® (the organization that develops the official GMAT exam):

The Official Guide for GMAT Review, 11th Edition &
The Official Guide for GMAT Quantitative Review

These two books contain quantitative questions that have appeared on past official GMAT exams. (The questions contained therein are the property of The Graduate Management Admission Council, which is not affiliated in any way with Manhattan GMAT.)

Although the questions in the Official Guides have been "retired" (they will not appear on future official GMAT exams), they are great practice questions.

In order to help you practice effectively, we have categorized every problem in The Official Guides by topic and subtopic. On the following pages, you will find two categorized lists:

(1) **Problem Solving:** Lists all Problem Solving GEOMETRY questions contained in *The Official Guides* and categorizes them by subtopic.

(2) **Data Sufficiency:** Lists all Data Sufficiency GEOMETRY questions contained in *The Official Guides* and categorizes them by subtopic.

Note: Each book in Manhattan GMAT's 8-book preparation series contains its own *Official Guide* lists that pertain to the specific topic of that particular book. If you complete all the practice problems contained on the *Official Guide* lists in the back of each of the 8 Manhattan GMAT preparation books, you will have completed every single question published in *The Official Guides*. At that point, you should be ready to take your Official GMAT exam!

Problem Solving

from *The Official Guide for GMAT Review, 11th edition* (pages 20-23 & 152-186) and *The Official Guide for GMAT Quantitative Review* (pages 62-85)

Note: Problem numbers preceded by "D" refer to questions in the Diagnostic Test chapter of *The Official Guide for GMAT Review, 11th edition* (pages 20-23).

Solve each of the following problems in a notebook, making sure to demonstrate how you arrived at each answer by showing all of your work and computations. If you get stuck on a problem, look back at the GEOMETRY strategies and content contained in this guide to assist you.

CHALLENGE SHORT SET
This set contains the more difficult geometry problems from each of the content areas.
> *11th edition*: D10, D20, D22, 30, 36, 45, 60, 89, 152, 176, 191, 206, 226, 227, 238, 248
> *Quantitative Review*: 123, 139, 175

FULL PROBLEM SET
Polygons
> *11th edition*: 3, 13, 16, 105, 112, 134, 238
> *Quantitative Review*: 12, 22, 139, 175

Triangles and Diagonals
> *11th edition*: D19, 45, 145, 147, 152, 176, 222

Circles and Cylinders
> *11th edition*: D5, D20, D22, 30, 160, 191, 206
> *Quantitative Review*: 31, 141

Lines and Angles
> *11th edition*: D10, 51, 60, 226
> *Quantitative Review*: 28

Coordinate Plane
> *11th edition*: 7, 23, 36, 89, 199, 227, 248
> *Quantitative Review*: 19, 123

Data Sufficiency

from *The Official Guide for GMAT Review, 11th edition* (pages 24-25 & 278-290) and *The Official Guide for GMAT Quantitative Review* (pages 149-157)

Note: Problem numbers preceded by "D" refer to questions in the Diagnostic Test chapter of *The Official Guide for GMAT Review, 11th edition* (pages 24-25).

Solve each of the following problems in a notebook, making sure to demonstrate how you arrived at each answer by showing all of your work and computations. If you get stuck on a problem, look back at the GEOMETRY strategies and content contained in this guide to assist you.

Practice REPHRASING both the questions and the statements by using your knowledge of geometric formulas and concepts. The majority of data sufficiency problems can be rephrased; however, if you have difficulty rephrasing a problem, try testing numbers to solve it.

It is especially important that you familiarize yourself with the directions for data sufficiency problems, and that you memorize the 5 fixed answer choices that accompany all data sufficiency problems.

CHALLENGE SHORT SET
This set contains the more difficult geometry problems from each of the content areas.
> *11th edition*: D39, D48, 15, 38, 41, 51, 113, 117, 136, 140, 152
> *Quantitative Review*: 58, 70, 87, 91, 109, 117

FULL PROBLEM SET
Polygons
> *11th edition*: D48, 38, 47, 102, 117
> *Quantitative Review*: 4, 59, 84

Triangles and Diagonals
> *11th edition*: D28, 27, 32, 51, 66, 108, 113, 152
> *Quantitative Review*: 19, 64, 87, 109, 117

Circles and Cylinders
> *11th edition*: D36, 39, 41, 76, 86, 136
> *Quantitative Review*: 57, 58, 91, 95

Lines and Angles
> *11th edition*: 6, 23, 72
> *Quantitative Review*: 70

Coordinate Plane
> *11th edition*: D39, 15, 78, 85, 124, 140
> *Quantitative Review*: 14

To waive "Finance I" at Harvard Business School you must:
  (A) Be a CFA
  (B) Have prior coursework in finance
  (C) Have two years of relevant work experience in the financial sector
  (D) Pass a waiver exam
  (E) None of the above; one cannot waive core courses at HBS

What are the requirements of an Entrepreneurial Management major at the Wharton School?
  (1) Completion of 5 credit units (cu) that qualify for the major
  (2) Participation in the Wharton Business Plan Competition during the 2nd year of the MBA program

(A) Statement (1) ALONE is sufficient, but statement (2) alone is not sufficient.
(B) Statement (2) ALONE is sufficient, but statement (1) alone is not sufficient.
(C) BOTH statements TOGETHER are sufficient, but NEITHER statement ALONE is sufficient.
(D) EACH statement ALONE is sufficient.
(E) Statements (1) and (2) TOGETHER are NOT sufficient.

Once You Ace the GMAT, Get Ready to Ace Your Applications!

To make an informed decision in applying to a school—and to craft an effective application that demonstrates an appreciation of a program's unique merits—**it's crucial that you do your homework.** Clear Admit School Guides cut through the gloss of marketing materials to give you the hard facts about a program, and then put these school-specific details in context so you can see how programs compare. In the guides, you'll find detailed, comparative information on vital topics such as:

- The core curriculum and first-year experience
- Leading professors in key fields
- Student clubs and conferences
- Full-time job placement by industry and location
- Student demographics
- International and experiential learning programs
- Tuition, financial aid and scholarships
- Admissions deadlines and procedures

Now available for top schools including:
Chicago, Columbia, Harvard, Kellogg, MIT, Stanford, Tuck and Wharton

A time-saving source of comprehensive information, Clear Admit School Guides have been featured in *The Economist* and lauded by applicants, business school students and MBA graduates:

"Purchasing the Clear Admit HBS School Guide was one of best decisions I made. I visited HBS three times and have every book and pamphlet that covers the top business schools, but nothing can compare to the Clear Admit guides in offering up-to-date information on every aspect of the school's academic and social life that is not readily available on the school's website and brochures. Reading a Clear Admit School Guide gives an applicant the necessary, detailed school information to be competitive in the application process."
—An applicant to Harvard

"I want to tip my hat to the team at Clear Admit that put these guides together. I'm a recent graduate of Wharton's MBA program and remain active in the admissions process (serving as an alumni interviewer to evaluate applicants). I can't tell you how important it is for applicants to show genuine enthusiasm for Wharton and I think the Clear Admit School Guide for Wharton captures many of the important details, as well as the spirit of the school. **This sort of information is a must for the serious MBA applicant.**"
—A Wharton MBA graduate

Question #1: (e) and Question #2 (a)

www.clearadmit.com/schoolguides

contact us at mbaguides@clearadmit.com

Finally, a GMAT* prep guide series that goes beyond the basics.

Reading Comprehension, 2007 Edition
ISBN: 978-0-9790175-6-8
Retail: $26

Critical Reasoning, 2007 Edition
ISBN: 978-0-9790175-5-1
Retail: $26

Word Translations, 2007 Edition
ISBN: 978-0-9790175-3-7
Retail: $26

Number Properties, 2007 Edition
ISBN: 978-0-9790175-0-6
Retail: $26

Geometry, 2007 Edition
ISBN: 978-0-9790175-4-4
Retail: $26

Equations, Inequalities, & VIC's, 2007 Edition
ISBN: 978-0-9790175-2-0
Retail: $26

Sentence Correction, 2007 Edition
ISBN: 978-0-9790175-7-5
Retail: $26

Fractions, Decimals, & Percents, 2007 Edition
ISBN: 978-0-9790175-1-3
Retail: $26

Published by

Manhattan GMAT* Prep

 You get many more pages per topic than found in all-in-one tomes.

 Only buy those guides that address the specific skills you need to develop.

 Gain access to Online Practice GMAT* Exams & bonus question banks.

COMMENTS FROM GMAT TEST TAKERS:

Now Available at your local bookstore!

"Bravo, Manhattan GMAT! Bravo! The guides truly did not disappoint. All the guides are clear, concise, and well organized and explained things in a manner that made it possible to understand things the first time through without missing any of the important details."

"I've thumbed through a lot of books that don't even touch these. The fact that they're split up into components is immeasurably helpful. The set-up of each guide and the lists of past GMAT problems make for an incredibly thorough and easy to follow study path"

*GMAT and GMAC are registered trademarks of the Graduate Management Admission Council which neither sponsors nor endorses this product.

S0-ADZ-972

RELEASING AN
INDEPENDENT
RECORD

RELEASING AN

HOW TO SUCCESSFULLY START AND RUN

INDEPENDENT

YOUR OWN RECORD LABEL

RECORD

SIXTH EDITION

BY GARY HUSTWIT

ROCKPRESS PUBLISHING

P.O.BOX 99090 SAN DIEGO CA 92169 USA

© 1998 Rockpress Publishing Company
All rights reserved

First printing

ISBN 1-884615-18-X

All rights reserved. No part of this publication may be reproduced, stored in a
retrieval system, or transmitted, in any form or by any means, electronic, mechanical,
photocopying, recording, or otherwise, without the prior written permission of the
copyright holder.

This publication is designed to provide accurate and authoritative information in
regard to the subject matter covered. It is sold with the understanding that the publisher is not engaged in rendering legal, accounting, or other professional service. If
legal advice or other expert assistance is required, the services of a competent professional person should be sought.

Every effort has been made to provide correct information, however, the publisher
does not guarantee the accuracy of the listings and does not assume responsibility
for listings included in or omitted from this publication. Listings in this publication do
not constitute an endorsement or recommendation from the publisher, except
where noted.

Cover and book design by Gary Hustwit.
Cover photo of Lucy's Fur Coat by Mark Waters.

Special thanks to: Denise Hustwit, William Hustwit, Donna Wingate, Paige Cowett,
Myka Carrol, Brad Smith, Hal Leonard Publishing, Consortium, Apple Computer,
aMINIATURE, SST Records, Cargo Records, Restless Records, The Charms.

Printed in the USA.

Contents

Introduction

Releasing An Independent Record is about exactly that: recording, manufacturing, distributing and selling music, yours or other people's. Perhaps you want to release music without having to bend to the creative whims of someone else's company. This book is for you. Maybe you're looking for MTV corporate mega-stardom, and you want to release a record to attract the attention of major labels. This book is for you. You may just want to sell your music in your region to fans and friends, or you may want to form a huge record label with global distribution. In either case, *Releasing an Independent Record* will give you valuable advice and instructions on how to achieve your goals.

What's In This Book?

This book is designed to give you step-by-step information on how to release an album, cassette or compact disc on a nationwide level. It is arranged into sections, each dealing with a topic involved in the process of releasing a record. Since I have no idea how much you know about this subject, or how far along you are with your own project, this book has been written for the person who is starting from scratch, with no previous knowledge of the music industry. Feel free to skip around the sections that do or do not apply to your particular situation. If you're starting from scratch, you should probably read the sections in order.

Throughout this book, I will be using the term "record" to signify all music formats: vinyl LPs & 7"s, cassettes, CDs, whatever. Here is a brief overview of the topics covered in this book:

Starting Your Label

How to deal with the business aspects of setting up your label. Business licenses, fictitious name statements, etc.

Recording & Production

This section covers recording your music, deciding on which format to release it, and arranging for the manufacture of your products. It also includes the copyright forms you need to protect your music and a list of record, tape and CD manufacturers.

Publishing & Performance Rights

Information on publishing, performance and mechanical rights and a directory of music publishers.

The Press

Reviews, good or bad, are free advertising. This section includes sample press releases, "one-sheets" and a list of music publications.

Distribution

Distributors will put your records in stores all over the country, but will they pay you? This section includes a list of independent distributors and store chain buyers.

Sales

Mail order? Direct to store? Selling your records to individual stores and consumers is tedious, but it's the best way to make your money back and reach your audience. Included is a directory of independent record stores.

Advertising

Advertisements will sell records and increase interest in your record. This chapter shows how to represent your release in print, and gives samples of good independent ads.

The Internet

Essentials about the Internet, and ways you can use it to promote your music.

Radio

Getting radio airplay is an important part of promoting your release, building a following and setting up tours. Here's some advice on how to get them to play your record.

Touring

Touring is the best promotional tool an independent band has. This section features instructions on how to plan a tour and includes a list of booking agents.

Record Label Directory

A list of major and independent labels in the USA, and guidelines for licensing your records and releasing other people's music.

Sample Contracts

A sample management agreement and an independent label recording contract.

A Word of Advice...

Forget sending demo tapes to major labels in an attempt to get signed. It's a waste of your time and money. It's physically impossible for them to listen to all the tapes they get sent, and, at best, some high school intern will listen to about five seconds of your tape and toss it in the trash. The best way for you to gain recognition is to become your own record label, release your own record, and send it to the contacts in this book. These are the addresses and phone numbers of people and companies who will be vital to the success of your release. Use them. You'll receive radio airplay, get some reviews, get your records into stores across the country, and create a nationwide audience.

The major labels are constantly monitoring the independent scene, looking for new bands. If your goal is to get signed by a major label, you'll have a much better chance if your band is successful in the independent industry, especially in college radio. The college charts serve as scouting lists for the major label A&R people. If you receive attention in the independent market, you'll have these people coming to you, like it or not.

Obviously, sending out records all over the country costs money, as does advertising, manufacturing, printing, phone bills, etc. When you do release your record, only give away copies to people who can actually help the band; the press, club bookers, industry people. I know it's hard to get money out of your friends, but you will have invested a lot of your own money in the project, and you need to recoup this money if you want to keep your record label going.

The sad but true fact is that the more money you've got, the more exposure you can give your music. This book was created in an attempt to help eliminate this rule, but you will still need money for postage and phone calls. If you have access to a postage machine or a company phone, you're in luck. The bottom line is to get your music out there, whatever the cost. If you don't have much money, but you believe in your music, you'll eventually succeed.

Believe in Your "Product"

Which brings us to the most important aspect of starting your own record label: belief in your product. If you're not enthusiastic and persistent about your record, then no one else will be. This book is not a guarantee of success, it is a tool for you to use to gain recognition for your music. It is intended to steer you through the proper channels to get your record seen, heard, reviewed and bought. If musical creativity is to survive, musicians must be able to release their own music, free from corporate censorship and control. By releasing your own records, you're helping keep the future of music out of the hands of hardened bureaucrats and into the hands of musicians, where it belongs.

Rockpress is always trying to make this book better by including new information, so if you have any suggestions, comments or would like to be included in one of our mailing lists, please write us. Thank you and good luck.

–Gary Hustwit

Starting Your Label

There are a few things you should take care of before you start releasing records. First, decide on a name for your record company (if you don't already have one) and get a business license. If your city won't allow you to run a business from your home address due to zoning, rent out a P.O. Box (suite) from a postal services business (Mail Boxes, Etc., etc.). Renting from the U.S. Post Office is cheaper, but you can't physically run a business from a Post Office Box. You can run one from a suite address, though, because in the eyes of the government you are actually renting out an office space. The downside to a suite address is that if you ever move, you have to keep paying monthly box rental and forwarding costs for as long as you want to keep receiving mail at your old address. Anyway, get a business license and then file a fictitious name statement at your county clerk's office in your record company's name, and if you're in a band, in your band's name also.

DBA Accounts

You should then open a DBA (Doing Business As) bank account; you may be able to modify your existing bank account by adding your business name to it. This enables you to cash checks made out to the label name; the type of checks you'll be getting from mail order customers, distributors, record stores, clubs, etc.

Sales Tax

The final step in setting up your business is obtaining a Resale Permit from your state's Board of Equalization. This allows you to buy the products that you intend to resell (the CDs you'll be making, posters, your catalogs, stickers, t-shirts, etc) without paying sales tax.

If you sell your records wholesale, either to a store or a distributor, these sales are exempt from sales tax. But, when you sell a record directly to a fan in your state, either in person or by mail, you are required to charge sales tax, and pay this tax to the Board of Equalization (usually annually). Again, sales tax does not apply when you're selling at wholesale, or if the sales are to a customer outside of your state. When you get your permit, they'll give you the sales tax guidelines for your state in detail.

You should also have letterhead and business cards printed, and get a rubber stamp with the label name and address. Depending on what formats you release, you'll need a ton of different sized envelopes, and stamping the return address is easier than having them printed or writing it by hand.

Bulk Mail

If you are going to be sending out large amounts of mail (and you *will* be), get a bulk rate permit from your post office. If you send out more than 200 pieces of mail at a time, you'll save some money.

Speaking of saving, save your receipts! If you're going to declare income from your band or label at tax time, you'll need receipts to document your deductions. If you start selling records in serious volume, definitely find a good accountant. Again,

All of the steps above, including the business license and fictitious name statement, should cost between $100 & $300. Having a professional (somewhat) look to your company can benefit it in many ways. It will give it viability and make people want to give you their hard-earned cash in exchange for your records.

You'll also need to set up some sort of publishing company for your label and pick a performance rights organization (see chapter on this elsewhere in this book).

The Outline

Here is a basic outline of the steps you'll be taking during the production and release of your record if you're starting from scratch. This is just a rough framework; depending on your situation, you may or may not be taking all of these steps.

1. **Establish business.**
2. **Record songs.**
3. **Send tape of songs and lyric sheets to Library of Congress.**
4. **Create artwork.**
5. **Have negatives or color separations made of the artwork (unless you're going to have the pressing plant do these)**
6. **Send master tape and art negatives to pressing plant.**
7. **Receive finished product.**
8. **Send out finished release and bio or one-sheet to the press.**
9. **Start selling records locally.**
10. **Send out to college radio.**
11. **Advertise in trades and consumer magazines, and on the Internet.**
12. **Obtain distribution & start selling direct to stores.**
13. **Tour.**
14. **Go to Step 2.**

Steps 10 through 13 should be done as close together as possible, even simultaneously, if you have the resources.

The Ideal Situation

The goal of every independent band or label is to have the press reviews coming out when the records get to the stores while radio is playing it and you're band is touring. Try to get as close as possible to this "holy grail" of indie music.

Recording & Production

Basement 4-track or 48-track to digital? Whatever you can afford. If you're truly happy with your recording, no matter what it was recorded on, release it. Poor recording quality will really stand out when transferred to a record, (especially CDs) but if that's your sound, fine. There have been a lot of technological advances recently, especially in the digital recording area, and an 8-track ADAT machine can make some very nice-sounding recordings. Compare your recording to other independent or major label releases. If you think it stands up to them, press it.

Copyrighting

After you've recorded your music, send a cassette and lyric sheet to the Library of Congress for copyright registration. Technically, the minute you record something it's considered copyrighted, but copyright registration is a way to establish the date of your copyright in case any future legal issues arise.

Following this chapter is an SR copyright form that you can cut out and use to register your material. Just follow the instructions to fill it out and send it, along with $20, to the Library of Congress. Before you fill it out, make copies of the form (double-sided) to use on later recording projects, or call the Library of Congress copyright forms hotline at 202-707-9100. This is a 24-hour recorded message that lets you leave your address and what forms you'd like sent to you. The forms are free, and if you want more copyright information, you can call 202-707-3000. You can copyright a whole group of songs by filing them as a "body of work" ("The Songs of Joe Blow, Volume One").

Trademarking

If you want to register your band or record label name as a trademark, you'll need to either talk to a trademark attorney or get a book on the subject. Most Public Libraries have computers that are hooked in to the national trademark database; this is a quick way to find out if your band or label name has been taken. Trademarking your name isn't cheap, but if you're serious about your band or label you should look into it. I've heard too many stories about bands having to change their names because another group in some other city had it as well. Usually, registering a trademark will cost you a few hundred dollars.

Deciding on a Format

What format should you release? This is a really tough question. CDs have become the dominant format, and you probably can't go wrong with a CD-only release. If you can afford it, do CDs and cassettes, and maybe even vinyl if your musical style warrants it. Here are some pros and cons to help you decide:

7" and 12" Vinyl

Pros: Sales still good for alternative, punk and dance music. Collectable. 7" are inexpensive to make. Sound quality good when new. 7" singles are a cheap way for a consumer check out new music. College radio still plays it.

Cons: Hardly anyone's making or buying turntables. CDs and cassettes sell better. Warpage. There are only a few distributors that will buy vinyl from unknown artists.

Cassettes

Pros: Good sales for all styles of music. Easy to bring and sell on tour. Can record over it. Car cassette decks are prevalent. Relatively inexpensive to make.

Cons: Poor sound quality. Short lifespan. Radio won't play them.

Compact Discs

Pros: Outsells all other formats. Biggest profit for your label. Easy to bring and sell on tour. Excellent (potential) sound quality. Friends think you've "made it." They make good coasters.

Cons: Expensive at retail. Consumers afraid of spending big $$$ on unknown band. Too easy for reviewers and DJs to trade for $$$ at local used CD store.

It's a decision that depends on your individual circumstances. If you can only afford to record a few songs, (or that's all you've written) then put out either a 7" single or a cassette. I think that CDs are a waste unless you have (at least close to) a full album's worth of material, unless you've got major money and want to send CD singles to radio.

If you want to make a nationwide splash, and you've got enough money, make CDs and cassettes, and vinyl as well if your musical style warrants it.

Manufacturing

As far as the actual manufacturing goes, on the next several pages is a list of record, tape, and CD masterers and manufacturers, or maybe you've already had records made before. These companies are a great source of information regarding record manufacturing, so call them and get their brochures and price lists. Most manufacturers offer packages that include mastering, artwork negatives, printing and pressing / duplication. If you don't have any previous experience in these fields, go for the package deal.

In most cases, you'll be providing the manufacturer with a DAT or a CD master of your recording, although most still accept 1/4 or 1/2 inch analog master tapes. Do you have a back-up copy of your master? You'd better have.

Estimating Production Time

A good rule of thumb is to take however long the pressing plant says your record will take to make, and add a few weeks to it. In other words, don't plan a record release party for the day after they tell you it should be ready. There are many situations that can and will occur that can add weeks (or months) to your project. You don't like how the test pressings sound, or the colors in the artwork aren't right, etc.

The fastest and probably the cheapest way to release your own record is to go to a tape duplicator and have a few hundred cassettes made. Many of these companies have package deals that include a label for the tape and a J-card insert for the case. This type of release will only be effective as a demo tape or just to sell at shows and to friends. Don't plan on selling these to distributors.

An even faster and even cheaper way is to get your sister's dual-dubbing cassette player and start dubbing them off. I have to admit, I've seen some really interesting tapes produced this way, but of course the sound quality is not going to be that good, so unless you're going for the lo-fi sound, forget it. The high-tech equivalent of this is using a recordable CD-ROM drive to burn individual CDs. At about $10 per disc, this could get very expensive, but if you only need a few copies it's an option.

Shipping Tips

Pressing plants usually sell cardboard mailers or envelopes for send-out purposes at decent prices. If you're sending vinyl, you must either use a cardboard mailer or put a cardboard insert in your envelope, or they'll get warped or broken every time. For CDs, use those bubble envelopes, don't just stick them in plain manilla-type envelopes. You'd be surprised how easily those CD jewel cases break.

While we're on the subject of send-outs, always ask for the special fourth class sound recording rate when you're mailing music. It's usually much cheaper than first class, and it gets anywhere in the country in about a week.

Artwork

Use your imagination. Some stores won't carry "obscene" or "racist" art or other artwork they deem controversial, but hey, it's your record. The more colors you want, the more it'll cost, for both printing and negatives.

Some pressing plants have package deals that include color separations and/or negatives, but usually it's usually cheaper to get a graphic designer (check your Yellow Pages) or a friend with a computer to layout the album digitally and have the negs output at a service bureau. You could also go to a lithographic negative company, but these days it's cheaper and easier to use a Macintosh for this sort of thing. With software like Adobe Photoshop and Quark XPress, you can easily create artwork that can be output to negatives and used for your project. If you've got no artistic talent visually, for god's sake get a "real" graphic designer to do the layout!

Get the printing specs from the pressing plant and give them to your graphics person, or have one call the other and let them work it out. The more colors you want on your covers, the more it'll cost. Full-color printing is known as four-color printing, because even the most colorful photo can be broken down into different mixes of four primary colors. Try using creative xeroxing tactics, or black & white photos with spot colors for low budget, interesting-looking graphics.

Barcodes

Should you put barcodes (Universal Product Codes) on your releases? The answer depends on the scale on which you plan to release them. If you want to get your records into the big retail chains, you're going to have to put barcodes on them. If you plan to sell them through independent stores, at shows, or to small distributors, you probably don't need them. If you manufacture your products without barcodes, then decide that you need them, you can always have small stickers made with the barcode on them. Many distributors will even put their own barcode stickers on your products (some may charge you for this, though). It costs about $300 to get registered for barcodes; for more information call the Uniform Code Council at 937-435-3870.

When you get the finished product back, you can proceed to your press send-out, trying to get radio airplay, sales and distribution. This is also time to start the advance publicity for your release.

Record, Tape & Compact Disc Manufacturers

A & R Record & Tape (TX)
214-741-2027
CD, cassette, vinyl mastering and manufacturing

ASR Recording Services of California
800-852-3124

A to Z Audio (OH)
216-333-0040

Abbey Tape Duplicators (CA)
818-882-5210

ADA
888-rubber-8
CD mastering, duplication

Alberti Record Manuf. Co. (CA)
213-283-5446
Vinyl pressing

Allied Audio (TN)
615-255-1000
Tape duplication

Alshire International (CA)
213-849-4671
CD, cassette, vinyl mastering and manufacturing.

Amalgamated Tape Duplications (TX)
214-644-0039

Americ Disc Inc (CAN)
819-474-2665
CD manufacturing

American Sound & Video (CA)
415-492-1300, 800-323-AAPX

AMtech
800-777-1927

Andol Audio (NY)
800-221-6578

Anza Records (CA)
619-268-9900
CD mastering, manufacturing

Audio Accessories Co. (CT)
860-741-6675
Reel and Cassette duplication

Audio Duplication (MO)
314-965-8895
CD & tape mastering & manufacturing, vinyl pressing

Audio Dynamix (NJ)
201-346-0374

Bauer Communications (CA)
800-627-7277

Bill Smith's Custom Records (CA)
310-322-6386
Vinyl pressing

BJM Duplication (CA)
818-761-2924

CD Labs (CA)
818-505-9581

Capitol Records Studios (CA)
213-871-5001
CD, cassette, vinyl mastering and manufacturing.

Carolina Custom Pressing (NC)
910-288-6929
Vinyl pressing

Cassette Productions (UT)
800-622-6036

CD Sonic
617-424-0670
888-237-6642
Cassette duplication, mastering

Chicago Master Works (IL)
815-356-9005

The Cloning Lab (MI)
616-929-1761

CMS Digital (CA)
818-405-8002
CD, tape mastering

Comp Disc (IL)
800-752-6754

Creative Digital Design (FL)
407-578-9540

Creative Sound Corp. (CA) & (NY)
800-323-PACK
Vinyl pressing, Cassette duplication

Creative Sound Prod. (TX)
713-777-9975
Tape mastering, tape & CD manufacturing.

CRT Custom Products (TN)
615-876-5490, 800-453-2533
Vinyl pressing

Crystal Clear Sound (TX)
214-630-2957
CD, tape mastering & manufacturing.

Custom Duplication (CA)
310-670-5575

Custom Tape Duplicators (TN)
615-256-1728

Debut Audio & Video (MA)
617-387-6477

Denon Digital (GA)
706-342-3425
CD manufacturing

Digidoc
800-digidoc
mastering, design, CD-rom dev., video

Digital Force (NY)
212-333-5953
CD mastering, replication

Digi Rom (NY)
212-730-2111
Tape duplication

Digital Bros. (CA)
714-645-9702
CD, CD-ROM, DAT, Cassette, mastering, manufacturing

Disc Factory (CA)
213-465-7522
CD ROM, cassette duplication, CD manufacturing

Disc Makers (NJ)
800-468-9353
CD, cassette, vinyl mastering and manufactuirng.

Disc Makers (CA)
510-226-0800
CD, tape mastering & manuf.

Disc Manufacturing Inc (CA)
818-411-3472
and
Disc Manufacturing Inc (NY)
212-599-5300

DiscTronics (TX)
972-881-8800
and
DiscTronics CA)
213-851-7300

Disques RSB Inc. (CAN)
800-361-8153
Tape duplication

DRT Studios (WI)
800-553-5176
Tape duplicators

The Dub-Train (WA)
206-523-8050

Duplicates (IL)
312-822-0305, 800-348-DISC
Vinyl pressing

Eastco Pro (NY)
800-365-8273

Eastern Standard (NY)
800-527-9225
716-691-7631
CD, cassette, vinyl mastering and manufacturing.

EMC Prod. (MN)
612-771-1555
CD, tape mastering & manufacturing.

Europadisk (NY)
212-226-4401
CD, cassette, vinyl mastering and manufacturing.

Eva-Tone (FL)
800-EVA-TONE
CD and Cassette mastering and duplication, flexible sound sheets.

EVERMARK (CA)
310-450-2898
CD and tape manufacturing

Ezee Tape To Tape Inc (CA)
310-358-9151

Fantasy Studios (CA)
510-486-2038
CD, cassette, vinyl mastering and manufacturing.

Fault Line Audio Prod. (CA)
408-338-6005
CD and Cassette

First Generation Audio (IL)
800-374-7131

Forge Recording (PA)
800-331-0405
CD, cassette mastering and manufacturing.

Future Disc Systems (CA)
213-876-8733

Good Vibrations (CA)
619-267-0307
CD, tape mastering and manufacturing.

Have Inc (NY)
800-999-HAVE
mastering, replication

Healey Disc Manufacturing
800-835-1362
CD, Cassette manufacturing

Hi-Speed Tape Duplicating Co. (CA)
415-543-7393

ICCA Inc. (NC)
800-624-5940
704-523-7219

Interstate Recording Services (WA)
509-547-8142

Imperial Tape Co. (CA)
310-396-2008

In Record Time(NY)
800-575-4414
212-262-4414
CD manufacturing, tape duplication, vinyl pressing

Jackson Sound Productions, Ltd. (CO)
800-621-6773, 303-761-7940

Jazzmin (FL)
904-641-3704
Cassette duplication

Jewell Records (OH)
513-522-9336
CD, cassette, vinyl mastering and manufacturing.

Jones Tape Duplicating (TX)
713-869-3327

James Lee Record Processing (CA)
213-321-2187
Loran Audio Products (PA)
800-633-0455

Joe's Production and Grille
800-688-4212
CD & Tape manufacturing

KABA Audio & Multimedia (CA)
800-231-TAPE, 415-883-5041
CD, tape mastering and manufacturing

Kewal Real Time Tape Duplicators (NY)
516-586-2486

Klarity Kassette (ME)
800-458-6405

The Lacquer Channel (Toronto)
416-444-6778
Vinyl pressing

Laughing Dog (NY)
718-720-9497
CD one off's, tape duplic.,mastering

LSP (MD)
410-269-8008, 800-886-8008

Master Track Prod. (NE)
402-474-4985
CD, tape mastering, manufacturing.

Masterwork Recording (PA)
215-423-1022
CD, cassette, vinyl mastering and manufacturing.

Maxi Cassette Prod. Inc. (CA)
818-358-1644
CD, cassette duplicating and packaging

Media Systems (CA)
800-848-TAPE
Audio & Video duplication

Media Works Int.(TN)
615-327-9114
CD, Vinyl manufacturing, cassette duplication

Miami Tape (FL)
305-558-9211
Tape duplication, vinyl pressing

Mirror Image (CA)
213-876-1666

The Monkeyhouse
888-Monkey-5
Mastering, CD, cassette duplication

Music Factory (WV)
304-428-7200
Tape duplication

National Multimedia Services (DE)
302-999-1110
Tape mastering & duplication.

Nashville Quality Duplicating (TN)
615-889-8000

National Tape & Disc (TN)
800-874-4174

Night Disc
612-784-9654

Nimbus Manufact. (CA)
800-292-0932
and
Nimbus Manufact. (VA)
800-782-0778
CD mastering & manufacturing.

Northeastern Digital (MA)
508-481-9322
CD mastering & manufacturing.

North Hollywood Tape Duplicating (CA)
818-985-9737

The Notepad (CA)
626-794-4322
CD, Tape manufacturing

Oasis Recording Inc. (MD)
800-697-5734
CD, Tape manufacturing

Optimax Disc (CA)
909-626-2180

Tom Parham Audio Prod. (CA)
714-871-1395
Cassette manufacturing

Penguin Digital Recording Co (CO)
303-755-9978, 800-783-7372

Pierce Recording (VA)
800-200-2629

Planet Dallas Recording Studios (TX)
214-521-2216
CD , Tape manufacturing

Premier Cassette (WA)
206-391-0590, 800-626-8661
CD, Tape manufacturing

Prodigital (MD)
202-319-5588
CD, tape mastering and manufacturing.

Progressive Music Studios (FL)
813-251-8093
Tape duplication

Project 70 Audio Services (GA)
404-875-7000
CD manufacturing, tape mastering & duplication.

Pro Sound Manufacturing (NY)
212-382-1234
Mastering, vinyl pressing, tape processing

Pro Tape Northwest (WA)
206-441-TAPE

Protosound (VA)
802-453-3334
CD, tape mastering and manufacturing.

Quad Teck Digital (CA)
213-383-2155
CD manufacturing

Quality Clones Tape
Duplication (CA)
213-464-5853

QCA Inc.(OH)
800-859-8401
513-681-8400
CD, cassette, vinyl mastering and manufacturing.

Rainbo Records & Cassettes (CA)
310-829-3476
CD, cassette, vinyl mastering and manufacturing.

Random Access Media
415-389-1959
800-684-8071

Record Factory
800-3record
CD & Tape duplication

Record Tech. Inc. (CA)
805-484-2747
805-987-0508 (fax)
Vinyl pressing

Reel Time Recording (FL)
904-238-7002

Reliance A/V Corp. (NY)
212-586-5000
Tape duplication

Royal Scanlon Real Time (KS)
913-262-5335, 800-776-4096

SAS Industries, Inc (MO)
800-955-7271
CD replication, duplication

Selcer Sound (MA)
617-547-7904

Sanyo Laser Products (IN)
317-935-7574
CD manufacturing

Smith/Lee Productions (MO)
314-647-3900
Tape mastering, duplication

Sonopress Inc. (NC)
704-658-2000
Vinyl pressing, CD manufacturing

Sony Music Studios (NY)
212-445-2958
CD, tape, disc mastering, tape duplication.

Sound-Arts Co. Inc. (NJ)
908-493-8666

Sound Concepts (CA)
800-524-5706
CD manufacturing

Sound Recorders, Inc. (TX)
800-880-0270, 512-454-8324

Sound Impression (TN)
800-489-7756, 615-244-3535

Spinner World Wide
800-582-3472
Digital Mastering

Sterling Audio Services (NJ)
908-647-0327

Studio Magnetics Co. Inc. (NY)
516-289-3400

Summit Sound (CAN)
613-273-2818
Tape duplication

Sun Plastics (NJ)
704-658-2000
Vinyl pressing

Tape Complex (MA)
617-437-9449

Tape Specialty, Inc. (CA)
818-786-6111

Tom Parham Audio Prod.(CA)
714-871-1395
CD mastering, cassette duplication

Trutone Records (NJ)
201-489-9180
CD, cassette, vinyl mastering and manufacturing.

Univenture CD Packaging & Storing (OH)
614-529-2100

US Optical Disc (ME)
207-324-1124

Vaughn Duplication (MN)
612-832-3150

Viscount Recording Studio (RI)
401-467-9362

The Warehouse (FL)
800-483-8273
Tape duplication

Wea Manufacturing (CA)
213-725-6900
CD pressing
and
WEA Manufacturing (CA)
818-543-6600
and
WEA Manufacturing (NY)
212-399-8831
CD, cassette, vinyl mastering and manufacturing.

West LA Studio Services (CA)
310-478-7917

WK Studios (NY)
212-473-1203

WMG, Inc (IN)
317-549-8484

World Class Tapes (MI)
313-662-0669

World Group (NY)
800-463-9493

Zomax Optical Media
612-553-9300
CD manufacturing

🖉 Filling Out Application Form SR

Detach and read these instructions before completing this form. Make sure all applicable spaces have been filled in before you return this form.

BASIC INFORMATION

When to Use This Form: Use Form SR for copyright registration of published or unpublished sound recordings. It should be used where the copyright claim is limited to the sound recording itself, and it may also be used where the same copyright claimant is seeking simultaneous registration of the underlying musical, dramatic, or literary work embodied in the phonorecord.

With one exception, "sound recordings" are works that result from the fixation of a series of musical, spoken, or other sounds. The exception is for the audio portions of audiovisual works, such as a motion picture soundtrack or an audio cassette accompanying a filmstrip; these are considered a part of the audiovisual work as a whole.

Deposit to Accompany Application: An application for copyright registration of a sound recording must be accompanied by a deposit consisting of phonorecords representing the entire work for which registration is to be made.

Unpublished Work: Deposit one complete phonorecord.

Published Work: Deposit two complete phonorecords of the best edition, together with "any printed or other visually perceptible material" published with the phonorecords.

Work First Published Outside the United States: Deposit one complete phonorecord of the first foreign edition.

Contribution to a Collective Work: Deposit one complete phonorecord of the best edition of the collective work.

The Copyright Notice: For sound recordings first published on or after March 1, 1989, the law provides that a copyright notice in a specified form "may be placed on all publicly distributed phonorecords of the sound recording." Use of the copyright notice is the responsibility of the copyright owner and does not require advance permission from the Copyright Office. The required form of the notice for phonorecords of sound recordings consists of three elements: (1) the symbol "℗" (the Letter "P" in a circle); (2) the year of first publication of the sound recording; and (3) the name of the owner of copyright. For example: "℗ 1989 XYZ Record Co." The notice is to be "placed on the surface of the phonorecord, or on the label or container, in such manner and location as to give reasonable notice of the claim of copyright." Works first published prior to March 1, 1989, must carry the notice or risk loss of copyright protection.

For information about notice requirements for works published before March 1, 1989, or other copyright information, write: Information Section, LM-401, Copyright Office, Library of Congress, Washington, D.C. 20559.

PRIVACY ACT ADVISORY STATEMENT Required by the Privacy Act of 1974 (P.L. 93-579)
The authority for requesting this information is title 17. U.S.C. secs 409 and 410 Furnishing the requested information is voluntary But if the information is not furnished, it may be necessary to delay or refuse registration and you may not be entitled to certain relief, remedies and benefits provided in chapters 4 and 5 of title 17. U.S.C.
The principal uses of the requested information are the establishment and maintenance of a public record and the examination of the application for compliance with legal requirements
Other routine uses include public inspection and copying, preparation of public indexes. preparation of public catalogs of copyright registrations, and preparation of search reports upon request
NOTE No other advisory statement will be given in connection with this application Please keep this statement and refer to it if we communicate with you regarding this application

LINE-BY-LINE INSTRUCTIONS

1 SPACE 1: Title

Title of This Work: Every work submitted for copyright registration must be given a title to identify that particular work. If the phonorecords or any accompanying printed material bear a title (or an identifying phrase that could serve as a title), transcribe that wording completely and exactly on the application. Indexing of the registration and future identification of the work may depend on the information you give here.

Nature of Material Recorded: Indicate the general type or character of the works or other material embodied in the recording. The box marked "Literary" should be checked for nondramatic spoken material of all sorts, including narration, interviews, panel discussions, and training material. If the material recorded is not musical, dramatic, or literary in nature, check "Other" and briefly describe the type of sounds fixed in the recording. For example: "Sound Effects"; "Bird Calls"; "Crowd Noises."

Previous or Alternative Titles: Complete this space if there are any additional titles for the work under which someone searching for the registration might be likely to look, or under which a document pertaining to the work might be recorded.

2 SPACE 2: Author(s)

General Instructions: After reading these instructions, decide who are the "authors" of this work for copyright purposes. Then, unless the work is a "collective work," give the requested information about every "author" who contributed any appreciable amount of copyrightable matter to this version of the work. If you need further space, request additional Continuation Sheets. In the case of a collective work, such as a collection of previously published or registered sound recordings, give information about the author of the collective work as a whole. If you are submitting this Form SR to cover the recorded musical, dramatic, or literary work as well as the sound recording itself, it is important for space 2 to include full information about the various authors of all of the material covered by the copyright claim, making clear the nature of each author's contribution.

Name of Author: The fullest form of the author's name should be given. Unless the work was "made for hire," the individual who actually created the work is its "author." In the case of a work made for hire, the statute provides that "the employer or other person for whom the work was prepared is considered the author."

What is a "Work Made for Hire"? A "work made for hire" is defined as: (1) "a work prepared by an employee within the scope of his or her employment"; or (2) "a work specially ordered or commissioned for use as a contribution to a collective work, as a part of a motion picture or other audiovisual work, as a translation, as a supplementary work, as a compilation, as an instructional text, as a test, as answer material for a test, or as an atlas, if the parties expressly agree in a written instrument signed by them that the work shall be considered a work made for hire." If you have checked "Yes" to indicate that the work was "made for hire," you must give the full legal name of the employer (or other person for whom the work was prepared). You may also include the name of the employee along with the name of the employer (for example: "Elster Record Co., employer for hire of John Ferguson").

"Anonymous" or "Pseudonymous" Work: An author's contribution to a work is "anonymous" if that author is not identified on the copies or phonorecords of the work. An author's contribution to a work is "pseudonymous" if that author is identified on the copies or phonorecords under a fictitious name. If the work is "anonymous" you may: (1) leave the line blank; or (2) state "anonymous" on the line; or (3) reveal the author's identity. If the work is "pseudonymous" you may: (1) leave the line blank; or (2) give the pseudonym and identify it as such (for example: "Huntley Haverstock, pseudonym"); or (3) reveal the author's name, making clear which is the real name and which is the pseudonym (for example: "Judith Barton, whose pseudonym is Madeline Elster"). However, the citizenship or domicile of the author must be given in all cases.

Dates of Birth and Death: If the author is dead, the statute requires that the year of death be included in the application unless the work is anonymous or pseudonymous. The author's birth date is optional, but is useful as a form of identification. Leave this space blank if the author's contribution was a "work made for hire."

Author's Nationality or Domicile: Give the country of which the author is a citizen, or the country in which the author is domiciled. Nationality or domicile must be given in all cases.

Nature of Authorship: Give a brief general statement of the nature of this particular author's contribution to the work. If you are submitting this Form SR to cover both the sound recording and the underlying musical, dramatic, or literary work, make sure that the precise nature of each author's contribution is reflected here. Examples where the authorship pertains to the recording: "Sound Recording"; "Performance and Recording"; "Compilation and Remixing of Sounds." Examples where the authorship pertains to both the recording and the underlying work: "Words, Music, Performance, Recording"; "Arrangement of Music and Recording"; "Compilation of Poems and Reading."

3 SPACE 3: Creation and Publication

General Instructions: Do not confuse "creation" with "publication." Every application for copyright registration must state "the year in which creation of the work was completed." Give the date and nation of first publication only if the work has been published.

Creation: Under the statute, a work is "created" when it is fixed in a copy or phonorecord for the first time. Where a work has been prepared over a period of time, the part of the work existing in fixed form on a particular date constitutes the created work on that date. The date you give here should be the date in which the author completed the particular version for which registration is now being sought, even if other versions exist or if further changes or additions are planned.

Publication: The statute defines "publication" as "the distribution of copies or phonorecords of a work to the public by sale or other transfer of ownership, or by rental, lease, or lending"; a work is also "published" if there has been an "offering to distribute copies or phonorecords to a group of persons for purposes of further distribution, public performance, or public display." Give the full date (month, day, year) when, and the country where, publication first occurred. If first publication took place simultaneously in the United States and other countries, it is sufficient to state "U.S.A."

4 SPACE 4: Claimant(s)

Name(s) and Address(es) of Copyright Claimant(s): Give the name(s) and address(es) of the copyright claimant(s) in this work even if the claimant is the same as the author. Copyright in a work belongs initially to the author of the work (including, in the case of a work made for hire, the employer or other person for whom the work was prepared). The copyright claimant is either the author of the work or a person or organization to whom the copyright initially belonging to the author has been transferred.

Transfer: The statute provides that, if the copyright claimant is not the author, the application for registration must contain "a brief statement of how the claimant obtained ownership of the copyright." If any copyright claimant named in space 4 is not an author named in space 2, give a brief statement explaining how the claimant(s) obtained ownership of the copyright. Examples: "By written contract"; "Transfer of all rights by author"; "Assignment"; "By will." Do not attach transfer documents or other attachments or riders.

5 SPACE 5: Previous Registration

General Instructions: The questions in space 5 are intended to find out whether an earlier registration has been made for this work and, if so, whether there is any basis for a new registration. As a rule, only one basic copyright registration can be made for the same version of a particular work.

Same Version: If this version is substantially the same as the work covered by a previous registration, a second registration is not generally possible unless: (1) the work has been registered in unpublished form and a second registration is now being sought to cover this first published edition; or (2) someone other than the author is identified as copyright claimant in the earlier registration, and the author is now seeking registration in his or her own name. If either of these two exceptions apply, check the appropriate box and give the earlier registration number and date. Otherwise, do not submit Form SR; instead, write the Copyright Office for information about supplementary registration or recordation of transfers of copyright ownership.

Changed Version: If the work has been changed, and you are now seeking registration to cover the additions or revisions, check the last box in space 5, give the earlier registration number and date, and complete both parts of space 6 in accordance with the instructions below.

Previous Registration Number and Date: If more than one previous registration has been made for the work, give the number and date of the latest registration.

6 SPACE 6: Derivative Work or Compilation

General Instructions: Complete space 6 if this work is a "changed version," "compilation," or "derivative work," and if it incorporates one or more earlier works that have already been published or registered for copyright, or that have fallen into the public domain, or sound recordings that were fixed before February 15, 1972. A "compilation" is defined as "a work formed by the collection and assembling of preexisting materials or of data that are selected, coordinated, or arranged in such a way that the resulting work as a whole constitutes an original work of authorship." A "derivative work" is "a work based on one or more preexisting works." Examples of derivative works include recordings reissued with substantial editorial revisions or abridgments of the recorded sounds, and recordings republished with new recorded material, or "any other form in which a work may be recast, transformed, or adapted." Derivative works also include works "consisting of editorial revisions, annotations, or other modifications" if these changes, as a whole, represent an original work of authorship.

Preexisting Material (space 6a): Complete this space **and** space 6b for derivative works. In this space identify the preexisting work that has been recast, transformed, or adapted. For example, the preexisting material might be: "1970 recording by Sperryville Symphony of Bach Double Concerto." Do not complete this space for compilations.

Material Added to This Work (space 6b): Give a brief, general statement of the **additional** new material covered by the copyright claim for which registration is sought. In the case of a derivative work, identify this new material. Examples: "Recorded performances on bands 1 and 3"; "Remixed sounds from original multitrack sound sources"; "New words, arrangement, and additional sounds." If the work is a compilation, give a brief, general statement describing both the material that has been compiled **and** the compilation itself. Example: "Compilation of 1938 Recordings by various swing bands."

7,8,9 SPACE 7, 8, 9: Fee, Correspondence, Certification, Return Address

Deposit Account: If you maintain a Deposit Account in the Copyright Office, identify it in space 7. Otherwise leave the space blank and send the fee of $20 with your application and deposit.

Correspondence (space 7): This space should contain the name, address, area code, and telephone number of the person to be consulted if correspondence about this application becomes necessary.

Certification (space 8): The application cannot be accepted unless it bears the date and the **handwritten signature** of the author or other copyright claimant, or of the owner of exclusive right(s), or of the duly authorized agent of the author, claimant, or owner of exclusive right(s).

Address for Return of Certificate (space 9): The address box must be completed legibly since the certificate will be returned in a window envelope.

MORE INFORMATION

"Works": "Works" are the basic subject matter of copyright; they are what authors create and copyright protects. The statute draws a sharp distinction between the "work" and "any material object in which the work is embodied."

"Copies" and "Phonorecords": These are the two types of material objects in which "works" are embodied. In general, **"copies"** are objects from which a work can be read or visually perceived, directly or with the aid of a machine or device, such as manuscripts, books, sheet music, film, and videotape. **"Phonorecords"** are objects embodying fixations of sounds, such as audio tapes and phonograph disks. For example, a song (the "work") can be reproduced in sheet music ("copies") or phonograph disks ("phonorecords"), or both.

"Sound Recordings": These are "works," not "copies" or "phonorecords." "Sound recordings" are "works that result from the fixation of a series of musical, spoken, or other sounds, but not including the sounds accompanying a motion picture or other audiovisual work." Example: When a record company issues a new release, the release will typically involve two distinct "works": the "musical work" that has been recorded, and the "sound recording" as a separate work in itself. The material objects that the record company sends out are "phonorecords": physical reproductions of both the "musical work" and the "sound recording."

Should You File More Than One Application?
If your work consists of a recorded musical, dramatic, or literary work, and both that "work," and the sound recording as a separate "work," are eligible for registration, the application form you should file depends on the following:

File Only Form SR if: The copyright claimant is the same for both the musical, dramatic, or literary work and for the sound recording, and you are seeking a single registration to cover both of these "works."

File Only Form PA (or Form TX) if: You are seeking to register only the musical, dramatic, or literary work, not the sound recording. Form PA is appropriate for works of the performing arts; Form TX is for nondramatic literary works.

Separate Applications Should Be Filed on Form PA (or Form TX) and on Form SR if: (1) The copyright claimant for the musical, dramatic, or literary work is different from the copyright claimant for the sound recording; or (2) You prefer to have separate registrations for the musical, dramatic, or literary work and for the sound recording.

✂

FORM SR

UNITED STATES COPYRIGHT OFFICE

REGISTRATION NUMBER

SR	SRU

EFFECTIVE DATE OF REGISTRATION

Month	Day	Year

DO NOT WRITE ABOVE THIS LINE. IF YOU NEED MORE SPACE, USE A SEPARATE CONTINUATION SHEET.

1

TITLE OF THIS WORK ▼

PREVIOUS OR ALTERNATIVE TITLES ▼

NATURE OF MATERIAL RECORDED ▼ See instructions.
- ☐ Musical   ☐ Musical-Dramatic
- ☐ Dramatic   ☐ Literary
- ☐ Other _____

2

a

NAME OF AUTHOR ▼

DATES OF BIRTH AND DEATH
Year Born ▼   Year Died ▼

Was this contribution to the work a "work made for hire"?
☐ Yes
☐ No

AUTHOR'S NATIONALITY OR DOMICILE
Name of Country
OR { Citizen of ▶ _____
     Domiciled in ▶ _____

WAS THIS AUTHOR'S CONTRIBUTION TO THE WORK
Anonymous?   ☐ Yes ☐ No
Pseudonymous? ☐ Yes ☐ No
If the answer to either of these questions is "Yes," see detailed instructions

NATURE OF AUTHORSHIP Briefly describe nature of the material created by this author in which copyright is claimed. ▼

NOTE

Under the law, the "author" of a "work made for hire" is generally the employer, not the employee (see instructions). For any part of this work that was "made for hire" check "Yes" in the space provided, give the employer (or other person for whom the work was prepared) as "Author" of that part, and leave the space for dates of birth and death blank.

b

NAME OF AUTHOR ▼

DATES OF BIRTH AND DEATH
Year Born ▼   Year Died ▼

Was this contribution to the work a "work made for hire"?
☐ Yes
☐ No

AUTHOR'S NATIONALITY OR DOMICILE
Name of country
OR { Citizen of ▶ _____
     Domiciled in ▶ _____

WAS THIS AUTHOR'S CONTRIBUTION TO THE WORK
Anonymous?   ☐ Yes ☐ No
Pseudonymous? ☐ Yes ☐ No
If the answer to either of these questions is "Yes," see detailed instructions

NATURE OF AUTHORSHIP Briefly describe nature of the material created by this author in which copyright is claimed. ▼

c

NAME OF AUTHOR ▼

DATES OF BIRTH AND DEATH
Year Born ▼   Year Died ▼

Was this contribution to the work a "work made for hire"?
☐ Yes
☐ No

AUTHOR'S NATIONALITY OR DOMICILE
Name of Country
OR { Citizen of ▶ _____
     Domiciled in ▶ _____

WAS THIS AUTHOR'S CONTRIBUTION TO THE WORK
Anonymous?   ☐ Yes ☐ No
Pseudonymous? ☐ Yes ☐ No
If the answer to either of these questions is "Yes," see detailed instructions

NATURE OF AUTHORSHIP Briefly describe nature of the material created by this author in which copyright is claimed. ▼

3

a **YEAR IN WHICH CREATION OF THIS WORK WAS COMPLETED** This information must be given in all cases.
_____ ◀ Year

b **DATE AND NATION OF FIRST PUBLICATION OF THIS PARTICULAR WORK**
Complete this information ONLY if this work has been published.
Month ▶ _____ Day ▶ _____ Year ▶ _____ ◀ Nation

4

See instructions before completing this space.

COPYRIGHT CLAIMANT(S) Name and address must be given even if the claimant is the same as the author given in space 2. ▼

TRANSFER If the claimant(s) named here in space 4 are different from the author(s) named in space 2, give a brief statement of how the claimant(s) obtained ownership of the copyright. ▼

DO NOT WRITE HERE OFFICE USE ONLY

APPLICATION RECEIVED

ONE DEPOSIT RECEIVED

TWO DEPOSITS RECEIVED

REMITTANCE NUMBER AND DATE

MORE ON BACK ▶
- Complete all applicable spaces (numbers 5-9) on the reverse side of this page
- See detailed instructions
- Sign the form at line 8

DO NOT WRITE HERE

Page 1 of _____ pages

			FORM SR
	EXAMINED BY		
	CHECKED BY		
	☐ CORRESPONDENCE Yes		FOR COPYRIGHT OFFICE USE ONLY
	☐ DEPOSIT ACCOUNT FUNDS USED		

DO NOT WRITE ABOVE THIS LINE. IF YOU NEED MORE SPACE, USE A SEPARATE CONTINUATION SHEET.

PREVIOUS REGISTRATION Has registration for this work, or for an earlier version of this work, already been made in the Copyright Office?

☐ Yes ☐ No If your answer is "Yes," why is another registration being sought? (Check appropriate box) ▼

a. ☐ This is the first published edition of a work previously registered in unpublished form.

b. ☐ This is the first application submitted by this author as copyright claimant.

c. ☐ This is a changed version of the work, as shown by space 6 on this application.

If your answer is "Yes," give: **Previous Registration Number** ▼   **Year of Registration** ▼

5

DERIVATIVE WORK OR COMPILATION Complete both space 6a & 6b for a derivative work; complete only 6b for a compilation.

a. **Preexisting Material** Identify any preexisting work or works that this work is based on or incorporates. ▼

b. **Material Added to This Work** Give a brief, general statement of the material that has been added to this work and in which copyright is claimed. ▼

6

See instructions before completing this space

DEPOSIT ACCOUNT If the registration fee is to be charged to a Deposit Account established in the Copyright Office, give name and number of Account.

Name ▼   **Account Number** ▼

7

CORRESPONDENCE Give name and address to which correspondence about this application should be sent. Name/Address/Apt/City/State/Zip ▼

Area Code & Telephone Number ▶

Be sure to give your daytime phone number ◀

CERTIFICATION* I, the undersigned, hereby certify that I am the

Check one ▼

☐ author

☐ other copyright claimant

☐ owner of exclusive right(s)

☐ authorized agent of _____
    Name of author or other copyright claimant, or owner of exclusive right(s) ▲

8

of the work identified in this application and that the statements made by me in this application are correct to the best of my knowledge.

Typed or printed name and date ▼ If this application gives a date of publication in space 3, do not sign and submit it before that date.

_____ date ▶ _____

Handwritten signature (X) ▼

MAIL CERTIFI-CATE TO

Certificate will be mailed in window envelope

Name ▼

Number/Street/Apartment Number ▼

City/State/ZIP ▼

• Complete all necessary spaces
• Sign your application in space 8

1. Application form
2. Nonrefundable $20 filing fee in check or money order payable to *Register of Copyrights*
3. Deposit material

Register of Copyrights
Library of Congress
Washington, D.C. 20559

9

* 17 U.S.C. § 506(e): Any person who knowingly makes a false representation of a material fact in the application for copyright registration provided for by section 409 or in any written statement filed in connection with the application, shall be fined not more than $2,500.

May 1991—75,000   ☆U.S. GOVERNMENT PRINTING OFFICE:1991-282-170/20,017

Publishing & Performance Rights

Performance Rights

Every time your record is played publicly, over the radio, television, at a nightclub, etc., you are entitled to payment from that business for the right to play your song. Performance rights organizations such as ASCAP and BMI collect this money on behalf of their members and distribute it accordingly.

Out of the money that you receive, half of it goes to the writer(s) of the song, and the other half goes to the publisher of the song. If you start your own publishing company, (which you'll be doing when you register as a publisher with ASCAP or BMI) and you write the songs, you'll get all of the money. You can also assign part of your publishing rights to another publishing company (called a co-publishing deal) or have a larger publishing company administer (keep track of) your publishing. In a co-publishing deal, the other company would get a percentage of your songs (usually 25%) for life. This includes performance and mechanical rights. In exchange, you'd get cash up front as an advance, and the potential to make more money, because a larger publishing company would be out there pitching your songs for movie sound-tracks, television shows, etc.

Mechanical Rights

When a record label releases an artist's music, they pay a mechanical rights fee of approximately 5¢ per song on the record to the artist's publishing company for every record sold. This is in addition to the standard sales royalty. Since you've started your own record label, and you're probably releasing your own music, you won't be paying yourself mechanical rights moneys. If you were getting signed to another label, they would be paying you these. If you're releasing your friend's band's 7" single, you're supposed to pay them mechanical rights, or work out some arrangement to waive them.

These are very simplified explanations; for more information, check out *The Musician's Business and Legal Guide* (Prentice Hall) or *Get It In Writing*, by Brian McPherson (Rockpress).

Performance Rights Organizations

A phone call or letter will get you more information on performance rights and how to register your music. These organizations also put on regional showcases for unsigned bands. Call for info.

ASCAP

1 Lincoln Plaza
New York NY 10023
212-621-6000

P.O. Box 11171
Chicago IL 60611
312-481-1194

7920 Sunset Bl. Ste. 300
Los Angeles CA 90046
213-883-1000

2 Music Square W.
Nashville TN 37203
615-742-5000

1519 Ponce de Leon Ave.
Ste.505
Santurce Puerto Rico 00909
809-725-1688

52 Haymarket
Stes. 10 & 11
London SW1 Y4RP
ENGLAND
011-44-71-973-0069

BMI

8730 Sunset Bl. 3rd Floor
Los Angeles CA 90069
310-659-9109

10 Music Square E.
Nashville TN 37203
615-291-6700

320 W. 57th St.
New York NY 10019
212-586-2000

SESAC, Inc

421 W. 54th St.
New York NY 10019
212-586-3450

55 Music Square E.
Nashville TN 37203
615-320-0055

Music Publishers Directory

Following this section is a directory of music publishers. If you're interested in co-publishing or having another company administer your publishing, call them and get more information.

Music Publishers

Ace Publishing
103 Fairmont Lane
Pearl, MS 39208
601-939-6868
Fax: 601-932-3038
All Styles

Alfred Publishing Co., Inc.
PO Box 10003
Van Nuys, CO 91410
818-891-5999
Fax:818-891-2182
All Styles
70740,475@compuserve.com

All Nations Music
8857 W. Olympic Bl #200
Beverly Hills, CA 90211
310-657-9814
Fax: 310-657-2331

Any Kind of Music Inc.
1119 N Wilson Ave
Teaneck, NJ 07666
201-836-5116
Fax: 201-836-0661
Dance Music

Avatar Publishing Group
1319 N La Brea
Los Angeles, CA 90028
213- 878-1100
Fax: 213- 878-1114
Rap, Street R&B, Dance, Hip-hop

Backbone Publishing/Edson Publishing/Sugo Recording Co./ElGranada
c/o Take Note
725 Washington St, Ste 211
Oakland, CA 94607
510-836-4554
Fax: 510-836-4580
Jazz,Latin, Classical, New Age

Beam of Light Publishing
3081 NW 24th St.
Miami, FL 33142
305-635-6782
Fax: 305-633-7127
All Styles

Bekool Music
PO Box 671008
Dallas, TX 75367
214-750-0720
Fax: 214-987-4638
Country, Gospel

Bekool Music
23Music Sq. E, Ste 101
Nashville, TN 37203
615-251-3128
Fax: 615-259-0656
Country, Gospel

Bill Butler Music
638 West Iris
Nashville, TN 37204
210-426-2112
Fax: Same as phone
Country

Biograph Records
35 Medford St, Ste 203
Somerville, MA 02143
617-627-9050
Fax: 617-627-9051
Jazz, Blues

BMG Music
1540 Broadway
New York, NY 10036
212-930-4000
Fax: 212-930-4096

BMG Music
1 Music Circle N
Nashville, TN 37203
615-780-5420
Fax: 615-780-5430

BMG Music
151 John St #307
Toronto, ONT M5V 2T2
CANADA
416-586-0850
Fax: 416-586-0853

Bob-A-Lew Music
11712 Moorpark Ave #111
Studio City, CA 91604
818-506-6331
Fax: 818-506-4735

Bok Music
3435 Stoneridge Ct.
Calabasas, CA 91302
818-222-9969

Bourne Company/Morbo
5 W 37th St
New York, NY 10018
212-391-4300
Fax: 212-391-4306
All styles

Bug Music Inc.
6777 Hollywood Bl 9th Fl
Hollywood, CA 90028
213-466-4352
Fax: 213-466-2366
All Styles

Bug Music Inc.
1026 16th Ave. S
Nashville, TN 37212
615-726-0782
Fax: 615-726-0784
All Styles

Cherry Lane Music
Publishing Co., Inc.
10 Midland Ave.
PO Box 430
Port Chester, NY 10573
914-937-8601
Fax: 914-937-0614

Chrysalis Music
8500 Melrose Ave, Ste 207
Los Angeles, CA 90069
310-652-0066
Fax: 310-652-2024
Country, Alternative, Urban

Chrysalis Nashville
1204 16th Ave. South
Nashville, TN 37212
615-327-4797
Fax: 617-327-1903
Country

Concrete Publishing
361 W Broadway, 2nd Fl.
New York, NY 10013
212-965-8530
Fax: 212-343-2198

Copperfield Music
54 Music Sq East, Ste 304
Nashville, TN 37203
615-726-3100
All styles

Cosmic Winds/Jazz Mania
270 W 19th St.
New York, NY 10011
212-989-7200
Fax: 212-633-8022
Jazz

Creativeman
1875 Century Pk. E #1165
Los Angeles, CA 90067
310-556-1325
Fax: 310-556-4617

Criterion Music
6124 Selma Ave.
Los Angeles, CA 90038
213-469-2296
Fax: 213-962-5751

Criterion Music
1025 17th Ave. S #C
Nashville, TN 37212
615-327-2146

Dancing Asparagus Prod.
505 S Beverly Dr. #238
Beverly Hills, CA 90212
310-285-7774
Fax: 310-843-3999

Demann Entertainment
8000 Beverly Blvd.
Los Angeles, CA 90048
213-852-1500
Fax: 213-852-1505

Edgewater Music Co.
437 N Rush St
Chicago, IL 60611
312-527-2003
Fax: 312-527-1291
All styles

El Gurren Music
16311 Askin Dr.
Pine Mtn Club, CA 93222
805-242-0125
Fax: 805-242-4313
Rap, Hip-hop

EMI Music
1290 Ave. of the Americas
43rd Fl
New York, NY 10104
212-492-1200
Fax: 212-245-4115

EMI Virgin Music
8730 Sunset Bl 5th Fl
Los Angeles, CA 90069
310-652-8078
Fax: 310-289-6486

EMI Music
35 Music Square E
Nashville, TN 37203
615-742-8081
Fax: 615-726-2394

Erikanian Music Inc.
853 W University Pkwy
Baltimore, MD 21210
410-467-4231
Fax: 410-467-4642
Folk, World, Jazz, New Age,
Industrial, Dance

Eyeball
1441 W Devon
Chicago, IL 60660
773-973-7736
Fax: 773-973-2088
Blues

Famous Music
10635 Santa Monica Bl.
Los Angeles, CA 90025
310-441-1300
Fax: 310-441-4722

Famous Music
65 Music Square E
Nashville, TN 37203
615-329-0500
Fax: 615-321-4121

Fiction Songs
1540 Broadway, 27th Fl
New York, NY 10036
212-930-4910
Fax: 212-930-4295
Alternative Pop

Frozen Inca Music
1800 Peachtree St NW, #333
Atlanta, GA 30309
404-355-5580
Fax: 404-351-2786
Blues, Jazz, Roots
mrland@mindspring.com

GEG
207 N Canon Dr, Ste 1164
Beverly Hills, CA 90210
310-552-3301
Fax: 310-659-8633
All styles except Country

Great Cumberland
914 18th Ave. South
Nashville, TN 37212
615-320-9971
Fax: 615-322-9288
Country

Hal Bernard Enterprises
2612 Erie Ave
Cincinnati, OH 45208
513-871-1500
Fax: 513-871-1510
Pop, Rock

Happy Valley Music
1 Camp St
Cambridge, MA 02140
617-354-0700
Fax: 617-491-1970
Alternative

H/B Webman and Co.
1650 Broadway, Ste 701
New York, NY 10019
212-586-0240
Fax:212-586-4306
Pop

Heart Music Inc
PO Box 160326
Austin, TX 78716
512-327-4649
Fax: 512-795-9573

Hit List Music
120 W 44th #404
New York, NY 10036
212-302-8544
Fax: 212-302-8584
All styles except Rap and
Country

Hit & Run Music
1325 6th Ave, 7th Fl
New York, NY 10019
212-956-2880
Fax: 212-956-2114
All styles

Imago Songs, Inc.
530 Broadway
New York, NY 10012
212-343-3400

Instinct Records
26 W 17th St #502
New York, NY 10011
212-727-1360
Fax: 212-366-5979

Interscope
10900 Wilshire Bl 10th Fl
Los Angeles, CA 90024
310-208-6547

Jamaal Entertainment
2825 Wilcrest Dr #415
Houston, TX 77042
713-781-7166
Fax: 713-781-7176

JATAP
Publishing/Lynnstrom
PO Box 10372
Sedona, AZ 83639
502-282-4394
Jazz

Jeneane Claps and Freeway Fusion
c/o JAJ Records
156 5th Ave, #434
New York, NY 10010
212-691-5630
Fax: 212-645-5038

Jobete Music
6255 Sunset Bl 18th Fl
Los Angeles, CA 90028
213-856-3507
Fax: 213-461-2785

Joey Boy Publishing
3081 NW 24th St.
Miami, FL 33142
303-635-6782
Fax:303-633-7127
House, Rap, Techno, Reggae

Justice Music Corp.
11586 Blix St.
N Hollywood, CA 91602
818-762-6850
Fax: 818-762-6747

Largo Music
425 Park Ave.
New York, NY 10022
212-756-5071
Fax: 212-207-8167
Pop, Alternative, Hard Rock

Leeds Entertainment
1007 Montana Ave, Ste 341
Santa Monica, CA 90403
310-440-0140
Fax: 310-440-0240
All styles

Lefrak Entertainment
40 W 57th St #1510
New York, NY 10019
212-586-3600
Fax: 212-307-7027

Leiber & Stoller
9000 Sunset Bl #1107
Los Angeles, CA 90069
310-273-6401
Fax: 310-273-1591

Leona Music/Miss Music
270 W 19th St
New York, NY 10011
212-989-7200
Fax: 212-633-8022
Pop
JMRecords@aol.com

Malaco Inc.
3023 W Northside Dr
Jackson, MS 39213
601-982-4522
Fax: 601-982-4528
Black Gospel, R&B

Maraville/Sonrisa
PO Box 69188
West Hollywood, CA 90069
213-876-1988
Fax: 213-876-7098

MCA Music Publishing
70 Universal City Pl #425
Universal City, CA 91608
818-777-4550
Fax: 818-777-1480

MCA Music Publishing
1755 Broadway 8th Fl
New York, NY 10019
212-841-8000
Fax: 212-582-7240

MCA Music
12 Music Circle
Nashville, TN 37203
615-248-4800
Fax: 615-248-9300

MCA Music
2450 Victoria Park Ave.
Willowdale, ONT N2J 4A2
CANADA
416-491-3000

Motown Music
11150 Santa Monica Blvd.
Los Angeles, CA 90025
310-996-7200

**Mucho Loco Music, Inc./
Loco de Amor Music, Inc.**
156 W 56th 5th Fl
New York, NY 10019
212-489-4820
Fax: 212-262-0043

Music Umbrella
PO Box 1067
Santa Monica, CA 90406
310-452-0116
Fax: 310-452-2585
Cutting Edge Country,
Americana,
Positive Hip-hop

Muskuser Publishing
15030 Ventura Blvd, Ste 425
Sherman Oaks, CA 91403
310-440-0140
Fax: 310-440-0240
All styles

NEM Entertainment
8730 Sunset Bl #485
Los Angeles, CA 90069
310-652-8320

Northcott Productions Ltd.
594 Broadway, Ste 1011
New York, NY 10012
212-343-2660
Fax: 212-343-2753
Dance

Old Boston Publishing
180 Pond St. Box 311
Cohasset, MA 02025
617-383-9494
Fax: same as phone
All styles

Only New Age Music
8033 Sunset Blvd
Los Angeles, CA 90046
213-851-3355
Fax: 213-851-7981
NAC, New Age

Peer Music Int'l
810 7th Ave. 10th Fl
New York, NY 10019
212-265-3910
Fax: 212-489-2465

Peer Music
8159 Hollywood Blvd.
Hollywood, CA 90069
213-656-0364
Fax: 213-656-3298

Peer Music
1206 16th Ave. S
Nashville, TN 37212
615-329-0603
Fax: 615-320-0409

PolyGram Music
Publishing Group
825 8th Ave.
New York, NY 10019
212-333-8000
Fax: 212-603-7973

PolyGram Music
Publishing Group
1416 N. La Brea Ave.
Los Angeles, CA 90028
213-856-2776
Fax: 213-856-2664

**PolyGram Music
Publishing Group**
54 Music Square E #200
Nashville, TN 37203
615-256-7648
Fax: 615-255-8549

**PolyGram Music
Publishing Group**
1345 Denison St., Markham
ONT L3R 5V2 CANADA
905-415-7314
Fax: 905-415-0850

Private Music
8750 Wilshire
Los Angeles, CA 90021
310-358-4500
Fax: 310-358-4501

Realization Music
559 Broome St.
New York, NY 10013
212-431-3676
Fax:212-431-3702
All styles

Rondor Music Int'l
360 N La Cienega Blvd
Los Angeles, CA 90048
310-289-3500
Fax: 310-289-4000
All styles

Rondor Music Int'l
1 S Green St, Ste 1102
New York, NY 10012
212-226-9800
Fax: 212-226-8550

Rondor Music Int'l
1904 Adelicia
Nashville, TN 37212
615-321-0820
Fax: 615-327-1018

Rustron Music Publishers
1156 Park Lane
W Palm Beach, FL 33417-5957
407-686-1354
Adult Contemp, Eclectic
Acoustic, Blues,
R&B, New Age

**September Music
Galahad Music**
250 W 57th St
New York, NY 10019
212-581-1338
Fax: 212-765-6703
Pop, MOR, Adult Contemporary

**Shankman DeBlasio Melina
Anderson Inc.**
740 N La Brea 1rst Fl
Los Angeles, CA 90038
213-933-9977
Fax: 213-933-0633

Skinny Zach Music
PO Box 570815
Tarzana, CA 91357
818-708-1300
Fax:818-705-6332
All styles

Slash Music
825 8th Ave
New York, NY 10019
212-603-3999
Fax: 212-333-8030
Alternative

Slash Music
7381 Beverly Blvd
Los Angeles, CA 90036
213-937-4660
Fax:312-933-7277
Alternative

Sony Music Publishing
550 Madison Ave 27th Fl
New York, NY 10022
212-833-4729
Fax: 212-833-5552

Sony Music Publishing
2100 Colorado Ave.
Santa Monica, CA 90404
310-449-2100
Fax: 310-449-2544

Sony/Tree International
8 Music Square W.
Nashville, TN 37203
615-726-8300

Starmaker Entertainment Group
3210 21st St.
San Francisco, CA 94110
415-282-3600
Fax: 415-282-4474
All styles

Threptos Music Inc,
101 B St.
Carboro, NC 27510
919-932-1882
Fax: 919-932-1885

To The Moon Music
11 Music Square W. #205
Nashville, TN 37203
615-251-3205

TriStar Music
79 Fifth Ave
New York, NY 10003
212-337-5400
Fax: 212-337-5433

Walrus Music Publishing
PO Box 11267
Glendale, CA 91226
818-242-2093
Jazz

Warner/Chappell Music
10585 Santa Monica Bl.
Los Angeles, CA 90025
310-441-8600
Fax: 310-470-3232

Warner/Chappell Music
1290 Ave of the Americas
New York, NY 10019
212-399-6910
Fax: 212-315-5590

White Cat Music
10603 N Hayden Rd, Ste 114
Scottsdale, AZ 85260
602-951-3115
Fax:602-951-3047
All except Rap and Metal

Windswept Pacific
9320 Wilshire Bl #200
Beverly Hills, CA 90212
310-550-1500
Fax: 310-247-0195

Wood Monkey Music/ Ellymay Music Co.
350 E 30th St, Ste 4D
New York, NY 10016
212-213-8787
Fax: 212-213-9797
Rock, Alternative, Pop

Yo-Yo Music
48-780 Eisenhower Dr.
La Quinta, CA 92253-0643
619-564-0559
All styles

Zomba Music Publishing
9000 Sunset Bl #300
Hollywood, CA 90069
310-247-8300
Fax: 310-247-8366

Zomba Music Publishing
137-139 W. 25th St.
New York, NY 10001
212-727-0016
Fax: 212-242-7462

Zomba Enterprises Inc.
914-916 19th Ave S
Nashville, TN 37212
615-321-4850

The Press

Before the Record Comes Out

Make up a press release or one-sheet (see examples) and send it to all local newspapers, music related magazines and record stores in your area, well in advance of the record's release. Set an "official" release date for the record that is about a month or two after the date the pressing plant says the record will be done. This gives you a buffer in case the pressing plant is late (happens very often) and lets you do some advance promotion, such as press releases, setting up a release party, etc. You can always sell your records locally before your "national" release date.

After You Get the Product

Send out as many records as you can to consumer press and trade publications. A good review in one of the radio trades such as *CMJ* or *Gavin* can mean the difference between a few stations playing your record and a few hundred stations. Likewise, good reviews in consumer music magazines can sell hundreds or thousands of records. Even a bad review is good, because it is space devoted to your band in that magazine.

Following this section is a list of music publications that will review independent bands' releases. With some of them, like *Rolling Stone*, *Musician* and *SPIN* for example, your chances of getting a review are rather slim. Send to them anyway, you never know. There are other magazines which are geared more towards independent and alternative bands, like *MAXI-MUMROCKNROLL*, *Flipside* and *Option*, to name a few. These magazines are great for independent bands because they will review the majority of the records they receive. Every time your record gets reviewed, thousands of people are at least seeing the name of your band, and some of them are going to write you for information or go to their local record store looking for your record.

Where to Send It

If you can afford it (there it is again) send a copy of your record to all of the following publications. If you can't, pick magazines you've heard of or ones that are in your area. It's important to send your review copies right when you get them back from the pressing plant. This should be your first priority once you receive them. Why? Because all of these magazines have lead times of a month or more, meaning reviews that they write today won't get published for at least a month, maybe two. And it may take a few weeks for your record to even make it into the hands of the reviewer. This means two to three months from the day you send your record to the day the review is published.

Advance Tapes

Most big labels send out advance cassettes months before the actual record comes out, so that the reviews are published close to the record's release date. For an unknown label,

HERE ARE THE FACTS YOU REQUESTED/1

BIOGRAPHY

Contrary to the popular wisdom, Pop is not obvious. Elevator recording artists *Here Are The Facts You Requested* discovers, excavates and refines the raw material of our pop-musical subconscious. Instruments as diverse as guitar-synthesizer and cello, interlocking guitar riffs, drums and samples populate an eclectic pop neighborhood which is simultaneously smart and fun. Like Romper Room rockers, Here Are The Facts You Requested makes sophisticated ideas the stuff of instantly accessible pop songs and groovy moving rhythms: your body feels good and you learned something new!

Influences range from the Beatles (melody and methods) to Talking Heads (integration), VU (tone) to Deee-Lite (fashion and fantasy), Joni Mitchell (intimacy) to Laurie Anderson (elevation), House Music (solidity) to Jazz (liquidity). This musical history is revisited in a manner which seeks to explore as well as celebrate. As a result, the songs are often improvised and abundant with samples, either digitally captured or re-performed (as in "Drone's" sample of "Groove Is In The Heart"). They are at once respectful of classical pop techniques but irreverent of any unnecessarily imposed rules for how these techniques should be employed or combined. This gives them the freedom to brilliantly overlay Ornette Coleman-style sax solos over techno synth and upright bass tracks in "Pretty Part." Both their recordings and performances utilize the power of imaginative improvisation to create compelling psychedelic environments. For Here Are The Facts You Requested, pop music is a narcotic of potentially profound effects, and these enigmatic leaders of mental experience drive the music which takes us on a soulful trip.

The spirit of total pop integration that begins with the music continues with their visual approach. Their concerts are a multimedia art form employing a subtextual light show, immersive set environments and dramatic song presentation. Their award-winning mailing list has confronted hundreds of fans with its DIY visual sampling style, and their product packaging resonates with themes rooted in the music. They do this to show that pop music is not a limited entertainment commodity, but rather an art form, whose full potential expands as far as you will it.

HISTORY

Here Are The Facts You Requested began their journey 10 years ago, when King Me and Max Love, long time best-friends, began taking their heretical ideas to guitar in several high school bands. In Baltimore, 1991, they found drummer L. Bill and immediately convinced his parents to buy him a drum machine for Christmas. Classical cellist Akire joined the trio after seeing them perform at a local club and added a layer of funk and femininity to their already densely-influenced music. With this group, Here Are The Facts You Requested performed to packed and loyal houses throughout the D.C. and Baltimore area. They also formed a collective of local bands which shared gigs, resources and distribution. In 1994, the band relocated to the Bay Area to join the ranks of other S.F. regional artists reaching national prominence. They preach directly to the people through their weekly radio show, "Talk About Pop Music," on Radio Libre, 103.3 FM San Francisco.

BIOLOGY

King Me guitar synthesizer, voice
Max Love guitar, voice
L. Bill electric and acoustic drums
Akire cello, voice
Boomerang projections, environment, ambient sound

PUBLICITY CONTACT

Eugene Chen, Elevator Pop Gallery
945 Vermont Street
San Francisco, CA 94107
hatfyr@violet.berkeley.edu
415.282.7456

B W glossy photo, cassette or DAT demo and video of band are available if not included.

Above: A sample one-sheet from an independent band.

it's better just to send the finished product. It looks better, and it'll get taken more seriously by the magazine. Besides, you can use this lag time to send out to college radio, get distribution, etc.

What To Send

As far as the format goes, send what you've got. If you made all three, I'd suggest sending cassettes to the smaller magazines and CDs to the larger ones. For important magazines, it's wise to send several copies to ATTN: REVIEWER (or better still, call the magazine and find out who you should address it to), and also send copies to random staff members. If someone in the office likes it or plays it a lot, chances are it'll get more attention.

Along with your record, you should send a bio or a one-sheet. (see examples) A one-sheet is a combination introduction, press release, past reviews, hype and biography. You should also write (or copy) a letter to each magazine requesting a sample issue, ad rates and ask them to notify you if and when your record is reviewed. Some publications do this automatically so that they can solicit ads from you, others won't do it at all. It's worth asking, though. If you want to include an 8" x 10" photo, go ahead, but it's not a must. In fact, the majority of the promo pictures that I've seen have looked pretty stupid, and do the band that sends them more bad than good. If you can have them made cheaply, and they look good, send them. If your band is planning to tour, include a list of dates.

You should also send review copies and information to all your local newspapers, weeklies and magazines. Mention that your group is available for interviews. Even if they don't normally write reviews of your style of music or any music, they may decide to do a story or mention of a "local" artist. It's not everyday that a band releases a record nationally, THIS IS NEWS!

After you send your review copies out, you can start working on advertisements and getting your record into stores.

CRUZ RECORDS

P.O. BOX 7756, LONG BEACH, CA 90807 USA
PHONE (213) 430-2077   FAX (213) 430-7286

```
BIG DRILL CAR
BATCH
CRZ 018 (LP/CA/CD)
Produced By: Stephen Egerton & Bill Stevenson
```

```
BAR CODE #: 31895-0018        Side 1               Side 2
RELEASE DATE: August 6, 1991  Take Away            In A Hole
TERRITORY: Worldwide          Restless Habs        Crust
                              If It's Poison       Freedom of Choice
MARK ARNOLD:     Guitar       Freep                Ick
FRANK DALY:      Vocals       Never Ending Endeavor  Faster
DANNY MARCROFT:  Drums
BOB THOMSON:     Bass
```

BIG DRILL CAR is a high-octane powered quartet from Orange County, CA that has
toured the United States and Canada extensively. BDC released their first LP on
CRUZ, ALBUM/TAPE/CD TYPE THING, late in 1989 to a groundswell of national media
reviews and solid college radio airplay in addition to spins at adventurous
commercial radio outlets. ALBUM/TAPE/CD TYPE THING landed on the cover of CMJ
as a Jackpot pick and Tower PULSE! magazine declared BDC as contenders for the
title of ". . . Heaviest Band On Earth." Last year CRUZ re-issued SMALL BLOCK,
the first EP from BDC that the band had originally released themselves. SMALL
BLOCK contains six gear-grinding tracks that manage to continuously playback in
the head. Earlier this year, BDC covered the Cheap Trick tune, "Surrender" on
a split single seven inch with labelmates, CHEMICAL PEOPLE, doing a version of
KISS' "Getaway."
With their new album, BATCH, BDC have whipped up a recipe of bombastic rock and
head-on pop hooks. Labelmates Stephen Egerton and Bill Stevenson (ALL) handled
the production on BATCH which features ten crashing originals along with a
pumped-up cover of Devo's "Freedom Of Choice."

```
TOUR                          RADIO                    BIG DRILL CAR discography
BDC will tour the United States and Canada  -Advance vinyl promo to key    CRZ 008   Album/Tape/CD Type Thing
starting in late August to support BATCH.    college, commercial radio.              (LP/CA/CD)
They will also do a European "Batch"        -CD service to all key         CRZ 014   Small Block (EP/CA EP/
type tour in Autumn.                         commercial radio, select               CD EP)
                                             college radio.                CRZ 701   "Surrender/Getaway"
RETAIL                                      -Extensive radio interviews             (Split 7" SNGL w/
-Advance CA serviced to key Mom and Pop      scheduled prior to tour.               CHEMICAL PEOPLE)
 retail.
-Advance CA serviced to key chains and      ADVERTISING                    CONTACT
 dist. sales staff.                         CO-OP advertising dollars      Promo/Marketing: Ron Coleman
-Instore copies to key accounts.            will be available to support             (213) 430-2077
-Color posters plus tour posters/           the release of BATCH in        Sales:           Chuck Dukowski
 flyers available.                          addition to the national                (213) 430-7687
                                            and trade slated for
                                            August, 1991.
PRESS
-Advance CA/LP service to key national,     VIDEO
 regional, and fanzine press.               A promotional video for the
-CD service to select press.                song,"Restless Habs,"
-Vinyl service to all national, regional    from BATCH will be serviced
 international, and fanzine press.           on an national and
                                            regional basis.
```

Above: A sample one-sheet from a large independent label.

Above: A sample band bio from an independent label.

Music Press

ALABAMA

Auburn Plainsman
Auburn University
Foy Union Bldg, B-100
Auburn, AL 36849
334-844-4130
Weekly on campus paper
www.auburn.edu/~plainsm

Black & White
PO Box 13215
Birmingham, AL 35202
205-933-0460
Monthly alternatve paper

fun & stuff
2829 2nd Ave S #310
Birmingham, AL 35233
205-252-0200
Monthly paper

The Harbinger
PO Box U-980
Mobile, AL 36688
334-476-0430
Biweekly alternative paper

ARIZONA

The Blast
2404 W Huntington Dr
Tempe, AZ 85282
602-438-8042
Biweekly magazine
www.playtimeusa.com

Country Spirit Magazine
P.O. Box 3174
Tempe, AZ 85280
602-966-6236

Fast Lane
5722 N. Black Lane
Canyon Hwy #25
Pheonix, AZ 85017
602-249-3342
All Styles

The New Times
1201 E Jefferson
Phoenix, AZ 85034
602-271-0040
Weekly paper
www.pheonixnewtimes.com

State Press Magazine
Arizona State University
P.O. Box 871502
Tempe, AZ 85287-1502
602-965-1695
Weekly paper

Whirlpool
P.O. Box 616
Tempe, AZ 85280
602-921-1185
whirl@primenet.com

ARKANSAS

Little Rock Free Press
824 W 7th St
Little Rock, AR 72201
501-372-4719
Biweekly alternative paper
www.aristotle.net/freep

Nightflying
PO Box 250276
Little Rock, AR 72225
501-664-5099
Fax: 666-2805
Monthly paper

Zassafras Music News
P.O. Box 1000
Gravette, AR 72736-1000
501-787-6629

CALIFORNIA

Album Network
120 N. Victory Blvd.
Burbank, CA 91502
818-955-4000
Fax: 955-8048
www.networkmags.com

The Angry Thoreauan
PO Box 2246
Anaheim, CA 92814
714-740-3063
Quarterly mag, all styles
revtinear@aol.com

Antidote
550 Guerrero
San Francisco, CA 94110
415-487-0639
Weekly on-line zine
watski@well.com

BAM (South)
6767 Forest Lawn Dr #110
Los Angeles, CA 90068
213-851-8600
Fax: 851-8303
www.musicuniverse.com

BAM (North)
Bam Publications
3470 Buskirk Ave.
Pleasant Hill, CA 94523
510-934-3700
Fax: 934-3958

Bass Player/Keyboard
The GPI Group
411 Borel #100
San Mateo, CA 94402
415-358-9500
Fax: 358-8728
www.mfi.com

Ben is Dead
Box 3166
Hollywood, CA 90028
213-960-7674
Fax: 479-2336
Alternative
benisdead@mrrogers.recordings
.com

Billboard
BPI Communications
5055 Wilshire Bl 7th fl
Los Angeles, CA 90036
213-525-2300
Fax: 525-2394
www.hollywoodreporter.com

**The Bomb Hip-Hop
Magazine**
4104 24th St. Ste. 105
San Francisco, CA 94114
415-826-9479
Hip-Hop, Heavy Metal,
Alternative, Jazz & Reggae

Bunny Hop
P.O. Box 42390
San Francisco, CA 94142
Indie, alternative zine

Caffeine
P.O. Box 4231-306
Woodland Hills CA 91365
213-468-1250
poetrymag@aol.com
Poetry and Alternative music

ChinMusic
P.O. Box 423657
San Francisco CA 94142
girlchin@sirius.com
Alternative music and baseball

City Revolt
190 Martha St., top floor
San Jose, CA 95112
408-971-8511
408-971-0139
revolt@ix.netcom.com

Electronic Musician
Act III Publishing
6400 Hollis St. Ste. 12
Emeryville, CA 94608
510-653-3307
Fax: 653-5142

Factsheet Five
P.O. Box 170099
San Francisco, CA 94117
415-668-1781
All styles
Monthly zine

Flipside
P.O. Box 60790
Pasadena, CA 91116-6790
818-585-0395
Punk Rock, Underground,
Industrial
Fax: 818-585-0395
flipside@ix.netcom.com

Fresh
215 E. Orangethorpe
Fullerton, CA 92632
714-632-3930
Fax: 714-632-3934
Hip-Hop

The Gavin Report
140 Second St
San Francisco, CA 94105
415-495-1990
Fax: 495-2580
Radio trade
www.gavin.com

Gearhead
P.O. Box 421219
San Francisco, CA 94142
415-668-7080
Punk, Indie

Genetic Disorder
PO Box 151362
San Diego, CA 92175
Music 'zine with lots of reviews

Girlyhead
P.O. Box 423657
San Francisco CA 94142
girlchin@sirius.com
A fun, cerebral, chick music mag

Good Times
P O Box 1885
Santa Cruz, CA 95061
408-458-1100
Weekly entertainment
www.goodtimes.com

The Grindstone Magazine
11288 Ventura Blvd., #450
Studio City, CA 91604
818-981-6252
Fax: 818-981-6149
Quarterly zine
grind55@aol.com

Guitar Player
411 Borel Ave. Ste. 100
San Mateo, CA 94402
415-358-9500
Fax: 415-388-9216
All Guitar-Intensive Releases
Regardless of Style
www.mfi.com

Hits Magazine
14958 Ventura Blvd.
Sherman Oaks, CA 91403
818-501-7900
Radio trade
www.dock@buzznetonline.com

Hot Lava
2060 Placentia, Ste. C4
Costa Mesa, CA 92627
714-574-8122
Fax: 714-574-8123
mikeatlava@ aol.com

Huh/Raygun
2812 Santa Monica Blvd.
Santa Monica, CA 90404
310-828-0522
Fax: 452-8076
huhcentral@aol.com

Keyboard
411 Borel Ave., Ste.100
San Mateo, CA 94402
415-358-9500
Fax: 415-358-9527
keyboard@well.sf.ca.us

Kulture Deluxe
715 J St. #306
San Diego CA 92101
619-531-7979
www.kulturedeluxe.com
Monthly, alternative

LA Weekly
6715 Sunset Bl
Hollywood, CA 90028
213-465-9909
Weekly free paper

Lounge Magazine
315 S. Willaman Dr., Ste. 1
Los Angeles, CA 90048
310-859-8665
310-475-1765
All styles except mainstream
lounge@netcom.com

Maximumrocknroll
P.O. Box 460760
San Francisco, CA 94146-0760
Punk, alternative

Mean Street
6481 Orangethorpe Ave., #10
Buena Park, CA 90620
714-521-1560
Fax: 714-521-1355
Alternative, punk mag
www. meanstreet.com

Metro
550 S first St
San Jose, CA 95113
408-298-8000
toddinoue@livewire.com
Weekly entertainment

Metro News
PO Box 11964
Fresno, CA 93776
209-445-4131
Weekly paper

Mondo 2000
PO Box 10171
Berkeley, CA 94709
510-845-9018

Music Connection
6640 Sunset Blvd., #201
Hollywood, CA 90028
213-462-5772
Fax: 462-3123
All Styles

Option
1522 B Cloverfield Blvd.
Santa Monica, CA 90404
310-449-0120
Fax: 449-1153
All Styles, mostly
alternative
optionmag@aol.com

Permission Magazine
1800 Market St., Ste.777
San Francisco, CA 94102
415-789-8583
Fax: 415-522-0703
Industrial, techno
submissions@permission.com

POPsided
614 Highlander ave
Placentia, CA 92870
714-524-9825
Pop
popsided@aol.com

Pulse!
2500 Del Monte St. Bldg. C
West Sacramento, CA 95691
916-373-2450
Fax: 373-2480
All styles
www.towerrecords.com

Rap Pages
8485 Wilshire, Ste.900
Beverly Hills, CA 90211
213-651-5400
Fax: 213-655-2339
Rap

Revolt In Style
4150 Mission Blvd. Ste. 210
San Diego, CA 92109
619-274-4954
Fax: 274-7418
All Styles

RIP Magazine
8484 Wilshire Bl #900
Beverly Hills, CA 90211
213-651-5400
Heavy Metal, Hard Rock

Rock City News
1452 N Martel Ave
Los Angeles, CA 90046
213-461-6600
Fax: 461-6622

San Diego Reader
PO Box 85803
San Diego, CA 92186
619-235-3000
Weekly alternative
www.sdreader.com

S.F. Bay Guardian
520 Hampshire St.
San Francisco, CA 94110
415-255-3100
www.sfbg.com

S.F. Weekly
185 Barry St., #3800
San Francisco, CA 94107
415-541-0700
weekly newspaper

Schlock
3841 4th Ave., #192
San diego, CA 92103
619-295-0085
Fax: 619-295-5845
Indie, alternative
newsline@thegroup.net

Short Cutz
1280 Santa Anita Court
P.O. Box 2057
Woodland, CA 95695
Alternative

Slamm Magazine
3530 Camino Del Rio N., #105
San Diego, CA 92108
619-281-7526
Monthly mag, all styles
slammsd@aol.com

Speak Magazine
301 8th St., #210
San Francisco, CA 94103
415-431-5395
Alternative, hip-hop

Strobe
P.O. Box 48558
Los Angeles, CA 90048
213-938-1243
strobe@strobe.com

Thicker
P.O. Box 882283
San Francisco, CA 94188
Fanzine

Thrasher
1303 Underwood Ave.
San Francisco, CA 94124
415-822-3083
All styles

Tongue Bath
P.O. Box 14067
Berkeley, CA 94712
510-251-8255
All styles
Quarterly zine

Unhappy Planet
25351 Kay Ave.
Hayward, CA 94545
510-887-6925
Fax: 510-887-0362

URB Magazine
168 N. Vine St., #1012
Hollywood, CA 90028
213-993-0291
Fax: 466-1207
Hip-Hop/Dance Music
urbmag@aol.com

Valley Music News
2740 Auburn Blvd.
Sacramento, CA 95281
916-484-7575
Fax: 484-7610

COLORADO

Boulder Weekly
690 S Lashley Ln
Boulder, CO 80303
303-494-5511
Weekly alternative
www.boulderweekly.com

Creative Insanity
P.O. Box 1341
Denver, CO 80201
303-784-5858
Punk, hardcore

Suburban Home
1750 30th St., #365
Boulder, CO 80301
303-449-3379
Punk, hardcore

CONNECTICUT

Chairs Missing
P.O. Box 522
Stratford, CT 06497
semi-annual zine

Country Music
1 Turkey Hill Road S.
Westport, CT 06880
203-221-4950
Fax: 221-4948
Country

New Haven Advocate
1 Long Wharf Dr
New Haven, CT 06511
203-789-0010
All styles
www.newhavenadvocate.com

Spectrum
P.O. Box 1308
Atwater, CT 95301
209-358-0028
Industrial, indie

Zentertainment
P.O. Box 220756
Newhall, CT 91322
805-255-6629
seanjordan@aol.com

DELAWARE

Big Shout
1120 West St
Wilmington DE 19801
302-888-2929
Monthly paper, lots of reviews
www.magpage.com/bigshout

The Bob
P.O. Box 7223
Wilmington, DE 19803
302-477-1248
Rock & Roll

FLORIDA

Aiding & Abetting
155 19th Ave SE
St. Petersburg, FL 33705
813-823-9830
Fax: 813-827-1697
Weekly on-line zine
jworley@cent.com

Amalgam
PO Box 612321
N Miami, FL 33261
305-895-9049
Fax: 305-948-3523
Quarterly zine

Fifty/Fifty
8851 Ridgeland Dr
Miami, FL 33157
305-378-4994
Quarterly zine
fifty50mag@aol.com

Florida Flambeau
P.O. Box 20287
Tallahassee, FL 32316
904-681-6692

Focus Magazine
687 Central Ave.
St. Petersburg, FL 33701
813-865-1801
813-823-2612
Fanzine

Ink Nineteen
P.O. Box 1947
Melbourne, FL 32902
407-253-0290
ink19@aol.com

Jam Magazine
P.O. Box 151720
Altamonte Springs, FL 37215
407-767-8377
Fax: 407-767-0533
jamnorth@digital.net

MOE
P.O. Box 320753
Tampa, FL 33679-2753
813-254-4858

Moon Magazine
14 E University #206
Gainesville, FL 32601
352-377-5374
editor@moonmag.com

Music Forum Magazine
1800 Drew St.
Clearwater, FL 34625
813-298-8838
Fax: 813-298-8938
All styles

New Times
P.O. Box 011591
Miami, FL 33101
305-372-0004
All styles
www.miaminewtimes.com

Rag Magazine
PO Box 6768
Lake Worth, FL 33466
561-968-1888
Monthly mag

Reggae Report
P.O. Box 2722
Hallandale, FL 33008
305-933-1178
Fax: 305-933-1077
Monthly paper

Sonic
2215 Silver Pines Place
Orlando, FL 32806
407-294-7047
Alternative

South Florida Music News
2215 S Federal Hwy #56
Ft. Lauderdale, FL 33316
305-658-4750
Monthly mag, lots of reviews

Thrust
P.O. Box 17446
Clearwater, FL 34622
813-547-1361
All styles

Weekly Planet
402 Reo St #218
Tampa, FL 33609
813-286-1600
All styles
Weekly paper

GEORGIA

baby sue music review
P.O. Box 8989
Atlanta, GA 30306
404-875-8951
All Styles
babysue@babysue.com

Chunklet
P.O. Box 2814
Athens, GA 30612
706-543-5318
Fanzine

Creative Loafing
750 Willoughby Way NE
Atlanta, GA 30312
404-688-5623
Weekly alternative

Flagpole Magazine
P.O. Box 1027
Athens, GA 30603
706-549-9523
Fax: 548-8981
All styles
www.flagpole.com

The Technique
353 First Drive #137
Atlanta, GA 30332-0290
404-894-2830

IDAHO

The Arbiter
Boise State University
1910 University Dr
Boise, ID 83725
208-345-8204

The Argonaut
U of Idaho
Student Media
301 Student Union
Moscow, ID 83844-4271
208-885-7825
Fax: 885-2222

Carpe Noctem Magazine
260 S. Woodruff Ave., #106
Idaho Falls, ID 83401
208-528-2367
carpenoc@carpenoctum.com

ILLINOIS

Chicago Reader
11 East Illinois St.
Chicago, IL 60611
312-828-0350
Weekly alternative
www.chireader.com

Common Heir
2008 Kingston Rd.
Waukegan, IL 60087
847-244-2834
Alternative

Immeasurable Difference
401 W. Springfield #A
Urbania, IL 61801
Punk, hardcore
bsland@prarienet.org

Industrial Nation
614 W. Belmont
Chicago, IL 60657
312-665-9016
in@ripco.com

New City
770 N Halsted #208
Chicago, IL 60622
312-243-8786
The home of supreme music
writer, Ben Kim.
www.newcitynet.com

Oil
PO Box 412
Moline, IL 61266-0412
309-764-0451
Alternative, indie focus
oilmag@aol.com

Over The Edge
975 Palace, Ste5
Aurora, IL 60506
708-585-3807
Fax: 708-897-8703
All styles
jgudenas@admin.aurora.edu

Speedkills
P.O. Box 14561
Chicago, IL 60614
Underground Drag Racing Snap
Crackle Punk
75111.645@compuserve.com

Stop Smiling
P.O. Box 2038
Darien, IL 60561
708-399-4357
Indie

Subnormal
Box 602
Normal, IL 61761
Punk, industrial, gothic

Velocity
321 S. Jefferson, 3rd Fl.
Chicago, IL 6060
312-913-7034
velocitymag@aol.com

INDIANA

Cranal Fracture
P.O. Box 86
Fort Branch, IN 47648
812-753-4598
Quarterly mag

Nuvo
811 E Westfield Bl
Indianapolis, IN 46220
317-254-2400
Weekly paper

Styzine
P.O. Box 2192
Bloomington, IN 47402
812-335-8439

IOWA

Icon
PO Box 3002
Iowa City, IA 52244-3002
319-351-1531
Biweekly paper
www.jeonet.com/icon

River Cities' Reader
PO Box 4927
Davenport, IA 52808
319-324-0049
www.rcreader.com

KENTUCKY

Ace
263 N Limestone
Lexington, KY 40507
606-225-4889
Alternative paper

Louisville Eccentric
Observer
3900 Shelbyville Rd #14A
Louisville, KY 40207
502-895-9770
Weekly alternative paper

Louisville Music News
7505 Cambridge Dr
Crestwood, KY 40014
502-241-2699
Monthly paper, all styles

Rifle Comics
c/o WRFL
Box 777 University Station
Lexington, KY 40506-0025
606-257-4636
www.uky.edu/studentorgs/wrfl

Subtones
P.O. Box 24927
Lexington, KY 40524

LOUISIANA

Gambit
3923 Bienville
New Orleans, LA 70119
504-486-5900
Weekly mag
www.bestofneworleans.com

Offbeat
333 St. Charles Ave #614
New Orleans, LA 70130
504-522-5533
www.offbeat.com

Off The Record
911 N. Hennessey St.
New Orleans, LA 70119
505-522-5979
Fax: 505-523-1836
Alternative, punk
xina1211@ix.netcom.com

Times Picayune
3800 Howard Ave
New Orleans, LA 70140
504-826-3470
Daily paper
www.neworleans.net

MAINE

Casco Bay Weekly
561 A Congress St
Portland, ME 04101
207-775-6601
Weekly paper
www.cascobayweekly.com

Cradle/Maine Music
Magazine
PO Box 4811
Portland, ME 04112
207-772-1711
Biweekly mag

Face Magazine
500 Forest Ave., #2
Portland, ME 04101
207-774-9703
All styles

MARYLAND

Ant
P.O. Box 70382
Baltimore, MD 21237
410-682-2739
Fax: 410-682-5229
Bimonthly indie mag

Banana Peel Buzz
11946 Beltsville Dr., #34
Beltsville, MD 20705
301-586-0111
Fax: 301-586-0222
Bimonthly zine

Bent
331 lincoln Ave.
Takoma Park, MD 20912
301-270-2869
Bimonthly mag
bent_page@aol.com

City Paper
812 park Ave.
Baltimore, MD 21201
410-523-2300
Weekly alternative
www.citypaper.com

Dameleche
18 S. Schroeder St.
Baltimore, MD 21223
410-528-1863
Quartery zine

Dirty Linen
P.O. Box 66600
Baltimore, MD 21239-6600
410-583-7973
Folk, Electric Folk, Traditional,
World Music
www.dirtylinen.com

The Foster Child
7635 Marcy Ct
Glen Burnie, MD 21060
410-766-5218
Quarterly zine

Jazz Times
8737 Colesville Rd., 5th Fl.
Silver Spring, MD
20910-4898
301-588-4114
Fax: 588-5531
www.jazzcentralstation.com

Melodia
7420 1/2 #3 Baltimore Ave.
College Park, MD 01821
301-864-7340
Fax: 301-864-7341
All styles
tmelodia@aol.com

Music Monthly
14 W Seminary
Lutherville, MD 21093
410-494-0566
Fax: 494-0565
All styles

Uno Mass
P.O. Box 1832
Silver Springs, MD 20915
301-946-5232
FAx: 301-770-3250
unomasmag@aol.com

Unstoppable News
8900 Orwood LAne
Laurel, MD 20708
301-776-3555
Fax: 410-486-5176
Rock, alternative

MASSACHUSETTS

Boston Phoenix
126 Brookline Ave
Boston, MA 02215
617-536-5390 x3345
Weekly paper

Boston Rock
Box 371 New Town Branch
Newton, MA 02258
617-244-6803
All styles

Cheeseball
510 Comm Ave., #123
Boston, MA 02215
617-433-7069

The Cool and The Crazy
P.O. Box 335
89 Mass Ave.
Boston, MA 02115
617-859-2923
Rockabilly zine

Forced Exposure
P.O. Box 9102
Waltham, MA 02254-9102
Good

Handful of Hate
553 Cooley St.
Springfield, MA 01128
413-782-9581
fax: 413-584-4267
Punk, hardcore

Instant Entertainment
Magazine
P.O. Box 2224
Woburn, MA 01888
617-246-0334
Rock
info@instantmag.com

Lollipop Magazine
P.O. Box 147
Boston, MA 02123
617-623-5319
Fax: 617-623-5103
Punk, alternative
feedback@lollipop.com

Metronome Magazine
P.O. Box 921
Billerica, MA 01821
508-957-0925
All styles

New England Folk Almanac
PO Box 336
Cambridge, MA 02141
617-661-4708

The Noise
74 Jamaica St.
Boston, MA 02130
617-524-4735
Monthly zine
tmaxnoise@aol.com

The Pit Report
PO Box 120905
Boston, MA 02112-0905
617-338-4849
Monthly review

Popwatch
PO Box 440215
Somerville, MA 02144
617-628-5333
Monthly zine

Stubble
P.O. Box 1420
Attleboro, MA 02703
508-396-4270
Quarterly zine

Stuff
126 Brookline Ave
Boston, MA 02215
617-859-3333
Fax: 617-536-1463
All styles
stuff@stuffmag.com

Suburban Voice
P.O. Box 2746
Lynn, MA 01903
617-596-1570
Punk Rock, Garage Hardcore,
Hard Alternative, Some Metal

You Could Do Worse
P.O. Box 649
Cambridge, MA 02238
617-666-4007
Indie

You Could Do Worse
P.O. Box 175
Concord, MA 01742
617-322-8589
Rock, Alternative

Zoom
107 Merrill Ave.
Lowell, MA 01850
508-452-1072
All styles

MICHIGAN

Detroit Monthly
1400 Woodbridge
Detroit, MI 48207
313-446-0330
www.crainsdetroit.com

Detroit Music Zine
DMA, P.O. Box 24323
Detroit, MI 48224
313-730-7664
Fax: 313-886-8479

Intrr Nrrd
P.O. Box 6765
East Lansing, MI 48826
517-333-0800
Punk
bri@nervecore.com

Jam Rag
PO Box 20076
Ferndale, MI 48220
810-542-8090
Biweekly alternative paper

Metro Times
733 St. Antoine
Detroit, MI 48226
313-961-4060
Weekly paper. Thom Jurek's the
Motor City authority

Orbit
919 S. Main St #2001
Royal Oak, MI 48607
810-541-3900
Fax: 810-541-4054
orbit@orby.com

MINNESOTA

Cake Magazine
2401 University Ave. NE
Minneapolis, MN 55418
612-788-2253
Fax: 781-9181
cake@bitstream.mpls.mn.us

City Pages
401 N 3rd St #550
Minneapolis, MN 55401
612-375-1015
Weekly paper with BUZZ, a
quarterly music pull-out section
www.citypages.com

Request
7630 Excelsior Blvd.
Minneapolis, MN 55426
612-932-7700

See You
P.O. Box 16120
St. Paul, MN 55105
612-699-8540
Punk

Servo
1043 Grand Ave., #350
St. Paul, MN 55105
612-292-9050
Fax: 612-225-1034
Jazz, alternative

The Skyway News
15 S. 5th St
Minneapolis, MN 55402
612-375-9222
Fax: 375-9208
Weekly paper

The Squealer
2500 University Ave W., #F1
St. Paul, MN 55114
612-649-0580
Fax: 612-649-0729
squeal2@bitstream.mpls.mn.us

Your Flesh
P.O. Box 583264
Minneapolis MN 55458
Finnicky Punk zine
612-871-6855
Fax: 612-871-6977

We Don't Know Yet
P.O. Box 16120
St. Paul, MN 55116
612-699-8540
Punk

MISSISSIPPI

Debaser
463 Old Canton Rd.
Jackson, MS 39211
601-956-0313

MISSOURI

The New Times
207 W. Port Rd #201
Kansas City, MO 64111
816-753-7880
Weekly alternative paper
www.kcnewtimes.com

Nightimes
P.O. Box 1838
Maryland Heights, MO 63043
314-542-9995
Fax: 314-542-0156

The Note
3535 Broadway #400
Kansas City, MO 64111
913-843-6561
www.pitch.com

Pitch
3535 Broadway #400
Kansas City, MO 64111
816-561-6061
Weekly arts and
entertainment
www.pitch.com

Riverfront Times
6358 Del Mar #200
St. Louis, MO 63130
314-615-6666
Weekly arts and
entertainment
www.rftstl.com

Sample
c/o KWUR Washington
University
Box 1182
1 Brookings Drive
St Louis, MO 63130
314-935-5952
Quarterly reviews, interviews
www. kwur.wustl.edu

Yellow Pills
4933 O'Dell, #1E
St. Louis, MO 63139
Alternative
yellowpilz@aol.com

MONTANA

The Exponent
Montana State U.
Strand Union Building #305
Bozeman, MT 59717
406-994-2611
Campus paper twice a week

Missoula Independent
115 S. 4th W.
Missoula, MT 59801
406-543-6609
Weekly alternative
www.everyweek.com

NEBRASKA

The Mouthpiece
7701 Pacific St.
Omaha, NE 68114

The Reader
1618 Harney St.
Omaha, NE 68102
402-341-7323
Fax: 341-6967
Paper every other Wed.

NEVADA

The New Times
3335 Winn Road
Las Vegas, NV 89102
702-871-6780
Weekly paper

Reno News & Review
708 N. Center Street
Reno, NV 89501
702-324-4440
Weekly paper, reviews

Scope
800 South Valley View
Las Vegas, NV 89107
702-256-6388
Monthly music alternative paper
www.scopemag.com

NEW HAMPSHIRE

IQ Demo Review
13 Roberts Rd Box #8
Brookfield, NH 03872
603-522-6290
Quarterly newsletter

NEW JERSEY

The Aquarian Weekly
P.O. Box 137
Montclair, NJ 07042
201-783-4346
Alternative, Metal, Rock, Pop,
Hip-Hop, Folk

BB Gun
P.O. Box 5074
Hoboken, NJ
07030
201-798-0945
bbgun96@aol.com

Black Moon Magazine
3587 Highway 9, #174
Freehold, NJ 07728
908-517-1409
Gothic & Industrial
Bimonthly mag

B-Side
P.O. Box 1860
Burlington, NJ 08016
609-387-9424
Alternative

Carnifex
1385 Route 35, Ste 169
Middletown, NJ 07748
908-517-1409
Metal

Consumable Online
409 Washington St., #294
Hoboken, NJ 07030
201-216-0969
gajarsky@pilot.njin.net

Fantastic Voyage System
P.O. Box 6126
Hoboken, NJ 07030
201-795-4337
tfvs@aol.com

The Hard Report, Inc.
708 Stokes Rd.
Medford, NJ 08055
609-654-7272
Rock AOR, Metal,
Alternative, & Triple A

Hudson Reporter
Hudson Current
1400 Washington St
Hoboken, NJ 07030
201-798-7800
Biweekly arts and
entertainment

Jersey Beat
418 Gregory Ave.
Weehawken, NJ 07087
201-864-9054
Alternative Rock, Rap, Metal,
Industrial
jimjbeat@aol.com

Metal-Core Magazine
13 Carriage Ln.
Marlton, NJ 08053
609-596-1975
Fax: 609-983-6288
Quarterly zine

Modern Musician Monthly
3587 Hwy 9 #212
Frehold, NJ 07728
908-409-3677
All styles
thenebula@pluto.skyweb.net

Oculus Magazine
P.O. Box 148
Hoboken, NJ 07030
201-963-6859
Fax: 201-222-0672

Science Geek
P.O. Box 8641
Trenton, NJ 08650
609-273-9089
Alternative

The Traditional Music Line
P.O. Box 10598
New Brunswik, NJ 08906
908-699-0665

Yeah, Yeah, Yeah
89 Grant St.
Boonton, NJ 07005
210-402-1876
Alternative, indie

NEW MEXICO

The New Mexican/
Pasatiempo
202 E. Marcy
Santa Fe, NM 87501
505-983-3303
Weekly arts and
entertainment
www.sfnewmexican.com

The Nucity
2118 Central SE #151
Albuquerque, NM 87106
505-268-8111
Weekly paper

Santa Fe Reporter
132 E marcy
Santa Fe, NM 87501
505-988-5541
Weekly paper

NEW YORK

Agent & Manager
Facilities Magazine
650 First Ave.
New York, NY 10016
212-532-4150
Fax: 213-6382

Alter Girl
85-53 116th St.
Richmond Hill, NY 11418
917-285-9695
Bimonthly zine

Art Voice
500 Franklin St.
Buffalo, NY 14201
716-881-6604
Bimonthly art and music

Big Takeover
249 Eldridge St. #14
New York, NY 10002
212-533-6057
Alternative, Some 50's & 60's,
Some Pop

Billboard
BPI Communications
1515 Broadway 14th Floor
New York, NY 10036
212-764-7300
Fax: 212-536-5358

Buzz
P.O. Box 3111
Albany, NY 12203
518-489-0658
Alternative, Metal

Canvas
2176 Turk Hill Road
Fairport, NY 14450
Quarterly zine
jkennard@skidmore.edu

Carib News
15 W. 39th St., 13th Fl.
New York, NY 10018
212-944-1992
Fax: 212-994-2089
Carribean Music

CMJ New Music Report
11 Middle Neck Rd.
Great Neck NY 11021-2301
516-466-6000
All Genres of Alternative
cmjmonthly@cmjmusic.com

Cover
P.O. Box 1215
Cooper Station
New York, NY 10276
212-673-1152
All styles

CREEM
12 W. 27th St.
New York NY 10010
212-481-3004
Fax: 647-0236

CVC Report
Creative Video Consulting
648 Broadway #700
New York, NY 10012
212-533-9870

Details
Conde Nast Publications
632 Broadway 12th Fl.
New York, NY 10012
212-420-0689
Fax: 228-0674
www.swoon.com

Extreme
2316 Delaware Ave., Ste. 210
Buffalo, NY 14216
716-874-1373
Fax: 905-935-1149
All styles
extreme@vaxxine.com

Fast Folk Musical Magazine
P.O. Box 938
Village Station
New York, NY 10014
212-274-1636
Folk

Fly
297 7th St.
Brooklyn, NY 11215
718-965-2559
Fax: 718-788-1348
R&B, rap

Foundations
Concrete Marketing, Inc.
1133 Broadway Ste. 1220
New York, NY 10010
212-645-1360
Fax: 245-2607
Heavy Metal

Good Times
P.O. Box 33
Westbury, NY 11590
516-334-9650
Biweekly paper, all styles

Interview
575 Broadway 5th Fl.
New York, NY 10012
212-941-2900
Fax: 941-2819
All styles

The Island Ear
2-12 West Park Ave.
Long Beach NY 11561
516-889-6045
Fax: 889-5513
All Styles
editor@islandear.com

Mixmag U.S
666 Broadway Ste.1200
New York, NY 10012
212-777-6676
212-777-7167
Alternative, techno, hip-hop
dmcusa@aol.com

Musician
1515 Broadway, 11th Fl.
New York NY 10036
212-536-5208
Fax: 536-6616
All styles

Musician's Exchange
The Music Paper
P.O. Box 304
Manhasset, NY 11030
212-614-0300
Fax: 516-883-2577

Pit Report
P.O. Box 1605
New York, NY 10009
212-529-9002
Monthly zine

Propaganda Magazine
PO Box 296
New Hyde Park, NY 11040
516-248-1795
Fax: 516-248-8143
Quarterly hardcore mag

Rolling Stone
1290 Ave. of the Americas
New York, NY 10104
212-484-1616

POPsmear
648 Broadway, #909
New York, NY 10012
212-477-4502
Fax: 212-477-4942
All Styles
jpopsmear@aol.com

Psychomotozine
45 Ave. B, #2
New York, NY 10009
212-979-8165
Alternative, punk

Reggae World
P.O. Box 74
Bronx, NY 10472
718-842-0428
Fax: 718-861-3400
All styles

Rythym Music
126 MacDougal St., Ste1C
New York, NY 10012
212-358-0954
World music
rhmu@aol.com

Smash
452 Amherst St.
Buffalo, NY 14207
716-874-2316
All styles

Smug magazine
155 E. 23rd, #303
New York, NY 10010
212-505-0119
Fax: 212-505-2094
Alternative
smugny@aol.com

Seconds
24 5th Ave. #405
New York, NY 10011
212-260-0481
Fax: 260-0440
Bimonthly arts mag
secondsmag@aol.com

Sound Views
96 Henry St. Ste. 5W
Brooklyn, NY 11201
718-797-5350
Fax: 718-982-4959
soundviews@aol.com

The Source
594 Broadway, Ste. 510
New York, NY 10012
212-253-8700
Fax: 212-253-9343
Monthly mag

Spin
6 W. 18th St. 11th Fl.
New York, NY 10011
212-633-8200
Fax: 633-2668
spin@aol.com

Stumble
59 Brentwood Lane
Farport, NY 14450
Fax: 401-874-4349
Indie pop, rock
spinachpie@aol.com

Swing Magazine
342 Madison Ave., #1402
New York, NY 10017
212-490-0525
Fax: 212-490-8073
All styles

Time and a Word
P.O. Box 296
Prince St. Station
New York, NY 10012
212-925-0621
Quarterly zine

The Weak in Rock
39 Claremont Ave., #64
new York, NY 10027
212-666-2823
Indie
wes1@cornell.edu

Under the Volcano
P.O. Box 236
Nesconset, NY 11767
516-781-1905
Semi monthly zine

Urban Rag
P.O. Box 100270
Brooklyn, NY 11210
718-859-0596
Most Except R&B, Soul, Etc.

Village Voice
36 Cooper Sq.
New York, NY 10003
212-475-3300
www.villagevoice.com

NORTH CAROLINA

Bees Make Honey Reader
P.O. Box 423
Wilmington, NC 28402
910-343-2952
bees@isaacnet.net

Crunchy
908 Spring Garden St
Greensboro, NC 28403
910-272-7883
Fax: 910-272-5994
Monthly zine
crunchy@nr.infi.com

The Independent
P.O. Box 2690
Durham, NC 27715
919-286-1972
Weekly alternative

Indie File
P.O. Box 31725
Charlotte, NC 28231
704-377-6500
Monthly paper

Juice Sound Surf & Skate
6766 G #214
Wilmington, NC 28403
910-256-4653
Monthly mag
www.juice.com

Out and About
PO Box 18434
Asheville, NC 28814
704-253-2366
Biweekly entertainment paper

The Spectator Magazine
P.O. Box 12887
Raleigh, NC 27605
919-828-7393
Weekly entertainment, reviews

Triad Style
P.O. Box 20007
Greensboro, NC 27420
910-373-7374
910-373-7359 calendar items

OHIO

Alternative Press
6516 Detroit Ave. #5
Cleveland, OH 44102-2350
216-631-1212
Fax: 631-1016
Alternative
altpress@aol.com

Everybody's News
1310 Pendleton #700
Cincinnati, OH 45210
513-381-2606
Biweekly arts paper

The Ledge
P.O. Box 9441
Cincinnati, OH 45209
513-961-0037
All styles
hubcap@iac.net

Moo
1688 Northwest Blvd.
Columbus, OH 43212
614-486-6669
Fax: 614-481-8038
mooohio@aol.com

Noisy Fans of America
P.O. Box 174
Niles, OH 4446
330-652-6719
Alternative, Rock

Ouch!
P.O. Box 23309
Cincinnati, OH 45223
513-541-8972
Fax: 513-577-7099
All styles
bkb949@optimum.com

Rock Out Censorship
Box 147
Jewett, OH 43986
614-946-6535
Quarterly zine

Scene Magazine
1375 Euclid Ave #312
Cleveland, OH 44115
216-241-7550
www.clevescene.com

US Rocker
6370 York Rd. #281
Cleveland, OH 44130
216-262-8387

OKLAHOMA

The Oklahoma Gazette
P.O. Box 54649
Oklahoma City, OK 73154
405-528-6000
Weekly entertainment paper

Parabrisas
PO Box 701416
Tulsa, OK 74170
918-743-1060
Fax: 918-749-8247
Bimonthly bilingual zine

Urban Tulsa
P.O. Box 50499
Tulsa, OK 74150-0499
918-592-5550
Monthly paper

OREGON

Elixir
P.O. Box 3273
Eugene, OR 97403
541-710-1602
Fax: 541-683-0747
All styles
xmag@e-volve.com

Multiball
P.O. Box 40005
Portland, OR 97240
503-460-3873
Quarterly zine
Garage Rock

PDXS
2305 NW Kearney
Portland, OR 97210
503-224-7316
Fax: 503-224-5772

Plazm
P.O. Box 2863
Portland, OR 97208
503-222-6389
503-222-6356
All styles
plazmedia@aol.com

Puncture
P.O. Box 14806
Portland, OR 97293
503-236-8270
Alternative
puncture@teleport.com

Snipehunt
P.O. Box 3975
Portland, OR 97208
503-331-0771
Quarterly zine, lots of reviews
snipehnt@teleport.com

Two Louies
2745 NE 34th
Portland, OR 97212
503-284-5931

PENNSYLVANIA

Audio-Gliphix
William Penn Annex
#53123
Ninth & Market Streets
Philadelphia, PA 19105
215-748-2037
Fax: 215-748-4193
All styles

Barfly Monthly
516 W. Orange St.
Lancaster, PA 17603
717-293-9772
Music listings
www.lancaster.net/barfly

Black To Comm
714 Shady Ave.
Sharon, PA 16146
412-347-3187
Garage Rock, Non-Pretentious
Rock

Carbon 14
P.O. Box 29247
Philadelphia, PA 19125
215-351-0909
All styles, no commercial rock
carbon@voicenet.com

Disgruntl TV
P.O. Box 394
Chatham College
Woodland Road
Pittsburgh, PA 15232
412-365-1505
Punk, ska, techno
judas@mistica.com

Ergo Magazine
342 Adams Ave
Scranton, PA 18503
717-963-2040
Monthly mag, reviews

Fright X
1041 Buttonwood St., 2nd Fl.
Philadelphia, PA 19123
215-235-0057
Fax: 215-236-0057
Alternative, Indie
frightx@aol.com

Magnet
358 W. Trenton Ave.
Morrisville, PA 19067
215-295-8885
Fax: 215-295-8818

MAPPS
623 Spring St
Bethlehem, PA 18018
610-838-2295
Monthly local musicians mag

The Open Mike Monitor
7815 Froebel Rd.
Laverock, PA 19138
215-848-5381
raysings@aol.com

Out on the Town
P.O. Box 39040
Philadelphia, PA 19136
215-338-3550
Bimonthly entertainment,
reviews
ootme2@aol.com

Pennsylvania Musician Magazine
PO Box 362
Millerstown, PA 17062
717-444-2423
Monthly reviews, profiles

Philly Zine
P.O. Box 11662
Philadelphia, PA 19116
215-676-0628
Local, Alternative, Grunge, Punk

Pittsburgh City Paper
911 Penn Ave., 6th fl
Philadelphia, PA 15222
412-560-2489
Weekly alternative paper
www.pghcitypaper.com

Rockpile
P.O. Box 258
Jenkintown, PA 19046
215-885-7625
Fax: 215-885-7161
rockpile@netaxs.com

Urban Rag
P.O. Box 2702
Center Valley, PA 18034
610-868-3330
jwment@fast.net

RHODE ISLAND

Artzine
P.O. Box 41234
providence, RI 02940
401-621-7835
Quarterly zine

College Broadcaster
NACB
71 George St.
Providence RI 02912-1824
401-863-2225
Radio trade

Providence Phoenix
150 Chestnut St.
Providence, RI 02903
401-273-6397
Weekly entertainment, reviews
www.providencepheonix.com

Whatever
Box 157
Providence, RI 02906
401-351-0782
Alternative, punk

SOUTH CAROLINA

The Charleston City Paper
54 John St.
Charleston, SC 29403
803-577-5304
Biweekly paper

Free Times
P.O. Box 8515
Columbia, SC 29202
803-739-2488
Weekly entertainment
www.free-times.com

Gamecock
U of South Carolina
1400 Greene St.
Columbia, SC 29208
803-777-7726
Weekly paper
www.gamecock.sc.edu

SOUTH DAKOTA

Venture/The Argus Leader
200 S. Minnesota Ave
Sioux Falls, SD 57102
605-331-2317
Weekly entertainment pull-out

The Tempest
3712 Dawley Ct.
Sioux Falls, SD 57103
605-334-4134
Biweekly entertainment paper
hudson@inst.augie.edu

TENNESSEE

Contemporary Christian Music
107 Kenner Ave.
Nashville, TN 37205
615-386-3011
Fax: 386-3380
Christian Music

The Ledge
210 Lewisburg Ave.
Franklin, TN 37064
Fanzine

Limp Zine
326 Santa Rosa Court
Old Hickory, TN 37138
Fanzine

Memphis Flyer
460 Tennessee St
Memphis, TN 38101
901-521-9000
Weekly entertainment
www.memhisflyer.com

Metropulse
505 Market St #300
Knoxville, TN 37902
615-522-5399
Weekly entertainment, reviews
www.metropulse.com

The Nashville Scene
209 10th Ave #222
Nashville, TN 37203
615-244-7989
Weekly entertainment listings, reviews

Times Mirror Tennessee
620 Dickerson Pike
Nashville, TN 37207
615-254-5176
Weekly black community paper

TEXAS

Austin American Statesman
305 S Congress
Austin, TX 78704
512-445-3500
Daily paper, reviews, profiles
www.austin360.com

Austin Chronicle
PO Box 49066
Austin, TX 78765
512-454-5766
Alternative weekly
www.auschron.com

Buzzmonger
P.O. Box 1205
Dallas, TX 75221
214-994-3425

Concert Circuit
P.O. Box 630372
Houston, TX 77263
713-277-6626
Monthly zine

Dream Whip Magazine
P.O. Box 53832
Lubbock, TX 79453
806-794-9263
Punk, folk, soul, jazz

HM
6614 Bradley
Austin, TX 78745
512-929-9279
Fax: 512-929-1950
Industrial, punk, metal, hard Christian
hmmag@aol.com

Indie Street
434 Coombs Creek
Dallas, TX 75211
214-337-7265
Indie

Jam Magazine
PO Box 852186
Mesquite, TX 75815
972-329-2241

Lil' Rhino Gazette
P.O. Box 14139
Arlington, TX 76094
817-794-0772
Quarterly zine

Music City Texas
620 Circle Ave
Round Rock, TX 78664
512-218-8055

Music News Magazine
1506 Pearl
League City, TX 77573
281-480-6397
www.neosoft.com/~musicnew

Performance
1101 University #108
Fort Worth, TX 76107
817-338-9444
Fax: 877-4273
www.performancemag.com

Pop Culture Press
P.O. Box 150423
Austin, TX 78715
512-445-3208
Alternative
pcp@monsterbit.com

Public News
2038 Lexington
Houston, TX 77098-4222
713-520-1520
pnews@sam.neosoft.com.
http://www.neosoft.com/
publicnews/
Weekly alternative chock full of
reviews, listings

Texas Beat Magazine
P.O. Box 4429
Austin, TX 78765-4429
512-441-2422
All Styles
www.texasbeat.com

Thora-Zine
PO Box 49390
Austin, TX 78765
512-453-6747
Quarterly alternative zine
tzine@eden.com

X-Cell
5228 Anchorage Ave
El Paso, TX 79924
915-759-0482
All styles

UTAH

Catalyst Magazine
362 E Broadway
Salt Lake City, UT 84111
801-363-1505
Monthly alternative

The Event Newspaper
362 E Broadway
Salt Lake City, UT 84111
801-363-1505
Biweekly arts paper

SLUG (Salt Lake Underground)
2120 S 700th E #H200
Salt Lake City, UT 84106
801-487-9221
Fax: 801-487-1359
slugmag@aol.com

VERMONT

The Vermont Cynic
U of Vermont
Billings Student Center
Burlington, VT 05405-0040
802-656-4413
Fax: 802-656-0337
Weekly on campus paper

Vox
PO Box 940
Shelburne, VT 05482
802-985-2400
Weekly arts, reviews
www.vermont/times.com

VIRGINIA

Country Plus Magazine
6933 Westhampton Dr.
Alexandria, VA 22037
703-765-7042
Monthly reviews, listings

Nervous Breakdown
9397 Tartanview, VA 22032
703-548-2248
Punk, ska, reggae
ssnake@erols.com

WASHINGTON

Blue Suede Shoes
P.O. Box 25
Duvall, WA 98019
206-788-2776
Quarterly paper

Fizz
1509 Queen Anne Ave. N #276
Seattle WA 98109
206-283-7042
Alternative monthly
fizzmag@aol.com

Pool Dust
P.O. Box 85664
Seattle, WA 98145
Skate punk fanzine

The Rocket Magazine
2028 5th Ave.
Seattle, WA 98121
206-728-ROCK
Fax: 728-8827
Alternative, Rap, Rock, Blues

Rockrgrl
7683 SE 27th St., #317
Mercer Island, WA 98040
206-230-4280
Fax: 206-230-4288
Alternative, rock
rockrgrl@aol.com

The Stranger
1202 E. Pike St. #1225
Seattle, WA 98122
206-323-7101
Fax: 206-323-7203
Weekly alternative paper
postmaster@thestranger.com

Swellsville
P.O. Box 85334
Seattle, WA 98145
All Styles

Ten Things Jesus Wants You to Know
1407 NE 45 St., #17
Seattle, WA 98105
206-547-9822
Punk, indie
ten@u.washington.edu

WASHINGTON DC

The City Paper
2390 Champlain St NW
Washington, DC 20009
202-332-2100
Weekly paper
www.washingtoncitypaper.com

WISCONSIN

Milk
4220 N. Ardmore
Milwaukee, WI 53211
414-961-7304
Fax: 414-332-8095
Alternative
jmodell@csd.uwm.edu

CANADA

Canadian Musician
Norris Publications
23 Hannover Dr.
St. Catherines, Ont L2W 1A3
CANADA
416-641-3471
Fax: 905-641-1648

Chart Magazine
PO Box 332
Willowdale Station A
No. York, ONT M2N5S9
416-363-3101
Monthly trade

Caustic Truths
146 Old Sheppard Ave.
North York, ON M2J 3L9
416-756-0362
Fax: 416-756-2107
Alternative, punk

Discorder Magazine
U of British Columbia
c/o CITR SUB #233
6138 "S" Blvd
Vancouver, BC V6T 1Z1
CANADA
604-822-3017
Monthly alternative music mag

Exclaim Magazine
7B Pleasant Bl #966
Toronto, ONT M4T1K2
416-535-9735
Monthly zine, all styles

Gee-Zuz
2043 E 23rd
Vancouver, BC V5N 2T9
604-879-9129
Punk

Georgia Straight
1235 W Pender 2nd Fl
Vancouver, BC V6E2V6
604-681-2000
Weekly entertainment

Hour
4130 St Dennis St
Montreal, QUE H2W2M5
514-848-0777
Weekly alternative

ID
69 Wyndham St N #211
Guelph, ONT N1H4E7
519-766-9891
Free biweekly, reviews, profiles

In Hell's Belly
Box 4, 199 W. Hastings St.
Vancouver, BC V6B 1H4
604-873-3765
All styles, no jazz

M.E.A.T Magazine
PO Box 35 Station O
Toronto, ONT M4A2M8
416-699-8486
Monthly music mag, alternative,
hard rock

Montreal Mirror
400 McGill St
Montreal, QUE H2Y2G1
514-393-1010
Weekly paper

NOW
150 Danforth Ave
Toronto, ONT M4K1N1
416-461-0871
Weekly entertainment

Peace
5334 Yonge St#1018
Toronto, ONT M2N6M2
416-504-0065
Every month and a1/2 rap, hip
hop

Terminal City
825 Granville St #203
Vancouver, BC V6Z1K9
604-669-6910
Weekly entertainment

The Voice
275 St Jacques #20
Montreal, QUE H2Y1M9
514-842-7127
Monthly reviews of
alternative/hip hop

Distribution

Distributors sell the releases of independent labels to record stores in their territory, and in some cases to other distributors. Good distribution increases your chances of selling a substantial amount of records. Getting a distributor to properly handle your release, if at all, is a difficult task for an emerging band/label. Getting them to actually pay you is an extremely difficult task.

Pricing

In order to get a distributor to carry your product, you'll have to convince them that your records are going to sell. This means sending them college radio playlists, good reviews, advertisements that (you say) you'll put out and touring. If a distributor agrees to stock your record, they'll ask for a wholesale price. You'll be pressed to find a distributor that will buy vinyl from an independent band, but for full-length cassettes the ballpark price is between $4.50 and $5.50; for full length CDs it's between $7.00 and $8.50. EPs (three to six songs) and extended length releases are slightly less and more, respectively.

Terms

Then there's the terms. Distributors are going to try to get the longest possible terms on which to pay you. First, you send them the goods (get them to pay the freight or designate the shipping company they use). Second, you invoice them (send them a bill). Depending on the terms you agree to, they are obligated to pay you before either 10, 30, 45, 60, 90 or 120 days after the date you invoice them. You want to have the shortest terms possible, so you can get your money and pay your bills. Your ability to get shorter terms will center on how badly the distributor wants to carry your record, if at all. Whatever terms you get, the distributor should pay you during that amount of time. Here's where the fun starts.

How To Survive

The rule of thumb for dealing with a distributor is to only give them as many records as you can afford to lose. Distributors are notorious for: not paying, losing your invoice, going out of business, etc. The best way to ensure payment is to have another record coming out the next month that the distributor wants, and not selling it to them until they pay you for the first one. If that's not the case, keep in constant contact with the distributor. When they place an order with you, always ask for a P.O. (Purchase Order) number. This is critical for tracking the order through their system, and for proving that they did in fact order the records.

Invoicing

If you have access to a computer, use it to make your invoice. The idea is to make it look like something that they should pay on time. No handwritten letters! Include their P.O.

number and your invoice number (make one up) on the invoice, and clearly state the terms agreed to and the due date for payment. You'll need to find out who handles the distributor's accounts payable and send your invoices to that person.

If they don't pay, tell them to send your records back. Then, threaten them with collection and call a few collection agencies in their area. If you've got the P.O. number and have properly invoiced the distributor, then you have a legitimate debt. A collection agency will simply tack on their fee and harrass said distributor.

When you ship them your records, use the delivery confirmation service where UPS or the post office sends you proof that the distributor received your package. Once they have your product, give them tour dates, band info., new reviews, playlists; anything that will help them sell your records and know where they have the best chance of selling them. If you stay in close touch with them, it'll reduce the chances of them blowing you off when pay time rolls around.

Returns

It is standard practice in the record industry for record companies to allow stores and distributors to return unsold records for credit against what they owe. If it's clear that a distributor is not going to pay you, demand that they return your goods. Most will probably want to return when it's time to pay you, anyway. Then, after they've sent them back, they'll turn around and order those same records back from you again! This is their way of avoiding spending cash on inventory that is sitting in their warehouse. When they re-order the records from you, they now have fresh 90-day (or whatever) terms to work with. One thing you must specify is that they pay freight on any returns.

The Bottom Line

You should try distributors one at a time, with small amounts of merchandise on the shortest terms possible. This way you can find out who will deal with you in good faith, and not risk a lot of your records. Sure, you'll be thrilled when they order 1000 CDs, but you won't be so happy when they stiff you.

How can you get your records to the consumers and not have to deal with distributors? Read the next chapter for some helpful ideas. For the brave: the following is a list of independent distributors. Where available, after each listing are the styles of music that the distributor handles. Call first before sending anything.

Distributor Directory Musical Styles

A - Alternative
B - Blues
BG - Bluegrass
C - Country
CH - Christian
CL - Classical
D - Dance
E - Ethnic (Zydeco, British Isles, Eastern European)
F - Folk
G - Gospel
I - Industrial

J - Jazz
M - Metal
NA - New Age
R - Rock
RA - Rap
R&B - Rhythm & Blues
RG - Reggae
SW - Spoken Word
T - Techno
W - Women
WB - World Beat

Distributors

3C Sales Corp
The Laurie Group
1411 W. Emily Ct.
Abingdon, MD 21009
410-676-2001
Fax: 410-676-2003

Abbey Road Distributors
15050 Schumaker Ave
Santa Fe Springs, CA 90670
310-802-2011
Fax: 800-959-3475

Action Music Sales, Inc.
6541 Eastland Rd.
Cleveland, OH 44142
216-243-0300
Fax: 216-243-4063
All

Action Music
14611 E. 9 Mile Rd.
E. Detroit, MI 48021
810-779-1380
Fax: 810-243-4063

African Record Centre Distributors
1194 Nostrand
Cleveland, OH 44142
718-493-4500
Fax: 718-467-0099
WB

Albany Music Distibution
P.O. Box 5011
Albany, NY 12205
518-453-2203
Fax: 518-453-2205
CL, J

Alcazar Mail Order
P.O. Box 429
Waterbury, VT 05676
802-244-7856
Fax: 802-244-6128

All Point Bulletin (APB)
138 Arena St., Suite A
El Segundo, CA 90245
310-333-1733
Fax: 310-333-1732
All

Allegro Corporation
14134 NE Airport Way
Portland, OR 97230
503-257-8480
Fax: 503-257-9061
All

Altavoz Distribution
108 N. Adams St.
Rockville, MD 20850
301-279-0286
FAx: 301-279-6837
All

American Gramaphone Records
9130 Mormon Bridge Rd.
Omaha, NE 68152
402-457-4341
Fax: 402-457-4332
NA,J,CL

Arc Distributing
580 Reading Rd.
Cincinnati, OH 45202
513-381-4237
Fax: 513-381-4260
All

Associate Distributors
3803 N. 36th Ave.
Phoenix, AZ 85019
602-278-5584
Fax: 602-269-6356
R,B,RG,J,D,M,F,BG,C,NA,
RA,WB

AudioQuest Music
P.O. Box 6040
San Clemente, CA 92674
714-498-2770
Fax: 714-498-8223
J, B

Austin
P.O. Box 312
Austin, TX 78767
512-451-9770
Texas Artists

Avant Gard
7500 St. Loius St.
Skokie, IL 60076
847-329-1925
A

Baker & Taylor
8140 N. Lehigh Ave.
Morton Grove, IL 60053
847-965-8060
Fax:847-965-8093
All

Balbos Records Co.
10900 Washington Blvd.
Culver City, CA 90230
310-204-3792
Fax: 310-204-0886
E

Bassin
4250 Coral Ridge Dr.
Coral Springs, FL 33065
954-346-4024
All Styles

Bayside
2609 Del Monte St.
West Sacramento, CA 95691
916-373-2548
Fax: 916-373-2511
All

Beacon Records
P.O. Box 3129
Peabody, MA 01961
508-762-8400
Fax: 508-762-8467

Belt Drive Records Ltd.
P.O. Box 101107
San Antonio, TX 78201-9107
800-846-5201

The Benson Music Group
365 Great Circle Rd.
Nashville, TN 37228
615-742-6881
Fax: 615-742-6911
G

Big Daddy
71 Newark Way
Maplewood, NJ 07040
201-761-7000
Fax: 201-761-7576
All

Big Easy
P.O. Box 26575
New Orleans, LA 70186
504-241-9800
Fax: 504-241-9866
bigeasydist@aol.com
All

Big Money, Inc.
P.O. Box 2483
Minneapolis, MN 55402
612-379-2614
R, A

Big Spazz
1614 1/4 Edgecliff Dr.
Los Angeles, CA 90026
213-661-5167
Fax: 213-660-5005
R,I, A

Big State
4830 Lakawana, #121
Dallas, TX 75247
214-631-1100
Fax: 214-630-2866
A, R,B,RG,BG,C,J,D,M,F,NA

CRD
255 Parkside Dr.
San Fernando, CA 91340
818-361-7979
Fax: 818-365-7328
A, R,B,RG,BG,C,J,D,M,F,NA,RA

C.W. Paas, Inc.
1039 West Lake St.
Chicago, IL 60607
312-733-1717
Fax: 312-733-5819
D

Cadence Jazz Records
Cadence Building
Redwood, NY 13679
315-287-2852
Fax: 315-287-2860
cjr@cadencebuiding.com
J

California Record
Distributors
255 Parkside Dr.
San Fernando, CA 91340
818-361-7979
Fax:818-365-7328
All

California Record Dist.
San Francisco
10th & Parker Streets 5th Floor
Berkeley, CA 94710
510-548-3203
Fax: 510 548-9354
All

Caltex Records
9045-A Eton Ave.
Canoga Park, CA 91304
818-700-8657
Fax: 818-700-0285
All

The Calvary Music Group
142 8th Ave. N
Nashville, TN 37203
615-244-8800
Fax: 615-242-6515
G

Cambridge
205 Fortune Blvd.
Milford, MA 01757
508-478-2031

Campus Records
874 Albany Shaker Rd.
Latham, NY 12110
518-783-6698
Fax: 518-783-6753
R,B,RG,BG,C,J,D,M,F,NA,RA

Cargo
7070 St. Urbain, Ste. 200
Montreal, Quebec H2S 3H6
Canada
514-495-1212
Fax: 514-495-1211
A, M, R

Cargo
4901-906 Morena Bl.
San Diego CA 92117
619-483-9292
www.cargomusic.com
A

Carmel Records
P.O. Box 50353
Palo Alto, CA 94303
415-856-3650
Fax: 415-856-0371
J

Caroline (West)
6161 Santa Monica Blvd.
Ste. 208
Los Angeles, CA 90038
213-468-8626
www.caroline.com
A, R,RG,J,D,M,NA,I,WB,F

Cexton Records
2740 S. Harbor Blvd. Ste. K
Santa Ana, CA 92704
714-641-1074
Fax: 714-641-1025
www.cexton.com
J

Cisco Music Inc.
6307 DeSoto Ave. Suite C
Woodland Hills, CA 91367
818-884-2234
Fax: 818-884-1268
www.superanalogue.com//suana
All

City Hall Records
25 Tiburon St.
San Rafael, CA 94901
415-457-9080
Fax: 415-457-0780
www.linex.com/cityhall
All

City Hall
3038 21st Ave.
W. Seattle, WA 98199
206-282-4820
B, RA, F, RG

Colorado One Stop
PO Box 460718
Aurora, CO 80046
303-766-2273
Fax: 303-766-2553

Com Four Distribution
7 Dunham Place
Brooklyn, NY 11211
718-599-2205
Fax: 718-599-1052
www.com4.com

Creative Musicians Coalition
1024 W. Wilcox Ave.
Peoria, IL 61604
309-685-4843
Fax: 309-685-4878
All

Curtis Wood
Rte. 1 Box 172-C
Telephone, TX 75488
903-664-3741
All

Dance Floor Distribution
111 Cedar Lane
Englewood, NJ 07631
201-568-7066
Fax: 201-568-2599
R&B, D, RA

Delos International Inc.
1645 N. Vine St. Suite 340
Hollywood, CA 90028
213-962-2626
Fax: 213-962-2636
www.delosmus.com
CL

The Dice Company
P.O. Box 60471
Palo Alto, CA 94306
415-326-4346
All

Digital Waves Corp.
1001 Biroso Dr.
Costa Mesa, CA 92627
714-650-7900
Fax: 714-651-1025
R, A

Direct Records
600 Pickard West, #101
Mt. Pleasant, MI 48858
800-770-6792
Fax: 517-773-2126

Disc-o-Rama Music
186 W. 4th St.
New York, NY 10014
212-206-8417
Fax: 212-741-0908
All

Distribution Fusion Inc.
5455 rue Pare Suite 101
Montreal, QUE H4P 1P7 Canada
514-738-4600
Fax: 514-737-9780

DNA/Distribution North America
1 Camp St.
Cambridge, MA 02140
617-661-4362
Fax: 617-354-4840
info@rounder.com
All

Dream Disc
222 W. north St.
Kendaville, IN 46755
219-347-8080
A, R, M

Dutch East India
125 Michael Drive
Syossett, NY 11791
516-677-6000
Fax: 516-677-6007
A, R, I, SW

Eastside Digital
530 N. 3rd St.
Minneapolis, MN 55401
612-375-0233
Fax: 612-359-9580
B, BG, C, E, F, R, WB, RG
www.noside.com

East Coast Music
311 Willowbrook Rd.
Staten Island, NY 10314
718-698-7552
B, BG, CL, J, F

Echo Records Inc./ Dancefloor
115 Cedar Ln.
Englewood, NJ 07631
201-568-7066
Fax: 201-568-2599
D, R&B, RG, J

Electronic Fetus
2000 4th Ave. South
Minneapolis, MN 55404
612-870-1747
Fax: 612-870-4664
All

EMC Rhythm Ltd., Inc.
P.O. Box 10167
Newark, NJ 07101
201-673-1375
Fax: 201-673-2326
J, R&B

Empire Music Group
170 W. 74th St.
New York, NY 10023
212-580-5959
Fax: 212-874-8605
CL, J, F

Essex Entertainment
560 Sylvan Ave.
Englewood Cliffs, NJ 07632
201-894-8700
Fax: 201-894-8630
All

Europac Warehouse Sales
9586 Distribution Ave. #M
San Diego, CA 92121
619-566-7662
Fax: 619-566-0750
All Styles
www.europac.com

Fantasy Inc.
2600 10th St.
Berkeley, CA 94710
510-549-2500
Fax: 510-486-2015
J

Feedback
524 Windy Point Dr.
Glendale Heights, IL 60139
708-545-9100
Fax: 708-545-9191
All

Festival Distribution
1351 Grant St.
Vancouver, BC V5L 2X7
800-633-8282
Fax: 604-253-2634
F, B, J

Fiebre Latina
7960 Silverton Ave. Suite 116
San Diego, CA 92126
619-695-8863
Fax: 619-695-3768
E

Final Decade
P.O. Box 1693
Old Chelsea Station
New York, NY 10011
212-929-5462
Fax: 212-929-0749
R,B,RG,J,D,M,NA,RA,WB,I

Flat Town Music Co.
P.O. Drawer 10
Ville Platte, LA 70586
318-363-2177
Fax: 318-363-2094
E

Folkcarft Records
P.O. Box 807
Winstead, CT 06098
860-379-9857
Fax: 860-379-7685
F, WB

Forefront
222 Monroe St. Apt. 2FN
P.O. Box 1964
Hoboken, NJ 07030-1308
201-653-1990
Fax: 201-653-2011
M

Frankies
1533 Corp. Dr.
Freeport, LA 71107
318-424-9441
Fax: 318-424-8223
All

Freckle
P.O. Box 4005
Seattle, WA 98104
206-323-6200
R,G,BG,C,J,M,F,NA,D,B,
R&B,WB

FTC
8306 Wilshire Blvd., #544
Beverly Hills, CA 90211
213-965-9585
Fax: 213-933-3118
J, WB

G.H.B. Jazz Foundation
1206 Decatur St.
New Orleans, LA 70116
504-525-1776
Fax: 504-525-0690
J

Global Pacific
P.O. Box 2001
Sonoma, CA 95476
707-996-2748
Fax: 707-996-2658
www.ninegaits.com/global.htm
E,NA,J,WB

Goldband Records
P.O. Box 1485
Lake Charles, LA 70601
318-439-8839
Fax: 318-491-0994
All, no rap

Goldenrod/Horizon
1310 Turner St.
Lansing, MI 48906
517-484-1712
Fax: 517-484-1771
www.goldenrod.com
W,B,E,F,NA,RG,WB

Gramavision Records
27 Congress St.
Shetland Park
Salem, Mass 01970
508-744-7678

Great Bay Music
1400 Alice Anna ST.
Baltimore, MD 21231
410-675-7855
Fax: 410-675-1102
All

H.L. Dist., Inc.
6940 SW 12th St.
Miami, FL 33144
305-262-7711
All

Hailing Frequency
Entertainment
7438 Shoshone Ave.
Van Nuys, CA 91406
818-881-9888
Fax: 818-881-0555

Happy Squid Records
P.O. Box 94565
Pasadena, CA 91109-4565
818-794-4225

Harmony House
1755 E. Maple
Troy, MI 48083
810-524-2800
Fax: 810-524-1266
All

Hired Gun
730 E. Elm St.
Conshohocken, PA 19428
610-825-9698
Fax: 610-825-7329
All

Hits Unlimited
2015 W. Irving Park Rd.
Chicago, IL 60618
312-296-4487
J, B, A

Horizons Records
8863 Burlington
Brookfield, IL 60513
708-387-0086
Fax: 708-387-0083
All, no CL

Horsehoe Distributors
2937 Harlin Drive
Nashville, TN 37211
615-331-1125
All, no rap

Ichiban Records
3991 Royal Dr., NW
Kennesaw, GA 30144
404-419-1414
Fax: 404-419-1230
All, no CL

Imaginary Records
5324 Buena Vista Pike
Nashville, TN 37218
615-299-9237
All

Impact
910 S. Hohokam Dr.
Tempe, AZ 85281
602-894-8550
FAx: 602-894-6640
All

I.N.D.I.
1231 E. 26th St.
Cleveland, OH 44144
216-696-2701
Fax: 216-696-2066
RA,R&B

Imperial Records, Inc.
P.O. Box 2642
Santa Maria, CA 93457
805-934-8400
NA

Instinct Entertainment
2700 Neilson Wy. Ste. 1521
Santa Monica, CA 90405
310-452-0354
Fax: 310-452-5936
All

International Marketing Group
1900 Elm Hill Pike
Nashville, TN 37210
615-889-8000
Fax: 615-871-4817
All

Intersound
P.O. Box 1724
Rosewell, GA 30077
770-664-9262
Fax: 770-664-7316
All

Irish Records International
P.O. Box 196 Accord Station
Hingham, MA 02018
617-878-7936
Fax: 617-878-9018

JDC
507 Pier Ave.
Hermosa Beach, Ca 90254
310-937-4455
Fax: 310-937-4456
D,RA,R&B,I

JFL
2500 NW 5th Ave
Miami, FL 33127
305-573-7800
Fax: 305-573-1006
All

Jay Jay Records
35 NE 62nd St.
Miami, FL 33138
305-758-0000

June Appal
306 Madison St.
Whitesburg, KY 41858
606-633-0108
appalshop@aol.com
F,BG,G

Just in Case
P.O. Box 944
Canton, CT 06019
203-693-9567
A, R

Justice Records
P.O. Box 980369
Houston, TX 77098-0369
713-520-6669
Fax: 713-526-7045
justice@justicerecords.com
J,R&B

K
P.O. Box 7154
Olympia, WA 98507
360-786-1594
Fax: 360-786-5024
A,R

K-Tel International, Inc.
2605 Fernbrook Lane North
Minneapolis, MN 55447
612-559-6800
Fax: 612-559-6826
All

Keeling
1342 St. Johns Pl.
Brooklyn, NY 11213
718-778-9470
Fax:718-778-8312
RG,R&B

Kandamerica, Inc.
134 La Porte East Street
Arcadia, CA 91006
818-445-7700
Fax: 818-445-1000
All

Koch International
Southwest Regional Office
1803 Westridge Drive
Austin, TX 78704
512-442-5570
Fax: 512-442-5730
austinkoch@aol.com
All

Kubaney
3016 NW 79th St.
Miami, FL 33122
305-591-7684
Fax: 305-477-0789
E,RA

Lady Slipper
3205 Hillsborough Rd.
Durham, NC 27705
919-683-1570
Fax: 919-383-3525
NA,W
www.ladyslipper.org

Liaison
9445 Washington Bl. North
Suite K
Laurel, MD 20723
410-880-6111
Fax: 410-776-4566
D,R,R&B

Lifedance
3479 NW Yeon Ave.
Portland, OR 9271
503-228-9430
Fax: 503-228-5039
BG,NA,C,J,F,W

The Local Music Store
2800 Juniper Street Suite 1
Fairfax, VA 22031
703-641-8995
Fax: 703-641-9254
www.localmusicstore.com
All

MS
7635 W. Oklahoma Ave., Ste. LL1
Milwaukee, WI 53219
414-329-3700
Fax: 414-329-3710
All

Macola Records
P.O. Box 3510
Redondo Beach, Ca 90277
310-937-3789
Fax: 310-937-3793
D,RA,WB,R&B

Malverne
275 Secaucus Rd
Secaucus, NJ 07094
201-865-4100
Fax: 201-865-4100
R,B,RG,C,J,D,M,NA,RA,WB

Malverne
329 Washington St.
Woburn, MA 01801
617-933-7346
Fax: 617-933-7459
All styles

Mammoth Distributed Labels
101 B Street
Carrboro, NC 27510
919-933-6890
Fax: 919-933-2206
E-mail: mammoth.com
All Styles

Ment Media Group
P.O. Box 272
Center Valley, PA 18034
610-868-3330
Fax: 610-868-3339
R, A

Metro
P.O. Box 10004
Silver Spring, MD 20914
301-622-2473
www.metromusic.com
A,R,M,F

Midnight
P.O. Box 390
Old Chelsea Station
N.Y.C., NY 10011
212-255-3892
Fax: 212-741-7230
www.midnightrecords.com
A,R,B,C,I,J,R&B

Mill City
3820 E. Lake St.
Minneapolis, MN 55406
612-722-6649
Fax: 612-722-2079
B,BG,E,J,NA,F,WB,SW

Modern Music Mailorder
2905 O'donnell St
Baltimore, MD 21224
410-675-2172
Fax: 675-2373
rise1@aol.com

Mordam Records
P.O. Box 420988
San Francisco, CA 94142
415-642-6800
All

Mosh Pit
P.O. Box 9545
Colorado Springs, CO 80932
719-633-5752
www.pitmagazine.com
M,I,R,A,SW

Music Center
1314 1st Ave. N
Birmingham, AL 35203
205-251-8252
Fax: 205-251-8253
B,C,J,R,R&B
1stopmusic@prodigy.net

Music City
P.O. Box 22773
Nashville, TN 37202
615-255-7315
All

Music Craft
P.O. Box 2839
Honolulu, HI 96819
808-841-6219
Fax: 808-842-0362
All

Music Design
4650 N. Port Washington Rd.
Milwaukee, WI 53212
414-961-8380
Fax: 414-961-8381
order@musicdesign.com
NA,J,WB,W

Music Distributors
6504 Midway #200
Fort Worth, TX 76117
817-831-2982
All Styles

Music Latina, Inc.
2360 W. Pico Blvd.
Los Angeles, CA 90006
213-385-2151
E

Music People, Inc.
1025 W. MacArthur Blvd.
Oakland, CA 94608
510-653-5811
Fax: 510-652-5058
All Styles

Music Town Record Distributors
159 Village Green Dr.
Nashville, TN 37217
615-361-7902
Fax: 361-7600
All

Music Video Distributors
P.O. Box 1128
Norristown, PA 19404
610-650-8200
Fax: 215-272-6074
musviddis@aol.com

Navarre
7400 49th Ave.
New York, NY 55428
800-728-4000
Fax: 612-332-2156
A,R,B,BG,VH,F,I,J,M,NA,R&B

Navarre
16820 Ventura Blvd.
Encino, CA 91436
818-380-6600
Fax: 818-380-6611
All Styles

Navarre
3228 13th Ave. W.
Seattle, WA 98119
206-285-9655

Naxos of America
1165 Marlkress Rd., #E&F
Cherry Hill, NJ 08003
609-751-4744
Fax: 609-751-7721
CL, J

Nimbus Records
P.O. Box 7427
Charlottesville, VA 22906
800-782-0778

North Country Record
Cadence Building
Redwood, NY 13679
315-287-2852
Fax: 315-287-2860
www.cadencebuiling.com
J,B,NA,E,I,R&B

Norwalk Record
1193 Knollwood Circle
Anaheim, CA 92801
714-995-8111
M,R,I

Northwest Alliance of Independent Labels
282 SE Oak St., #100
Portland, OR 97214
503-736-3261
Fax: 503-736-3264
A, R, M

Note-Ably Yours
6865 Scarff Rd.
New Carlisle, OH 45344
512-845-8232
Fax: 513-845-3773
NA,F

O.R Records
6304 Guilford, Ste. C
Indianapoils, IN 46220
317-466-1352
Fax: 317-466-0494
A

Old Fogey
1100 N. Washington
P.O. Box 14210
Lansing, MI 48901
517-372-7888
Fax: 517-372-5155
F,BG,J,B,RG,C,WB,E,G,W, R&B

Orbius Distribution
16007-859 Dundas St. W
Toronto, ON M6J 3W2
416-530-0709
Fax: 416-530-0735
D, RA

PPI Entertainment
88 St. Francis St.
Newark, NJ 07105
201-344-4214
Fax: 201-344-0465

Pacific Coast One-Stop
9158 Eton Ave.
Chatsworth, CA 91311
818-709-3640
Fax: 818-709-7722
All

Pain
18758-6 Bryant St.
Northridge, CA 91324
818-772-6589
Fax: 818-772-2140
A, WB

Parasol
905 S. Lynn
Urbana, IL 61801
217-344-8609
Fax: 217-344-8652
All

Passport
2335 Delgany
Denver, CO 80216
303-292-9333
Fax: 303-292-3030
All

Paul Starr
1660 Lake Drive W.
Chanhassen, MN 55317
612-361-6667
Fax: 612-361-6936
All

Performance Distributors
2 Oak St.
P.O. Box 156
New Brunswick, NJ 08901
908-545-3004
Fax: 908-545-6054
A, B

Phantom CD
1001 Brioso Drive
Costa Mesa, CA 92067
800-533-9963
All

Phillips Enterprises
113 B Woodwinds Dr.
Cary, NC 27511
919-460-8686
Fax: 919-782-7037
All

Pigeon Neck
P.O. Box 9450
Denver, CO 80209
303-973-8236
Fax: 303-973-8236
A

Plug Productions
273 Chippewa Dr.
Columbia, SC 29210
803-750-5391
All

PPI Entertainment
88 St. Francis St.
Newark, NJ 07105
201-344-4214
Fax: 201-567-1565
R, J

Pravda
3823 N. Southport Ave.
Chicago, IL 60613
312-549-3779
A, R

Pricerite
P.O. Box 408
Freeport, NY 11520-0408
516-867-3770
Fax: 516-867-3774
All

Priority Records
6430 Sunset Blvd., #900
Hollywood, CA 90028
800-253-2300
Fax: 213-856-8796
RA, R, R&B

Profile
740 Broadway 7th Floor
N.Y.C., NY 10003
212-529-2600
Fax: 212-420-8216
RG,D,E,RA,WB,I, T

Qualiton Imports
24-02 40th Ave
Long Island City, NY 11101
718-937-8515
FAx: 718-729-3239
All

R.O.W. Entertainment
255 Shields Ct.,
Markham, ONT L3R 8V2
Canada
905-475-3550
Fax:905-475-4163
All

RAS
P.O. Box 42517
Washington, DC 20015
301-588-9641
Fax: 315-588-7108
R,RG

Red Distribution
79 5th Ave.
New York, NY 10003
212-337-5200
212-337-5252
All

Rediscover Music
705 S. Washington St.
Naperville, IL 66540
708-305-0770
Fax: 708-305-0782
F

Rep
9650 Newton Ave.
Bloomington, MN 55431
612-948-3700
Fax: 612-948-3790
All

ROIR International
611 Broadway Ste. 411
New York, NY 10012
212-477-0563
Fax 212-505-9908
RG,R,B

RRRecords
23 Central Street
Lowell, MA 01852
508-454-8002
R,I, A

Records Ltd.
1314 S. Hobart Blvd.
Los Angeles, CA 90006
213-737-2611
Fax: 213-737-0206

Rego Irish Records, Inc.
64 New Hyde Park Rd.
Garden City, NY 11530
800-854-3746
Fax: 516-354-7768
kellsmus@pipeline.com

R.E.D. Distribution
3420 Ocean Park Blvd
Suite 3050
Santa Monica, CA 90405
310-581-8205
Fax: 310-581-8200
All

Relix
P.O. Box 92
Brooklyn, NY 11229
718-258-0009
Fax: 718-692-4345
www.gibson.com/fog/relix
/records
All

Ripete
1111 S. Main St.
Elliott, SC 29046
803-428-3358
Fax: 803-428-6434
www.ripete.com
All

Roblan
274 Church St.
Toronto, ON M5B 1Z5
416-977-6490
Fax: 416-977-7565
All

Rock Bottom
6900 SW 21st St., #11
Davie, FL 33317
754-474-1114
Fax: 754-474-4079
All

ROIR International
611 Broadway Suite 411
New York, NY 10012
212-477-0563
Fax: 212-505-9908

Rotz Records
2211 N. Elston
Chicago, IL 60614
312-862-6500
Fax: 312-862-6295
A, R

RRRecords
151 Paige St.
Lowell, MA 08152
508-454-8002
T, R

Rounder
1 Camp St.
Cambridge, MA 02140
617-354-0700
Fax: 617-491-1970
www.rounder.com
All

Scorpio
P.O. Box A
Trenton, NJ 08691
609-890-6000
Fax: 609-890-0247
scorpiomus@aol.com
All

Scott's One Stop
2507 Roosevelt Ave.
Indianapolis, IN 46218
317-639-5491
Fax: 317-639-5573
All

Select-O-Hits Corp.
1981 Fletcher Creek Dr.
Memphis, TN 38107
901-388-1190
Fax: 901-388-3002
All

Silo
P.O. Box 429
S. Main St.
Waterbury, VT 05676
802-244-51 78
Fax: 802-244-6128
All

Smash
1636 W. 139th St.
gardena, CA 90249
310-352-3055
FAx: 310-352-4209
A

Smash Record Distribution
3402 W. Wilshire Dr., #24
Pheonix, AZ 85009
602-278-9285
R&B, C

Sparrow
P.O. Box 5010
Brentwood, TN 37024-5010
615-371-6800
Fax: 615-371-6999
CH

Square Deal
303 Higuera St.
San Luis Obispo, CA 93401
805-543-3636
Fax: 805-543-3938
sdrc@aol.com
All

St. Clair Entertainment
5905 Thimens Blvd.
St, Laurant, PQ H4S 1V8
514-339-2737
All

Stackhouse
232 Sunflower Ave.
Clarksdale, MS 38614
601-627-2209
Fax: 601-627-9861
B,R&B,G,J

Stanton Park Records
P.O. Box 58
Newtonville, MA 02160
617-527-7739
Fax: 617-527-7739
R, A

Strawberries Inc.
205 Fortune Blvd.
Milford, MA 01757
508-478-2031
Fax: 508-634-1145
All

Sub Pop
1932 !st Ave. #1103
Seattle, WA 98101
206-441-8441
Fax: 206-441-8245
www.subpop.com
R, A

Subterranean
P.O. Box 2530
Berkeley, CA 94702
415-821-5880
Fax: 415-647-0678
R,D,E,F,SW,I,J,M

Super Marketing Distributors
65 Richard Rd.
Ivyland, PA 18974
215-674-5410
All

Surefire
186 Lincoln St., 2nd Fl.
Boston, MA 02111
617-542-2929
FAx: 617-542-2421
R, A

T.C.I.
1263 Donahue Ave. W.
St. Paul, MN 55104
612-645-0227
Fax: 612-645-1592
A, R

Tant Enterprises
4319 Fruitvalle Rd.
Montague, MI 49437
616-894-9063
Fax: 616-894-4164
B,BG,E,F,G,J,RG,R&B, SW,WB

Tim Sweeney & Assoc./TSA
21213-B Hawthorne Blvd
Suite 5255
Torrance, CA 90503
310-542-6430
Fax:310-542-1300
All

Transcontinent
1762 MAin St.
Buffalo, NY 14208
716-883-9520
FAx: 716-884-1432
All

Trauma Records
15165 Ventura Blvd.
Suite 320
Sherman Oaks, CA 91403
818-382-2515
Fax: 818-990-2038
I, R, T, A

TRC
850 Stanton Rd.
Burlingame, CA 94010
415-692-2800
A, D, T

Tronic One Records
332 Prospect
Perth Anthony, NJ 08861
908-324-1191
Fax: 908-324-1195
All

Twin City International
1263 Donahue Ave
St. Paul, MN 55104
612-645-0227
Fax: 612-645-1592
R, A

Twinbrook Music
227 W. 29th St., 5th Fl.
New York, NY 10001
212-947-0440
Fax: 212-947-4567
All

Unique
110 Denton Ave.
New Hyde Park, NY 11040
516-294-5900
Fax: 516-741-3584
All

United
1420 Donelson Pike, Ste.A22
Nashville, TN 37217
615-399-2844
Fax: 615-399-2852
All

Universal
2055 Richmond St.
Philadelphia, PA 19125
215-426-3333
Fax: 215-426-2667
All

Valley
P.O.Box 2057
Woodland, CA 95965
916-661-6600
Fax: 916-661-5472
All Styles

VP
8905 138th St
Jamaica, NY 11435
718-291-7058
Fax: 718-658-3573
www.vprecords.com
RG, RA

Venture Beyond Records
P.O. Box 3662
Santa Rosa, CA 95402-3662
707-528-8695
Fax: 707-576-7041
R, A

Vista Sounds
95 Cedar Ln.
Englewood, NJ 07631
201-568-0040
RG, J, D, RA, I, T

Watts Music Ltd.
500 Ocean Ave.
East Rockaway, NY 11518
516-596-1888
Fax:596-0961
www.watts.com
D, T

Waxworks
325 E. 3rd St.
Owensboro, KY 42301
502-926-0008
Fax: 502-685-0563
All

Welk Music Group
1299 Ocean Ave. Ste. 800
Santa Monica, CA 90401
310-451-5727
Fax: 310-394-4148
All

West Coast Sales
P.O. Box 20832
Los Angeles, CA 90006
213-731-8115
Fax 213-731-2982

Western Merchandisers
4105 Holly St.
Denver, CO 80216
303-320-4660
Fax: 303-321-6908

Western Record Sales
226 Linnuspolling Drive
Hercules, CA 94547
510-741-8840
Fax:510-741-7060
B, J

Worldtone Music
230 7th Ave.
New York, NY 10011
212-691-1934
Fax: 212-691-2554
F

Zim Records
P.O. Box 158
Jericho, NY 11753
516-681-7102
FAx: 516-822-7952
B, J

Sales

There are several ways for independent labels to sell their records. One is through distributors, which we covered in the last chapter. The other ways are direct to store and direct to consumer, either through the mail or face to face.

Sales at the Show

Selling your records directly to the public can be as simple as setting up a table and selling them at your band's show. A lot of band members are uncomfortable about trying to get money from their "fans"; if this is the case, hire someone else to do the selling. You should price your records cheaper when you're selling them at a show. This will give people the incentive to buy them now instead of waiting and maybe getting them at a record store. Why wait for these people to wander into a store weeks later? Sell them the record now.

Mail Order

When you take out any advertisements, always include information on how to buy your records through the mail. Hopefully you'll have filed a fictitious name statement so you won't have to write "Please make checks payable to Joe Blow." Don't forget to include postage costs in your mail order info. Also, when you go on tour, make up some kind of catalog sheets with band propaganda and ordering information, and give them out at shows. If a new fan didn't buy your record at the gig, at least he or she can get it directly from you through the mail weeks or months later.

Mailing Lists

If you have a mailing list of fans and friends, you can mail them catalogs or postcards that announce your new record and give instructions on how to order it. If you don't have a mailing list, you should probably start one. A computer comes in handy here, but you can also write or type the addresses onto a piece of paper and photocopy this onto adhesive label stock that you can get at any stationery store. Also, if you have a computer you should put together an e-mail mailing list (see the Internet chapter for more info). E-mail will save you money on postage, but they won't get to see your stunning flier artwork. Get other people's mailing lists. Get subscriber lists from magazines. Mail order can supply a needed stream of cash to your label effort; don't overlook it.

Direct to Stores

Following this section is the largest list of independent record stores ever published. It should provide you with plenty of potential buyers for your record. These are stores that will buy independent releases directly from labels.

Direct Pricing

As far as pricing is concerned, the lower the better. These stores will be taking a risk buying records from an unknown band. Your records might never sell in their stores. It's up to you to convince them that they will sell, and to price them as low as possible. Your prices to direct stores should be comparable to your distributor prices. Assure the stores that your records are 100% returnable.

UPS It

The way you want to sell to these stores is UPS COD cash. This means if a store orders from you, you will have to go to a UPS office (or arrange for a pickup) to ship the records. UPS charges around $5 for a COD collection, which you will tack on to the store's order total in addition to the freight charges. When UPS delivers the records, they will collect the money from the store and return it to you. This is the best way to get your goods out to the stores and get paid for them. Make sure you specify COD CASH. If you don't do this, stores will be able to write a check for payment, and who needs the hassle of dealing with somebody's bounced check half-way across the country. Actually, passing bad checks across state lines is a major crime, so if anyone ever does this to you, bust 'em.

Store Strategy

You can't just randomly call a store and try to get them to buy your record. There has to be a reason for them to want it. Besides the stores in your immediate area, stores that will potentially be interested in your release are:

– **stores in cities where your record is receiving college radio airplay**

– **stores in cities where your band will be touring or has recently toured**

– **stores in cities where you have received reviews the press.**

Only call stores where there is a valid reason, like any of the above, for them to need your record. Otherwise, you will waste a lot of time and money and you won't sell any product. If you don't have any of the above valid reasons, make up a few valid reasons. You may want to send all of the stores a flier announcing your new release and telling them how they can buy it direct from you. When you get a store account, you should send them P.O.P. (Point of Purchase) displays, such as posters, fliers, etc. These will generate interest from store customers who have never heard of your band. Your posters should have a blank space at the bottom, so that you or the store can add tour information or a sale price.

Co-op Advertising

You can also do co-op advertising with stores. This is a great idea if you are on tour; you should try to arrange co-op ads with a store in each of the tour cities. Here's how it works: the store places, and pays for, an ad announcing your show. The ad would also read, "Their new record on sale now at Joe's Records!" You would then reimburse the store for the cost of the ad in free goods (your records). If the ad cost $50, you'd give the store $50 worth of your records at wholesale prices, say, 10 records at $5 each) Those records only cost you $1.50 to make, so the ad ends up costing you $15. You'll have more people at the show (buying your T-shirts) due to increased advertising, and there will be more people in that town who own your record, and come to your next show, and buy your next record, etc. You have to try to build a base of fans in every city, and the $15 you spend on that co-op ad will pay off in the long run.

Also, record stores report their top selling records to the trade publications such as *CMJ* and *Billboard*. Concentrating your promotional and P.O.P. efforts on these stores is a good idea. If a store is selling your release, make sure they are reporting it.

If you can set up a good network of direct stores in your area and all over the country, you'll be getting paid cash for your records, and you won't find yourself at the mercy of the distributors.

When calling these stores, (and distributors) ask for the independent record buyer. Sell, sell, sell.

Record Stores

ALABAMA

Big Beat Records
129 E Magnolia Ave.
Auburn, AL 36830
334-887-8890

Charlemagne
1924 1/2 11th Ave. S
Birmingham, AL 35205
205-322-5349

Magic Platter
106 Centre at Riverchase
Birmingham, AL 35216
205-823-0040

Oz Music and Other Stuff
518 14th St.
Tuscaloosa, AL 35401
205-758-3953

Satori Sound
5460 Old Shell Rd
Mobile, AL 36608
334-343-6677

Sunburst
4001 Holmes Ave Bldg A
Huntsville, AL 35816
205-830-8079

T&L
4710J University Dr.
Huntsville, AL 35816
205-837-4022
Fax: 205-837-4033

Triangle Compact Disc
3419 Colonnade Pky #1200
Birmingham, AL 35243
205-967-1699

Vinyl Solution
1207 University Bl
Tuscaloosa, AL 35401
205-758-3710

Whirligig
2111 University Blvd.
Tuscaloosa, AL 35401
205-758-0690

Wild Man Steve's
114-B W. Magnolia Ave.
Auburn, AL 36830
334-821-6622

ALASKA

Hoitt's Music
1698 Airport Way
Fairbanks, AK 99701
907-456-4144

Mammoth Music
2906 Spenard Rd
Anchorage, AK 99503
907-258-3555

ARIZONA

Eastside
217 W. University
Tempe, AZ 85281
602-968-2011

Hear's Music
2508 N Campbell Ave.
Tucson, AZ 85719
520-795-4494
Fax: 520-795-1875

Memory Lane
1940 E University Dr.
Tempe, AZ 85281
602-968-1512

Replay Records
4910 East Ray Rd. #23
Phoenix, AZ 85044
602-496-0100

Rockaway
1310 W. Southern #3
Mesa, AZ 85202
602-964-6301

Sounds Like Music
2734 W Bell Rd, Ste 1306
Phoenix, AZ 85023
602-993-3351
Fax: 602-993-6960

Stinkweeds
1250 East Apache #109
Tempe, AZ 85281
602-968-9490

Tower Records
3 E 9th St.
Tempe, AZ 85281
602-968-7774

Zia
3370 East Speedway
Tucson, AZ 85716
520-327-3340
Fax: 520-327-4535

Zia
105 W. University
Tempe, AZ 85282
602-829-1967

ARKANSAS

Arkansas Record & CD
4212 MacArthur
North Little Rock, AR 72118
501-753-7877

Been Around
1216 S University
Little Rock, AR 72204
501-663-8767

Disc-Jockey
Northwest Arkansas Mall
Hwy 71 B
Fayetteville, AR 72703
501-442-3788

Electric Moo
301 W. Main
Russleville, AR 72801
501-968-3337

Sound Warehouse
401 W Watson #2
Fayetteville, AR 72701
501-442-4822

CALIFORNIA

Aaron's
1150 N. Highland Ave
Los Angeles, CA 90038
213-469-4700

Amoeba Music
2455 Telegraph Ave.
Berkeley, CA 94704
510-549-1125

Aquarius
1055 Valencia St
San Francisco, CA 94110
415-647-2272
Fax: 415-647-3447

Barney's Good Times Music
15 W Main St.
Woodland, CA 95695
916-662-6376
Fax: 916-662-4813

Barton's Records
4018 Buckingham Rd.
Los Angeles, CA 90008
213-298-9338

The Beat Records
1700 J Street
Sacramento, CA 95814
916-446-4402

Benway Music
1600 Pacific Ave
Venice, CA 90291
310-396-8898

Bionic Records
9549 Valley View
Cypress, CA 90630
714-828-4225

Bleecker Bob's
7454 Melrose Ave
Los Angeles, CA 90046
213-951-9111

Blue Meanie
916 Broadway
El Cajon, CA 92021
619-442-2212

Scooter's
200 Pier Ave, Ste 1
Hermosa Beach, CA 90254
310-372-1666

CD Research
407 G St, Ste 1
Davis, CA 95616
916-756-0499

Cheap Thrills
563 Higuera
San Luis Obispo, CA 93401
805-544-0686

Compact Disc Warehouse
125 N. Tustin Ave. Ste. D
Orange, CA 92666
714-771-6646

Compact Disc Warehouse
470 E. El Camino Real
Sunnyvale, CA 94087
408-730-0991

Cymbaline
435 Front St
Santa Cruz, CA 95060
408-423-3949
Fax:408-423-3993

Danny's
432 E. Bullard
Fresno, CA 93710
209-447-5447

Digital Ear
17602 E. 17th
Tustin, CA 92680
714-544-7903

Dimple Records
1701 Santa Clara Dr.
Roseville, CA 95661
916-781-2800

Epicenter Zone
475 Valencia 2nd Fl.
San Fransisco, CA 94103
415-431-2725

Esoteric Records
3413 El Camino Ave
Sacramento, CA 95821
916-488-8966
http://www.cdealer.com

Go-Boy
1310 PCH
Redondo Beach, CA 90277
310-316-1957

Green Hell
14551 Ventura Blvd
Sherman Oaks, CA 91403
818-784-5127
Fax: 213-461-3535

The Hindenberg/The Loft
1114 21st St., Ste 666
Sacramento, CA 95814
916-443-4034

Lou's
434 N. Hwy. 101
Encinitas, CA 92024
619-632-5959

Metro CD's & Tapes
858 G St
Arcata, CA 95521
707-822-9015

Moby Disc
6850 Canby Ave #105
Reseda, CA 91335
818-881-9906

Mod Lang
2136 University Ave.
Berkeley, CA 94704
510-486-1880

Music Exchange
210 W Colorado
Glendale, CA 91204
818-240-6539

Music Trader
6663 El Cajon Blvd, Ste A
San Diego, CA 92115
619-753-1382
Fax: 619-462-6557

No Life Records
7209 Santa Monica Blvd
Los Angeles, CA 90046
213-845-1200

Noise Noise Noise
1505 Mesa Verde Dr E
Costa Mesa, CA 92626
714-55NOISE

Off The Record
3865 5th Ave
San Diego, CA 92103
619-298-4796

Off The Record
6130 El Cajon Bl
San Diego, CA 92115
619-265-0507

Open Mind Music
342 Divisidero St
San Francisco, CA 94117
415-621-2244

Paramount
455 Meridian Ave
San Jose, CA 95126
408-286-9839

Peer
2301 W. Balboa Bl
Newport Beach, CA 92663
714-675-3752

Poobah
1101 E. Walnut
Pasadena, CA 91106
818-449-3359

Rasputin's
2401 Telegraph Ave
Berkeley, CA 94704
510-848-9005

Reckless
1401 Haight St
San Francisco, CA 94117
415-431-3434

Record Finder
258 Noe St
San Francisco, CA 94114
415-431-4443

Rhino
1720 Westwood Bl
Los Angeles, CA 90404
310-474-8685

Rockaway Records
2395 N. Glendale Blvd.
Los Angeles, CA 90039
213-664-3232

Round World Music
593-A Guerrero St
San Fransisco, CA 94110
415-255-8411

Saturn
5488 College Ave.
Oakland, CA 92618
510-654-0335

Soundsations
8734 S. Sepulveda
Los Angeles, CA 90045
310-641-8877

Star Records
311C N Capitol Ave
San Jose, CA 95133
408-926-5200

Street Light
2350 Market St.
San Francisco, CA 94114
415-282-8000
Fax: 415-282-2090

Street Light
3979 24th St.
San Francisco, CA 94114
415-282-3550
Fax: 415-621-4075

Street Light
980 S Bascom Ave
San Jose, CA 95128
408-292-1404

Street Sounds
7751 Melrose Ave.
Hollywood, CA 90046
213-651-0630

Tower Records
5611 N Blackstone Ave
Fresno, CA 93710
209-431-4700

Tower Records
1028 Westwood Blvd
Los Angeles, CA 90024
310-208-3061
Fax: 310-208-3230

Tower Records
2514 Watt Ave
Sacramento, CA 95821
916-482-9191

Tower Records
6405 El Cajon Blvd
San Diego, CA 92115
619-287-1420
Fax: 619-287-4524

21st Century CD's
924 Soquel Ave
Santa Cruz, CA 95062
408-426-5480

Vinyl Fetish
7305 Melrose Ave
West Hollywood, CA 90046
213-935-1300

Vinyl Solution
18822 Beach Bl. #104
Huntington Bch., CA 92648
714-963-1819

Zed
1940 Lakewood Bl
Long Beach, CA 90815
310-498-2757

COLORADO

Albums on the Hill
1128 13th St.
Boulder, CO 80302
303-447-0159

JB&H
11961 W. Alameda Pkwy
Lakewood, CO 80228
303-989-3210

Jerry's Record Exchange
312 E. Colfax
Denver, CO 80203
303-830-2336

Pirate Records
2139 S. Sheridan Blvd.
Denver, CO 80227
303-763-8773

Recycle Records
6739 W. Colfax
Lakewood, CO 80214
303-238-4289

Twist & Shout
724 S. Pearl St.
Denver, CO 80209
303-722-1943

Twist & Shout
300 E Alameda
Denver, CO 80209
303-722-1943
Fax: 303-733-8191

Wax Trax
1143 13th St.
Boulder, CO 80302
303-444-9829

Wax Trax
1220 Pennsylvania Ave.
Boulder, CO 80302

Wax Trax
638 E. 13th Ave
Denver, CO 80203
303-831-7246

CONNECTICUT

Brass City
489 Meadow St.
Waterbury, CT 06702
203-574-7805

Cutlers
33 Broadway
New Haven, CT 06511
203-777-6271

Disc Place
221 Danbury Road
New Milford, CT 06776
860-335-0311
Fax: Same

Exile On Main St.
267 E Main St
Branford, CT 06405
203-483-6228
Fax: 203-483-6864

Johnny's
45 Tokeneke Rd
Darien, CT 06820
203-655-0157

Macaw Music
1391 Boston Post Rd.
Old Saybrook, CT 06475
203-388-4662

Mystic Disc
10 Steamboat Wharf
Mystic, CT 06355
203-536-1312

Phoenix Records
384 Stillson Rd.
Waterbury, CT 06705
203-756-1617

Record Breaker
2453 Berlin Turnpike
Newington, CT 06111
203-666-0696

Record Express
71 Pratt St.
Harford, CT 06103
203-522-8060

Record Express
80 Plaza Ct.
Groton, CT 06340
860-446-1277

Trash American Style
12 Mill Plain Rd.
Danbury, CT 06811
203-792-1630

University Music
42 Town St
Norwich, CT 06230
860-886-5800

University Music
University Plaza Rt 195
Storrs, CT 06268
860-429-7709

DELAWARE

Bert's
90E Main St
Newark, DE 19711
302-454-1064
Fax: 302-478-4875

Disc Go Round
45 E Main St
Main Street Galleria
Newark, DE 19711
302-369-3334
Fax: 302-369-3336

Jeremiah's
246 Phila. Pike
Wilmington, DE 19809
302-762-2155

Planet of Sound
1606 Delaware Ave
Wilmington, DE 19806
302-655-4013
Fax: 302-655-4162

Rainbow
3654 Concord Pike
Wilmington, DE 19803
302-479-7738

Wonderland
110 W Main St
Newark, DE 19711
302-738-6856
Fax: 302-738-6872

FLORIDA

Ace's Records
1518 E Fowler Ave
Tampa, FL 33612
813-978-9655
Fax: 813-977-6094

Alternative Records
11900 N. Nebraska Ave.
Tampa, FL 33612
813-977-6383

Asylum
6566 Central Ave
St Petersburg, FL 33707
813-384-1221

Bananas
1401 Pasadena Ave
St. Petersburg, FL 33707
813-343-4013

Blue Note Records
16401 NE 15th Ave.
N. Miami, FL 33162
305-940-3394

Bubaloo's Records
1634 NW First Ave.
Gainesville, FL 32602
904-371-6310

Daddy Kool
5900 S. Tamiami Trail # K
Sarasota, FL 34231
813-921-7271

East West Records
4895 S. Orange Ave.
Orlando, FL 32806
407-859-8991

East West Records
240 N. Orlando Ave.
Winter Park, FL 32789
407-647-3655

Groove Tube
980 N Hwy A1A
Indealantic,
FL 32903
407-723-5267
Fax: 407-951-3982

Hyde & Zeke
1620 W. University
Gainesville, FL 32603
904-376-1687

Park Ave. CD
528 Park Ave South
Winter Park, FL 32789
407-629-5293

Planet Grooves
2000 Gulf-to-Bay Blvd
Clearwater, FL 34625
813-442-4655

Play It Again
3148 W. New Haven
Melbourne, FL 32904
407-724-5685

Record Exchange
6702 Central Ave.
St. Petersburg, FL 33707
813-343-5845

Sound Box
6707 Plantation Rd
Pensacola, FL 32504
904-477-7729

Sound Splash
2118 Okeechobee Blvd.
W. Palm Beach, FL 33409
407-478-7133

Theory Shop
1051 Park St
Jacksonville, FL 32204
904-355-6620
theoryshop@aol.com

Uncle Sam's
4580 N. University Dr.
Lauderhill, FL 33351
305-742-2466

Vinyl Fever
2033 W. Pensacola St
Tallahassee, FL 32304
904-576-4314

Vinyl Fever
2307 S. Dale Mabry Hwy
Tampa, FL 33629
813-251-8399

Wax Tree Records
3092 Aloma Ave.
Winter Park, FL 32792
407-677-8897

GEORGIA

Big Shot
164 E Clayton
Athens, GA 30601
706-543-6666

Bloskbuster Music
1995 Barnett Shoals Rd
Athens, GA 30605
706-546-5626

Blockbuster Music
122 Alps Rd
Athens, GA 30606
706-549-3404

The Book
3342 Clairmont Rd
Atlanta, GA 30329
404-633-1328
Fax: 404-633-8677

Criminal Records
466 Moreland Ave NE
Atlanta, GA 30307
404-215-9511
eric@criminal.com

Dreamweaver
306 W. St. Julian St.
Savannah, GA 31401
912-236-9003

Eat More Records
1210 Rockbridge Rd,Ste K
Norcross, GA 30093
770-717-8111

Rainy Day Records
3005 N. Druid Hills Rd.
Atlanta, GA 30329
404-636-6166

Wax 'N' Facts
432 Moreland Ave. NE
Atlanta, GA 30307
404-525-2275

Wuxtry
197 E. Clayton
Athens, GA 30601
706-369-9428

Wuxtry
2096 N. Decatur Rd
Decatur, GA 30033
404-329-0020

IDAHO

CD Merchant
601 Main St
Boise, ID 83702
208-331-1200
Fax: 208-331-1203

Record Exchange
1105 West Idaho
Boise, ID 83702
208-343-8010

ILLINOIS

Blackout Records
3729 N. Southport
Chicago, IL 60613
312-296-0744

Discount Den
206 E Center
Leroy, IL 61752
309-962-2601

Hear-N-There
619 2nd St
La Salle, IL 61301
815-223-1062

Music Warehouse
7317 S Lamont Rd
Downers Grove, IL 60516
630-963-3410

Plaza
825 S. Illinois Ave
Carbondale, IL 62901
618-549-5423

Reckless
3157 N. Broadway
Chicago, IL 60657
312-404-5080

Record Revolution
817 W. Lincoln
Dekalb, IL 60115
815-756-6242

Record Service
621 E. Green
Champaign, IL 61820
217-344-6222

Record Swap
16 W Chicago Ave
Naperville, IL 60540
630-527-0999
Fax: 708-527-0981

Vintage Vinyl
925 Davis St.
Evanston, IL 60201
708-328-2899

INDIANA

Karma
116 S. Indiana Ave.
Bloomington, IN 47408
812-336-1212

Kemp Music
14 N. 2nd
Vincennes, IN 47591
812-886-9667

Orbit Music
2564 Miracle Ln
Mishawaka, IN 46545
219-256-5898

Rick's Records
2186 E 54th St
Indianapolis, IN 46220
317-259-4087
Fax: 617-259-0190

Streetside
421 Kirkwood Ave.
Bloomington, IN 47401
812-323-0551

Tracks
415 E. Kirkwood
Bloomington, IN 47408
812-332-3576

Tracks
5485 82nd st
Indianapolis, IN 46250
317-576-0404

IOWA

Apollo
13 S Linn, Ste 7
Iowa City, IA 52240
319-354-9341

BJ Records
6 1/2 S. Dubuque St.
Iowa City, IA 52240
319-338-8251

Compact Disc Shoppe
3761 NW 86th St
Urbandale, IA 50322
515-270-8774
Fax: 515-270-9322

Co-op Music
2801 Grand Ave
Ames, IA 50010

Co-op Tapes
422 E. Locust
Davenport, IA 52803
319-324-8522

Disc Go Round
2188 W Kimberly
Davenport, IA 52806
319-386-8632

People's Music
4040 University Ave, Ste F
Des Moines, IA 50311
515-255-5839

Real Records
130 E. Washington St.
Iowa City, IA 52240
319-354-0158

Record Collector
4 1/2 S. Linn
Iowa City, IA 52240
319-337-5029

KANSAS

Alley Cat
717 Massachusetts St.
Lawerence, KS 66044
913-865-0122

Hastings
1900 W. 23rd
Lawrence, KS 66046
913-832-0817

Kief's
2429 Iowa St
Lawrence, KS 66046
913-842-1544
www.idir.net/kief-sav/

Love Garden
936 1/2 Mass. Ave
Lawrence, KS 66044
913-843-1551

The Music Exchange
207A Westport Rd.
Kansas City, KS 64111
816-931-7560

Streetside
1403 W. 23rd St.
Lawrence, KS 66046
913-842-7173

KENTUCKY

Bear's Wax Exchange
371 S. Limestone
Lexington, KY 40508
606-253-3035

Better Days
1591 Bardstown
Loisville, KY 40205
502-456-2394

Cut Corners
377 S. Limestone St
Lexington, KY 40508
606-273-2673

Ear X-tacy
1534 Bardstown Rd
Louisville, KY 40205
502-452-1799
Fax: 502-459-8130

Phil's
2345 Buttermilk Crossing
Crescent Springs, KY 41017
606-344-9191

Recordsmith
415 Leigh Way
Richmond, KY 40475
606-623-5058

Underground Sounds
2003 Highland Ave
Louisville, KY 40204
502-485-0174
Fax: 502-485-0975

LOUSIANA

Brown Sugar Records
2334 Louisiana Ave.
New Orleans, LA 70115
504-895-8087

The Compact Disc Store
684 Jefferson Hwy
Baton Rouge, LA 70806
504-928-5706
Fax: 504-925-9722

Louisiana Music Factory
210 Decantur St
New Orleans, LA 70130
504-586-1094
Fax: 504-586-8818

Mushroom
1037 Broadway
New Orleans, LA 70118
504-866-6065

Odyssey Records & Tapes
Carrollton Shopping Center
3920 Dublin
New Orleans, LA 70118
504-486-8108

Paradise Records
226 W State St
Baton Rouge, LA 70802
504-344-2324
Fax: 504-344-2613

Record Ron's
239 Chartres St
New Orleans, LA 70116
504-524-9444

Underground Sounds
3336 Magazine St
New Orleans, LA 70115
504-897-9030

MAINE

Amadeus Music
332 Fore St.
Portland, ME 04101
207-772-8416

Borders Books and Music
430 Gorham Rd
South Portland, ME 04106
207-775-6110

Bull Moose
151 Main st.
Portland, ME 04011
207-725-1289

Enterprise Records
613 A Congress St.
Portland, ME 04101
207-773-7672

Newberry Comics
220 Main Mall Rd
South Portland, ME 04106
207-874-6788

Record Connection
254 Main St.
Waterville, ME 04901
207-873-1798

MARYLAND

An Die Musik
1 Investment Pl. Aneex Bldg.
Towson, MD 21204

Modern Music
2905 O'Donnell St
Baltimore, MD 21224
410-675-2172

Music Machine
11459 Cronhill Dr., Ste. O
Owings Mills, MD 21117
410-356-4567

Musical Exchange
422 N. Charles St.
Baltimore, MD 21201
410-528-9815

Normal's
425 E 31st St.
Baltimore, MD 21218
410-243-6888

Phantasmagoria
11309 Elkin St
Wheaton, MD 20902
301-949-8886

Record & Tape Trader
10435 Reistertown Rd.
Owings Mills, MD 21117
410-654-0510

Record Masters
711 W. 40th St.
Baltimore, MD 21211
410-366-1250

Reptilian
403 S. Broadway
Baltimore, MD 21231
410-327-6853

Vinyl Ink
955 Bonifant St
Silver Spring, MD 20910
301-588-4695

Yesterday & Today
1327 J Rockville Pike
Rockville, MD 20852
301-279-7007

MASSACHUSETTS

About Music
298 Main St.
Greenfield, MA 01301
413-772-6767

B-Side Records
4 Conz St
Maplewood Shops
Northampton, MA 01060
413-586-9556

Disc Diggers
401 Highland Ave.
Somerville, MA 02144
617-776-7560

Dynamite
150 Main St
Northampton, MA 01060
413-584-1580
Fax: 413-584-9952

For The Record
104 N. Pleasant St.
Amherst, MA 01002
413-256-6134

Harvard Co-op
1400 Mass. Ave
Cambridge, MA 02238
617-499-2000

HMV
1 Brattle Sq.
Cambridge, MA 02138
617-868-9696

In Your Ear
957 Comm. Ave
Boston, MA 02215
617-787-9755

Looney Tunes
1106 Boylston St.
Boston, MA 02115
617-247-2238

Mars
842 Mass. Ave
Cambridge, MA 02139
617-441-0307

Media Play
341 Russel St
Hadley, MA 01035
413-582-0410

Mystery Train
306 Newbury St
Boston, MA 02115
617-497-4024

Mystery Train
96 N Pleasant Ave
Amherst, MA 01002
413-253-4776

Newbury Comics
50 Main St
Amherst, MA 01002
413-256-8840

**Newbury Comics
Exec. Office**
38 Everett St
Allston, MA 02134
617-254-1666 x228

Nuggets
486 Comm. Ave
Boston, MA 02215
617-536-0679

Planet Records
536 Commonwealth Ave.
Boston, MA 02215
617-353-0693

Rockit
124 Broadway
Saugus, MA 01906
617-233-7805

Second Coming
1105 Mass. Ave
Cambridge, MA 02138
617-576-6400

Skippy White's
315 Centre St.
Jamaica Plain Plaza
Jamaica Plain, MA 02130

Spinnaker
596 Main St
Hyannis, MA 02601
508-778-4122

Stereo Jacks
1686 Mass Ave
Cambridge, MA 02138
617-497-9447
Fax: 617-864-3248

Tower Records
360 Newbury St
Boston, MA 02115
617-247-5900
Fax: 617-247-5980

Turn it Up!
5 Pleasant St
Northampton, MA 01060
413-582-1885
Fax:413-587-9726
turnitup@javanet.com

Twisted Village
12 B Eliot St
Cambridge, MA 02138
617-354-6898
Fax: 617-354-6899

MICHIGAN

Beat Hotel
3185 West Twelve Mile Rd
Berkley, MI 48072
810-544-2485

Car City Records
21918 Harper Ave.
St. Clair Shores, MI 48080
810-775-4770

Dearborn Music
220 Michigan Ave
Dearborn, MI 48124
313-561-1000

Desirable Discs II
13939 Michigan Ave
Dearborn, MI 48126
313-581-1767
Fax: 313-581-1194

Flat, Black & Circular
541 E. Grand River
E. Lansing, MI 48823
517-351-0838

Flipside
309 N. Burdick
Kalamazoo, MI 49007
616-343-5865

Michigan Where House Records
515 E Grand River
E Lansing, MI 48823
517-332-3525

New Moon
240 E. Front St
Traverse City, MI 49684
616-941-1035

Off The Record
401 S Washington
Royal Oak, MI 48068
810-398-4436

Play It Again
234 West 9 Mile
Ferndale, MI 48220
810-542-7529
Fax: 810-542-9312

Record Collector
28143 W. 8 Mile
Livonia, MI 48152
810-473-8350

Record Exchange
13064 Eureka Rd
Southgate, MI 48195
313-282-8750

Record Time
27360 Gratiot Ave.
Roseville, MI 48066
810-775-1550

Repeat The Beat
1116 N. Telegraph
Dearborn, MI 48128
313-562-6318

Repeat The Beat
520 S. Washington
Royal Oak, MI 48067
810-543-4310

Rock Cafe
647 Capital Ave
Battle Creek, MI 49015
616-962-6622

Rock of Ages
31015 Ford Rd.
Garden City, MI 48135
313-522-4590

Schoolkids
523 E. Liberty
Ann Arbor, MI 48104
313-994-8031

Vinyl Solution
2035-A 28th St SE
Grand Rapids, MI 49508
616-241-4040

Wazoo
336 1/2 S. State St
Ann Arbor, MI 48104
313-761-8686

MINNESOTA

Aardvaark Records
8913 Penn Ave S
Bloomington, MN 55431
612-885-9737
Fax: 612-884-8275

Cheapo Records
80 North Snelling Ave
St. Paul, MN 55104
612-644-8981
Fax: 612-644-6120

Disc & Tape
815 Main Ave.
Moorehead, MN 56560
218-236-7708

Electric Fetus
2000 4th Ave. S
Minneapolis, MN 55404
612-870-9300

Electric Fetus
28 S 5th Ave
St. Cloud, MN 56301
320-251-2569

Electric Fetus
12 E. Superior
Duluth, MN 55802
218-722-9970

Extreme Noise
3525 Nicolett Ave
Minneapolis, MN 55404
612-821-0119

Garage D'or
2548 Nicollet Ave. S
Miineapolis, MN 55404
612-871-0563

Let It Be
1001 Nicollet Mall
Minneapolis, MN 55403
612-339-7439

Oar Folkjokeopus
2557 Lyndale Ave. S
Minneapolis, MN 55405
612-872-7400

Roadrunner
4304 Nicollet Ave S
Minneapolis, MN 55409
612-822-0613

MISSISSIPPI

Be-Bop
900 E. County Line, Ste. 140
Ridgeland, MS 39157
601-977-0899

Little Big Store
P.O. Box 921
Raymond, MS 39154
601-857-8579

MISSOURI

Disc Connection
7253 Manchester
St. Louis, MO 63143
314-644-1171

Euclid
4906 Laclede Ave
St. Louis, MO 63108
314-361-7353

Groove Farm
827 Westport Rd
Kansas City, MO 64111
816-531-8800

The Music Exchange
207A Westport Rd
Kansas City, MO 64111
816-931-7560
Fax: 816-931-8422

Pennylane
4128 Broadway
Kansas City, MO 64111
816-561-1580

Recycled Sounds
3941 Main St.
Kansas City, MO 64111
816-531-4890

Salt of the Earth
573 S. 9th St
Columbia, MO 65201
314-874-0045

**Sight & Sound
Streetside Records**
(24 locations)
2055 Walton Rd
St Louis, MO 63114
413-426-2388(main office)

Seventh Heaven
7621 Troost Ave
Kansas City, MO 64131
816-361-9555

Sound Revolution
7751 N. Lindbergh
Hazelwood, MO 63042
314-839-3520

Streetside
2055 Walton Rd.
St. Louis, MO 63114
314-426-2388

Streetside
4128 Broadway
Kansas City, MO 64111
816-561-1580

Vintage Vinyl
6610 Delmar Bl
St. Louis, MO 63130
314-721-4096

West End Wax
389 N. Euclid
St. Louis, MO 63108
314-367-0111

MONTANA

Cactus Records
29 W. Main St.
Bozeman, MT 59715
406-587-0245

Rockin' Rudy's
237 Blaine
Missoula, MT 59801
406-542-0077

NEBRASKA

The Antiquarium
1215 Harney St.
Omaha, NE 68102
402-341-8077

Backtracks
3833 S. 48th St.
Lincoln, NE 68506
402-489-3817

Dirt Cheap Records
1026 Jackson St.
Omaha, NE 68102
402-341-9500

Drastic Plastic
1209 Howard St.
Omaha, NE 68102
402-346-8843

Homer's
1114 Howard St
Omaha, NE 68102
402-346-0264

Homer's
1339 O St.
Lincoln, NE 68508
402-434-2500
Fax: 402-434-2526

Recycled Sounds
824 P St.
Lincoln, NE 68508
402-476-8240

Stage Door Music
1415 Farnam St
Omaha, NE 68102
402-341-1502

Tunes Music & Video
7926 S. 84 St.
La Vista, NE 68128
402-339-3577

NEVADA

Mirabelli Music City
154 E. Plumb Ln.
Reno, NV 89502
702-825-7210

The Music Trader
565 Keystone
Reno, NV 89503
702-324-6344
Fax: 702-324-6180

Odyssey Records
1600 S Las vegas Blvd
Las Vegas, NV 89104
702-384-4040
Fax: 702-384-8563

Recycled Records
4934 S. Virginia
Reno, NV 89502
702-826-4119

Soundwave CD's
940 W. Moana St. #105
Reno, NV 89509
702-825-5044

Underground
1164 E. Twain St
Las Vegas, NV 89109
702-733-7025

NEW HAMPSHIRE

Bull Moose
82 Congress St
Portsmouth, NH 03801
603-422-9525

Dartmouth Bookstore
33 S. Main St
Hanover, NH 03755
603-643-3616

Lost Chord Records
489 Central Ave.
Dover, NH 03820
603-749-3859

Newbury Comics
777 S Willow St Plaza
Manchester, NH 03103
603-624-2842

Rock Bottom Records
86 Pleasant St.
Portsmouth, NH 03801
603-436-5618

Rock Bottom Records
140 Flett St
Portsmouth, NH 03801
603-436-5618

Rockit Records
293 Daniel Webster Hwy
Nashua, NH 03060
603-888-8441

Sessions Music
10 Congress St.
Portsmouth, NH 03801
603-431-8244

NEW JERSEY

Crazy Rhythms
561 Bloomfield Ave
Montclair, NJ 07042
201-744-5787

Flipside
120 Wanaque Ave
Pompton Lakes, NJ 07442
201-835-8448

Jack's Music Shop
30 Broad St.
Red Bank, NJ 07701
908-842-0731

Pranzatellis
1 E. Main St
Bound Brook, NJ 08805
908-356-1143

Princeton Record Exchange
20 S. Tulane St.
Princeton, NJ 08542
609-921-0881

Sound Effects
174 Main St
Hackettstown, NJ 07840
908-850-0688

Sound Exchange
1482 Route 23
North Wayne, NJ 07470
201-694-6049

Tower Records
809 Rte 17 S
Paramus, NJ 07652
201-444-7277
Fax: 201-612-0877

Vintage Vinyl
51 Lafayette Rd
Forbes, NJ 08863
908-225-7717

NEW MEXICO

Bow Wow
3103 Central NE
Albuquerque, NM 87106
505-256-0928

Mind Over Matter
1710 Central Ave SE
Albuquerque, NM 87106
505-842-5922

Natural Sound
3500 Central Ave Se
Nob Hill Shopping Center
Albuquerque, NM 87106
505-255-8295
Fax: 505-256-9219

The Rare Bear
1716 St Michael Dr
Santa Fe, NM 87505
505-474-3980

We Buy Music
3025 Central Ave NE
Albuquerque, NM 87106
505-256-2524

NEW YORK

Adult Crash
66 Ave A
New York, NY 10009
212-387-1558

Apollo Records
P.O. Box 1700
Buffalo, NY 14213-1700
716-883-7040

Bleecker Bob's
118 W 3rd St.
New York, NY 10012
212-475-9677

Borders Books and Music
5 World Trade Center
New York, NY 10048
212-839-8049

Brigade Records
47 E Houston St, 2nd Fl
New York, NY 10012
212-431-5138

Coconuts
Stuyvesant Plaza
Albany, NY 12203
518-438-3003

Doris Records
286 E. Ferry St.
Buffalo, NY 14208
716-883-2410

Downtown Music Gallery
211 E 5th St
New York, NY 10003
212-473-0043
Fax: 212-533-5059

Etherea
441 E 9th St
New York, NY 10009
212-358-1126

Finyl Vinyl
204 E 6th St
New York, NY 10003
212-533-8007

Footlight
113 E 12th St
New York, NY 10003
212-533-1572
http://www.footlight.com

Generation
210 Thompson St
New York, NY 10012
212-254-1100

Home of the Hits
1105 Elmwood Ave
Buffalo, NY 14222
716-883-0330

House of Guitars
645 Titus Ave.
Rochester, NY 14617
716-544-3500

Kim's Underground
144 Bleeker St
New York, NY 10012
212-387-8250
Fax: 212-260-1736

Knuckleheads
306 S Main St
N Syracuse, NY 13212
315-452-5572

The Last Unicorn
1907 Genese St
Utica, NY 13501
315-724-0007
unicorn@borg.com

Last Vestige
173 Quail St
Albany, NY 12203
518-432-7736
http://www.lastvestige.com

Loony Tunes
31 Brookvale Ave
W. Babylon, NY 11704
516-587-7722

Midnight Records
263 W 23rd St
Old Chelsea Station, NY 10113
212-675-2768

Midnight Records
263 W 23rd
New York, NY 10011
212-675-2768
Fax: 212-741-7230

Music Shack
65 Central Ave.
Albany, NY 12206
518-436-4581

Music Shack
295 River St.
Troy, NY 12180
518-273-1400

New World
512 Elmwood Ave.
Buffalo, NY 14222
716-882-4004

NYCD
426 Amsterdam Ave
New York, NY 10024
212-724-4466
Fax: 212-724-3790

Oliver's
107 Marshall St
Syracuse, NY 13210
315-471-2275

Other Music
15 E 4th St
New York, NY 10003
212-477-8150

Rebel Rebel
319 Bleeker St
New York, NY 10014
212-989-0770

Rebop
409 College Ave
Ithaca, NY 14850
607-273-0737

Record Archive
1394 Mt. Hope Ave
Rochester, NY 14620
716-473-3820

Record Runner
5 Jones St.
New York, NY 10014
212-255-4280

Record Stop
254 S Healy Ave
Scarsdale, NY 10583
914-949-6769

Record Theater
3500 Main St.
Buffalo, NY 14208
716-881-0654

Record Theater
227 Midtown Plaza
Rochester, NY 14604
716-262-3415

Records 'N' Such
Stuyvesant Plaza
Albany, NY 12203
518-438-3003

Rhino
188-D Main St
New Paltz, NY 12561
914-255-0230

Rocks in Your Head
157 Prince St
New York, NY 10012
212-475-6729

Second Coming
235 Sullivan St
New York, NY 10012
212-228-1313

Slipped Disc
68 Rockaway
Valley Stream, NY 11581
516-872-0516

Smash CD's
33 St. Marks Pl
New York, NY 10003
212-473-2200

Sounds
20 St. Mark's Pl.
New York, NY 10003
212-677-3444

Sounds Fine
171 E. State St. Box 111
Ithaca, NY 14850
607-277-4766

Stooz
122 E 7th St
New York, NY 10009
212-979-6294
Fax: 212-677-5003

Subterranean
5 Cornelia St.
New York, NY 10014
212-463-8900

Throb
211 E 14th St
New York, NY 10003
212-533-2328

Twisted Disque
222-01 Hempstead Ave
Queens Village, NY 11429

Venus
13 St. Marks
New York, NY 10003
212-598-4459

Vinyl Solution
33 N. Main
Portchester, NY 10573
914-939-5769

World's Records
132 Central Ave.
Albany, NY 12206
518-462-5271

NORTH CAROLINA

CD Alley
8 Market St
Wilmington, NC 28401
910-762-4003
Fax: 910-763-3886

Crunchy Music
908 Spring Garden St
Greensboro, NC 27403
910-272-7883
Fax: 910-272-5994
crunchy@spyder.net

Ernie's Records
4129 Park Rd
Charlotte, NC 28209
704-525-2271

Manifest
North 17 Shopping Center
4314 Market St
Wilmington, NC 28403
910-251-8499

Mighty Quinn Music
3722 Reynolda Rd.
Winston-Salem, NC 27106
910-922-2919

Mighty Quinn Music
179 E Franklin St
Chapel Hill, NC 27514
910-720-6592

Mighty Quinn Music
2008 Hillsboro St #8
Raleigh, NC 27607
910-720-6592

Milestone
1711 Central Ave
Charlotte, NC 28205
704-377-2350

Monster
144 E Franklin St
Chapel Hill, NC 27514
919-929-7766
Fax: 919-942-7766

Poindexter
718 Ninth St
Durhamm, NC 27705
919-286-1852

Record Exchange
1532 E Blvd
Charlotte, NC 28203
704-343-9400
fax: 704-364-9452

Record Exchange
2403-8 Battleground Ave
Greensboro, Nc 27408
910-288-2300
Fax: 910-545-1689

Record Exchange
Silas Creek Crossing
3254 Silas Creek Pkwy
Winston-Salem, NC 27103
910-768-0600

Record Exchange
2109-144 Avent Ferry Rd
Raleigh, NC 27606
919-831-2300
Fax: 919-839-1295
www.mal.com/~mmonitor

Repo CD
5640 South Blvd
Charlotte, NC 28210
704-523-7376

Repo Records
2516 Central Ave.
Charlotte, NC 28205
704-334-7376

Schoolkids
2316-104 Hillsborough St
Raleigh, NC 27606
919-821-7766

Schoolkids
1015 S Kerr Ave
Wilmington, NC 28403
910-791-0860

Selecter
2126 Hwy 70 SE
Hickory, NC 28602
704-322-6002

Skylly's
200 E 5th St
Greenville, NC 27858
919-758-4298

Spinning Mule
3114 Hillsborough St
Raleigh, NC 27605
919-828-7454

Spins
2144 Lawndale Dr.
Greensboro, NC 27408
910-274-8530

NORTH DAKOTA

Discontent
4101 13th Ave S
Fargo, ND 58103
701-282-5624

Mother's Records
542 6th Ave. N
Fargo, ND 58102
701-241-9601

OHIO

Bent Crayon
11600 Detroit Ave
Cleveland, OH 44102
216-221-9200
www.bentcrayon.com

Boogie Records
3301 W Central Ave
Toledo, OH 43606
419-536-5683
Fax:419-536-3217

Camelot Music
8000 Freedom Ave NW
N Canton, OH 44720
216-494-2284

CD Warehouse
5206-B Monroe St
Toledo, OH 43623
419-843-7348
Fax:419-843-7349

Chris' Warped
13383 Madison Ave
Lakewood, OH 44107
216-521-4981

Circle
5975 Glenway Ave
Cincinnati, OH 45238
513-451-9824

Co-op Book Store
37 W. College St.
Oberlin, OH 44074
216-774-3741

Digital Daze
1893 Brittain Rd
Akron, OH 44310
330-630-3600

Everybody's
6106 Montgomery Rd
Cincinnati, OH 45213
513-531-4500

Gem City Records
318 E 5th St
Dayton, OH 45402
937-223-8011

Heartbeat Records
430 E Main St
Kent, OH 44240
330-687-6371

Johnny Goes House O'Music
1900 N High St
Columbus, OH 43201
614-291-6133

Madhatter Music
143 E Wooster St
Bowling Green, OH 43402
419-353-3555

Magnolia Thunderpussy
1591 N. High St.
Columbus, OH 43201
614-421-1512

My Generation
25947 Detroit Ave
Westlake, OH 44145
216-871-5586

Perry's Rockpile
7425 York Rd
Parma, OH 44310
216-884-7755

Platterpuss
15601 Detroit Ave
Lakewood, OH 44107
216-221-7050

Quonset Hut
3235 Cleveland Ave NW
Canton, OH 44709
330-492-1293

Record Revolution
1828 Coventry Rd
Cleveland, OH 44118
216-321-7661

Schoolkids
12 S. Court St.
Athens, OH 45701
614-592-6140

Shattered
12414 Lorain Ave
Cleveland, OH 44111
216-941-5813

Singing Dog
1630 N High St
Columbus, OH 43201
614-299-1490

Time Traveler
2615 State Rd
Cuyahoga Falls, OH 44223
330-923-4408

Trader Vic's Music Emporium
1043 Brown St
Dayton, OH 45409
513-223-1333
Fax: 513-223-3388

Used Kids
1992B N. High St.
Columbus, OH 43201
614-294-3833

Wizard Records and The Cave
2612 Vine St
Cincinnati, OH 45219
513-961-6196

OKLAHOMA

Mohawk Music
6157 E. 51 Pl.
Tulsa, OK 74135
918-664-2951

Rainbow
2401 N. Classen Bl.
Oklahoma City, OK 73106
405-524-4682

Shadowplay
737 Asp St
Norman, OK 73069
405-364-1670

Starship
2813 E. 11th
Tulsa, OK 74104
918-583-0638

OREGON

D'Jangos
1111 SW Stark
Portland, OR 97205
503-227-4381

Everyday Music
1313 W Burnside
Portland, OR 97209
503-274-0961
allydark@aol.com

Local's Only
916 W Burnside
Portland, OR 97205
503-227-5000

Music Millenium
3158 E. Burnside
Portland, OR 97214
503-231-8943

Ozone
1036 W. Burnside
Portland, OR 97209
503-226-0249

Ranch Records
456 Court NE
Salem, OR 97301
503-362-8515

Second Ave Records
400 SW Second Ave
Portland, OR 97204
503-222-3783

Tower Records
1307 NE 102 Ave
Portland, OR 97220
503-253-1314

PENNSYLVANIA

Arboria
119 E Beaver Ave
State College, PA 16801
814-237-3808

BBC
315 N. Queen St.
Lancaster, PA 17603
717-394-1145

Boro Tunes
106 Meadville St.
Edinboro, PA 16412
814-734-4175

CD To Go
3417 Spruce St
Philadelphia, PA 19104
215-573-5714

City Lights
316 East College
State College, PA 16801
814-237-6623

3D Compact Discs
2549 S Queen St
York, PA 17402
717-845-5285

Digital Underground
526 S. 5th St.
Philadelphia, PA 19147
215-925-5324

Eide's
1111 Penn Ave.
Pittsburgh, PA 15222
412-261-0900

Encore Books and Music
4850 Carlisle Pike
Hampden Center
Mechanicsburg, PA 17055
717-761-2665
Fax: 717-761-6657

Gallery of Sound
180 Mundy St.
Wilkes-Barre, PA 18702
717-829-3603

HMV
1510 Walnut St
Philadelphia, PA 19103
215-875-5100

It's Only Rock & Roll
855 Market St.
Lemoyne, PA 17011
717-737-6399

K & K
53 Chambersburg St.
Gettysburg, PA 17325
717-337-1049

Noise Pollution
619 S 4th St
Philadelphia, PA 19147
215-627-7246

Paul's CD's
4526 Liberty Ave
Pittsburgh, PA 15224
412-621-3256

Phila. Record Exchange
608 S. 5th St.
Philadelphia, PA 19147
215-925-7892

Plastic Fantastic
26 W. Lancaster Ave
Ardmore, PA 19003
215-896-7625

Pop Bus
5879 Darlington Rd
Pittsburgh, PA 15217
412-422-8864
manny@dhp.com

Randy's Alternative Music
1210 E Carson St
Pittsburgh, PA 15203
412-481-7445
Fax: 412-481-7743

Record Castle
1118 Cottman Ave
Philadelphia, PA 19111
215-745-4151
rcastle@inet.net

Record-Rama Sound Archives
4981 McKnight Rd.
Pittsburgh, PA 15237-0595
412-367-7330

Siren
25 W. State St
Doylestown, PA 18901
215-348-2323

Sound City USA
5709 N Broad St
Philadelphia, PA 19141
215-424-0888

Sounds of Market
15 S 11th St, 2nd Fl
Philadelphia, PA 19107
215-925-3150

Spinster's
110 S. Main St
New Hope, PA 18938
215-862-2700

Spruce Street
4004 Spruce St.
Philadelphia, PA 19104
215-382-4554

Third Street Jazz & Rock
20 N. Third St
Philadelphia, PA 19106
215-627-3366

Tower Records
610 South St
Philadelphia, PA 19147
215-574-9888

RHODE ISLAND

Fast Forward
5 Steeples St.
Providence, RI 02903
401-272-8866

In Your Ear
286 Thayer St
Providence, RI 02906
401-861-1515

Newbury Comics
1500 Bald Hill Rd
Warwick, RI 02886
401-821-3170

Sound Wave
91 Pt. Judith Rd
Narragansett, RI 02882
401-789-9570

Tom's Tracks
281 Thayer St
Providence, RI 02906
401-274-0820

SOUTH CAROLINA

BJ's Music
1430 Augusta St.
Greenville, SC 29605
803-242-0500

52.5
52 1/2 Wentworth St.
Charleston, SC 29401
803-722-3263

Manifest Disc & Tapes
946 Orleans Rd.
Charleston, SC 29407
803-571-4657

Manifest Disc
1563A Broad River Rd.
Columbia, SC 29210
803-798-2606

Papa Jazz Records
2014 Green St.
Columbia, SC 29205
803-256-0095

Sounds Familiar
4420 Rosewood Extension
Columbia, SC 29209
803-776-7208

X Records
600 Laurens Rd.
Greenville, SC 29607
803-370-1919

SOUTH DAKOTA

Disc Jockey
1250 Empire Mall
Sioux Falls, SD 57116
605-361-9554

Ernie November's
1801 W 12th St
Sioux Falls, SD 57104
605-334-6455

Herb's
104 E. Main St
Vermillion, SD 57069
605-624-3027

TENNESSEE

Audiomania
1698 Madison
Memphis, TN 38104
901-278-1166

Blockbuster Music
2121 Cumberland Ave
Knoxville, TN 37916
423-522-3733

Blockbuster Music
2715 S Perkins Rd
Memphis, TN 38118
901-362-3191
Fax: 901-363-0781

Boss Ugly Bob's
726 E. McLemore Ave.
Memphis, TN 38106
901-774-6400

Cat's Compact Discs
3249 Austin Peay Hwy.
Memphis, TN 38128
901-385-2287

Cat's Records
7337 Kingston Pike
Knoxville, TN 37919
423-584-2933

Cheapskates
1576 Getwell Rd
Memphis, TN 38111
901-744-1312

The Disc Exchange
2615 Chapman Hwy.
Knoxville, TN 37920
615-573-5710

The Great Escape
1925 Broadway
Nashville, TN 37203
615-327-0646

Lucy's Record Shop
1707 Church St.
Nashville, TN 37203
615-321-0882

Phonoluxe
2609 Nolensville Rd
Nashville, TN 37211
615-259-3500

Pop-Lar Tunes
308 Poplar Ave.
Memphis, TN 38103
901-525-6348

Shangri-La
1916 Madison Ave.
Memphis, TN 38104
901-274-1916

The Sound Shop
1000 Two Mile Pkwy
Goodlettsville, TN 37072
615-859-0850

TEXAS

ABCD's
4631 Airport Blvd, Ste 110
Austin, TX 78751
512-454-1212
abcds@bga.com

Antone's Record Store
2928 Guadalupe
Austin, TX 78705
512-322-0660

Bill's Records
8118 Spring Valley Rd.
Dallas, TX 75240
214-234-1496

Cactus Music & Video
2930 S. Shepherd
Houston, TX 77098
713-526-9272

CD Source
5500 Greenville Ave #201
Dallas, TX 75206
214-890-7614

Collector's Records
10616 Garland Rd
Dallas, TX 75218
214-327-3313

Ellipse
6557 San Pedro
San Antonio, TX 78216
210-344-0093
Fax: 210-366-0574

Ernest Tubb Record Shop #6
140 E Exchange, Ste B604
Ft Worth, TX 76106
817-624-8449
Fax: 817-624-8451

Good Vibrations
910 Oblate
San Antonio, TX 78216
210-828-3472

Hogwild Records and Tapes
1824 N Main St
San Antonio, TX 78212
210-733-5354
Fax: 210-736-2371

Infinite Records
7100 A Ertel
Houston, TX 77040
713-466-6727
Fax: 713-466-5468

Inner Sanctum Records
504 W. 24th
Austin, TX 78705
512-472-9459

Last Beat Records
2639 A Elm St
Dallas, TX 75226
214-748-5600
Fax: 214-748-5632

Musicmania
3909-D N I-H-35 #1
Austin, TX 78722
512-451-3361

Pagan Rhythms
5409 Greenville Ave.
Dallas, TX 75206
214-739-6331

RPM
565 W Oates, Ste 110
Garland, TX 75043
972-681-8441
Fax: 214-681-9486

Record Rack
3109 S. Shepard
Houston, TX 77098
713-524-3602

Sound Exchange
1718 Westheimer
Houston, TX 77098
713-666-5555

Sound Exchange
2100-A Guadalupe
Austin, TX 78705
512-476-8742

Sound Plus
1403 Westheimer Rd.
Houston, TX 77006
713-520-7323

Sound Revolution
1312 FM 1690
Houston, TX 77096
713-444-5454

Sundance
202-B University Dr.
San Marcos, TX 78666
512-392-7084

University
2414 Broadway #b
Lubbock, TX 79401
806-741-0150

Vinyl Edge
13171 Veterans Memorial
Houston, TX 77014
713-537-2575

Waterloo
600 N. Lamar Bl #A
Austin, TX 78703
512-474-2500

The X
105 N Welch
Denton, TX 76201
817-387-8439

Yellow Rose
1805 S. Lincoln
San Angelo, TX 76904
915-944-7455

UTAH

Audio Works
149 E 2nd St.
Salt Lake City, UT 84111
801-364-9999

Blockbuster Music
2107 S 700 E
Salt Lake City, UT 84106
801-484-9131
Fax: 801-484-0674

Gray Whale CD
248 S 1300 E
Salt Lake City, UT 84102
801-583-3333

The Heavy Metal Shop
1074 E 2100 S
Salt Lake City, UT 84106
801-467-7071

Raunch
1121 Wilmington Ave.
Salt Lake City, UT 84106
801-484-3778

Raspberry
4844 Highland Dr
Salt Lake City, UT 84117
801-278-4629

VERMONT

Harlequin
PO Box 308
Rutland, VT 05702
802-775-1823

Pure Pop Records
115 S. Winooski Ave.
Burlington, VT 05401
802-658-2652

Sound Barrier
52 Center St
Rutland, VT 05701
802-775-4754

Tones Music and Art Inc.
Rte 15
Johnson, VT 05656
802-635-2223

Vibes Music
92 Church St
Burlington, VT 05401
802-864-5646

Yesterday & Today
200 Main St 2nd Fl.
Burlington, VT 05403
802-862-5363

VIRGINIA

Birdland
957 Providence Sq.
Virginia Beach, VA 23464
804-495-0961

Blockbuster Music
7544 Granby St
Norfolk, VA 23505
757-480-2851
Fax:804-583-2327

Books, Strings & Things
202 Market Sq
Roanoke, VA 24011
540-342-5511
Fax: 540-951-5034

Fantasia Comics & Records
1419 1/2 Universtiy Ave.
Charlottesville, VA 22901

Fantasy
9823 Jefferson Ave.
Newport News, VA 23605
804-595-1259

Gary's Stereo & Video
6017 W Broad St.
Richmond, VA 23230
804-288-1945

Half Moon Music
1511 Pacific Ave.
Virginia Beach, VA 23451
804-428-4072

Peaches Music & Video
8018 W Broad St
Richmond, VA 23294
804-747-1755
Fax: 804-747-1867

P&L Compact Discs
153 Glyndon
Vienna, VA 22180
703-281-7575

Plan 9
3002 W. Cary St
Richmond, VA 23221
804-353-9996

Plan 9
1325 W. Main St.
Charlottesville, VA 22903
804-979-9999

Record Convergence
4005 Chestnut St
Fairfax, VA 22030
703-385-1234

The Record Exchange
302A N Main St
Blacksburg, VA 24060
540-961-2500

Record Mart
217 King St.
Alexandria, VA 22314
703-683-4583

Skinnies
814 W. 21st St
Norfolk, VA 23517
804-622-2241

Unicorn Records
3214 Academy Ave.
Portsmouth, VA 23703
804-483-0774

WASHINGTON

2nd Time Around
4209 University Way NE
Seattle, WA 98105
206-632-1698
secndtme@dwolfe.net

Backstage Music & Video
2232 NW Market ST.
Seattle, WA 98107
206-784-9517

Bedazzled Discs
911 E Pine St
Seattle, WA 98122
206-329-6500

Bud's Jazz Records
102 S. Jackson St
Seattle, WA 98104
206-628-0445

Cellophane Square
4538 University Way NE
Seattle, WA 98105
206-634-2280
music@cellophane.com

Easy Street
4559 California Ave SW
Seattle, WA 98116
206-938-3279

Exotique Imports, Inc.
2400 3rd Ave.
Seattle, WA 98121
206-448-3452

Fallout
1506 E. Olive Way
Seattle, WA 98122
206-323-2662

Hot Poop
210 E. Main
Walla Walla, WA 99362
509-525-9080

Orpheum
618 Broadway E
Seattle, WA 98102
206-322-6370

Singles Going Steady
2219 2nd Ave
Seattle, WA 98121
206-441-7396

Sounds Great
3007 Judson
Gig Harbor, WA 98335
206-851-8986

WASHINGTON D.C.

Melody
1623 Connecticut Ave. NW
Washington, DC 20009
202-232-4002

Olsson's
1239 Wisconsin Ave NW
Washington, DC 20052
202-333-2650

Orpheus
3249 M St. NW
Washington, DC 20007
202-337-7970

Phantasmagoria
1619 Connecticut Ave
Washington, DC 20009
202-462-8886

Smash
3279 M St NW
Washington, DC 20007
202-337-6274

Tower Records
2000 Pennsylvania Ave NW
Washington, DC 20006
202-331-2400
Fax: 202-463-2172

WEST VIRGINIA

2nd Time Around
1208 4th Ave
Huntington, WV 25701
304-523-0299

Backstreet
370 High St.
Morgantown, WV 26505
304-296-3203

Davidson's
932 4th Ave
Huntington, WV 25701
304-522-0228
mail@davidsonsmusic.com,
www.davidsonsmusic.com

Groove Music
264 High St
Morgantown, WV 26505
304-296-1622

Music Box
300 S. 2nd
Laramie, WY 82070
307-742-3774

Now Hear This
1101 4th Ave
Huntington, WV 25701
304-522-0021

Top Notch
212 Ivinson St.
Laramie, WY 82070
307-742-7270

WISCONSIN

Atomic
1813 E. Locust St.
Milwaukee, WI 53211
414-332-3663
www.atomicrecords.com

B-Side
436 State St.
Madison, WI 53703
608-255-1977
Fax: 608-255-5102

Imports Plus
233 Broadway
Green Bay, WI 54303
414-435-4700

Mad City
600 Williamson
Madison, WI 53703
608-251-8558
Fax: 608-251-8668

Rush-Mor Records
2660 S KK Ave
Milwaukee, WI 53207
414-481-6040

WYOMING

Ken's Music Box
300 S 2nd St
Laramie, WY 82070
307-742-3774
Fax: 307-742-3775

Top Notch Records
212 Ivinson St
Laramie, WY 82070
307-742-7270

Advertising

Advertising your release in trade and consumer music publications is a way to get radio airplay, sell records and announce tours. Advertising can get very expensive, very quickly, and for the independent band this could mean a lot of wasted money. Obviously, it all depends on how much money you have to spend.

Ad Cost vs. Sales Potential

Before taking out any ad, ask yourself how many records can this ad realistically sell? If you don't think it'll make more money than it will cost, you probably shouldn't take out the ad. If you don't have nationwide distribution, don't take out a $1000 ad in a national publication unless you honestly think you can make that off mail-order alone. No matter how great your release is, if people haven't heard of you they most likely will not be shelling out 15 bucks for your CD. That $1000 could pay for dozens of co-op ads with local record stores, or smaller ads in regional music magazines. You've got to think about where your advertising dollar will do the most good. Wherever you place your ads, to release any record successfully you are going to have to spend at least a few hundred dollars on some sort of advertising.

Placement

Where should those ads be placed? First, get ad rate information from magazines in which you're interested in advertising (this is also a great way to get free subscriptions to your favorite magazines). The cost of the ad space will probably be the deciding factor. If you have local music magazine or entertainment weekly in your area, that'd be a good place to start.

You may be surprised to find that the smallest, cheapest ad you placed got the biggest response. Targeting the ads specifically to the audience you're trying to reach is the key here. Even a cheap, catchy classified ad offering a free catalog may get a response from hundreds of interested music fans. If it's possible, taking out an ad in an issue in which a review of your record will appear is always nice. It's kind of the one-two punch effect.

If you're going to be sending your release out to national radio, a radio send-out can be maximized by a few, well-placed ads in the college trade publications such as *CMJ*. These ads get music directors and DJs interested in your record.

Indie Discount

Many publications offer discounts to independent labels and bands. ASK FOR IT! Also, if you can, get terms with the magazine rather than pay cash in advance. If you can defer paying for the ad for a few months, you may be able to make enough money selling your releases through mail-order to cover the cost of the ad.

As far as the content of the ad is concerned, this is another chance to use your

MORE NEW SLUDGE FROM THE MOTOR CITY...

The EXCEPTIONS
No Shoes. No Shirt. No Exceptions CD (IC120) ($10)
~Ska/Ska-core - Motor City style~

ZUG ISLAND QUARTET
Two Beat / My Island 7" (IC121)
~ Industrial punk sludge~

The MANGOS
Diane Linkletter/Fly Me 7" (IC119)
~ Pop punk with big crunch ~

MOL TRIFFID
In Larry's Living Room - LTD. EDITION Double7" (IC118) ($6)
~Soft & crunchy NoCal style~

EL SMASHO!
Foster Brooks 3 Song 7" (IC117)
~ Punk rock from E. Lansing ~

The GOLDENTONES
"IN STEREO" 5 Song 7" (IC116)
~ Surf from the city ~

The VOLEBEATS
Knowing Me Knowing You/First TimeLast Time 7" (IC114)
~Folk rock plus ABBA cover ~

The EXCEPTIONS
Flowering Scrunch/Exceptionally Horny 7" ($4) (IC113)
~ Ska w/ instrumental B-side ~

OTHER ICON RELEASES: -IC115 BIGGER THAN MASS - Cansmacker / Magic Fingers 7" -IC111 MOL TRIFFID - Media Clowns / I. Caligula 7" -IC109 JESUS MANSON - Run Girl / Down 7" - IC108 INSIDE OUT (Detroit) - Cesspool / Mirrors 7" The EXCEPTIONS LOGO T-SHIRT - XLOnly. Black On White - $10 -ICON RECORDS T-SHIRT -2 Sided XL Only - $8 -For Mail Order Send: $3 For Singles, $10 For CD (ppd.)

ICON RECORDS
P.O. BOX 1746,
ROYAL OAK, MI 48068

NERVE SHATTERING HORROR!

THE MORTALS
"BULLETPROOF!" LP/CD
12 doses of full-bore guitar explosives...shaken, not stirred.
ES1216 $8.00 LP/$12.00 CD

MAN OR ASTRO-MAN?
"DESTROY ALL ASTRO-MEN!"
23 reverb drenched blasts of lethal, all-instro RayGun Rock!
ES1215 $8.00 LP/$12.00 CD

THE MONO MEN
"SIN & TONIC" LP/CD
Twelve booze fueled doses of loud and lewd no-brow rock!
ES1218 $8.00 LP/$12.00 CD

OUT NOW: The Woggles "Zontar Sessions" LP/CD, Jack O' Fire "Destruction of Squaresville" CD, Man Or Astro-Man? "Astro-Launch" 7" ep, The Mono Men "Mystery Girl" 7" ON THE BURNER: The Nomads 7", The Apemen 7", Galaxy Trio 10"/CD and lots more trash for yer can! We also carry loads of cool and hard to find non-Estrus stuff.......WRITE FOR A FREE CATALOG!

JOIN THE ESTRUS CRUST CLUB: 6 SINGLES $25 ($30 CANADA/$35 FOREIGN)
You'll get the next six limited edition color vinyl singles, a 15% discount on mail-order and more "members-only" bonuses...so what'cha waitin' for?

Distributed Worldwide by Mordam Records...stores call (415) 575-1970
Estrus Records PO Box 2125 Bellingham WA 98227

Above: Sample independent label ads.

Above: Sample indie labels ads. Note catalog offers.

imagination. The key to getting your message across is to get people to actually look at the ad, so make it as blatant and eye-catching as possible. I've included some samples from successful independent labels, and there are samples of radio-specific ads in the radio section.

Make a Catalog

Always include contact information and a free catalog offer. Even if you only have one release, you can make some sort of propaganda sheet to send to people who respond. You should also include information on how a reader can order your record through the mail, and if your band is touring, include the dates. If you've got a website (see the next chapter) that features an online catalog, always include the address in your ads. This is an easy way for people all over the world to get more information about you and your release.

The newest, and possibly the best new advertsising medium for independent musicians is the Internet. We'll look at ways it can help your cause in the next chapter.

The Internet

There's been plenty of talk about how the Internet is revolutionizing the music industry, and guess what? It's true. The Internet, the international computer network, has become a great way for musicians to network and promote their music. There are dozens of online discussion groups (called "newsgroups") that deal with issues facing independent labels and musicians, and all the big commercial on-line services (American Online, Compuserve, etc.) have music forums. If you have access to a computer, get Internet access! Here are a few ways the Internet can help you:

The Internet as Promotional Tool

There are several ways the Internet can help you promote your music. E-mail mailing lists, the World Wide Web, and newsgroups are your main tools.

World Wide Web

The World Wide Web is an area of the Internet that links computer (thousands of them) all over the world. Each of these computers (called "servers") contains graphic and text-based information, which can be "browsed" by anyone connected to the Internet (using browser software, such as Netscape Navigator or Microsoft Explorer). There are thousands of bands and labels who have "pages," or sites, on the Web, where people worldwide can view photos, watch full-motion video, download songs or read information about the particular bands. Websites also feature "links" which can take the browser to other related websites anywhere in the world.

A sample indie label website.

World Wide Web pages are written in a software language called HTML, it's fairly easy to learn, and if you ask around (especially on-line) you should be able to find someone who can help program a web page for you, and get it on the Web. Most internet service providers (including the large ones like America Online) offer free web space for their subscribers. Just think of the web as a global, 24-hour-a-day advertisement for your music. You can use it to list upcoming shows, offer CDs or merchandise for sale, or give people a taste of your music with a digitized sample. Once you get a website, you've got to publicize your address (called a URL) in order to attract visitors. Put the web address on your fliers, mailers, CDs, t-shirts, whatever. There are many web indices (like Yahoo!) and search engines that you can submit your site to, free, so that interested music fans can find you.

America Online's music section.

Also, if you know other musicians with sites, get them to put a link to your page on their site, and vice-versa. Again, the key to having any kind of success with your website is to get as many people as possible to check it out. You'll often hear people talking about "hits," as in how many hits their site gets. Anytime anyone views any page of your site, this counts as a hit. If one person looks at ten different pages on your site, that's ten hits. This is just a way of measuring how much traffic a particular site is getting.

IUMA hosts hundreds of band sites.

If you don't have any computer knowledge, there are many services that will make a website for your band or label. One is IUMA, the Internet Underground Music Archive, which houses information and music from hundreds of bands and dozens of indie and major labels. People can log onto the site for free and browse your band photo, read bio info or download one of your songs. IUMA gets over 100,000 hits per day. You'll pay a fee (around $200) to get your band on IUMA (http://www.iuma.com), but it's probably worth it, especially if you don't know anything about the web. The advantage of going with a service like IUMA is that people (lots of them) are already visiting this site, looking for new music. Call 408-426-IUMA for more information. There are other sites that offer this kind of service, so look into it.

E-mail Mailing Lists

You can put together an e-mail mailing list the same way you would a normal mailing list. Get e-mail addresses from other labels and bands you know, and with the click of a button you can send press releases, tour schedules or show announcements to hundreds or thousands of people at a time, free. The savings over traditional flier mailings will add up really quick.

Newsgroups

Newsgroups are online discussion groups or message boards stored on servers all over the world. You can "subscribe" to these newsgroups through your internet service provider using a news reader program (like Netscape News). The subjects covered by individual newsgroups are endless, from guitars to Kurt Cobain to Cocker Spaniels. There are newsgroups devoted to hundreds of different famous (and non-famous) bands. People "post" messages or questions on these newsgroups, and then other people read them and respond, and then other people respond to those responses, and so on.

Check out alt.music.independent for questions and advice about putting out your own music. Got a question about an indie label? Need information on cheap CD manufacturing? Need a place to play in Topeka? You can get these answers and lots more by subscribing to music-related newsgroups.

The Internet as Reference Tool

Almost every major label and large independent label has a website, as do most music-related organizations. ASCAP (http://www.ascap.com) and BMI (http://www.bmi.com) both have sites that can give you information on performance rights and music publishing. CMJ also has a website you can use to view their college radio charts at http://www.cmjmusic.com.

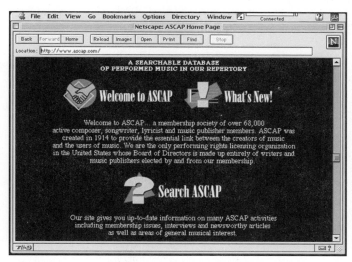

ASCAP's site lets you search their song title database.

If you're new to the Net, a good place to start is the music section at Yahoo! (http://www.yahoo.com). It's a pretty comprehensive directory of music-related websites, broken down into dozens of categories. There are also several sites devoted solely to musicians who are releasing their own music. One is Outersound (http://www.outersound.com), which is set up like a city for independent musicians, featuring areas on recording, touring, manufacturing records, and lots more. A good site for touring bands is WILMA, the Worldwide Internet Live Music Archive (http://www.wilma.com). Its "Search-O-Matic" feature is an interactive database of artists, venues and concert listings from thousands of clubs. Again, check Yahoo! under the "Independent Music" category for more useful music sites.

Internet Radio

Many college and commercial radio stations also broadcast over the Internet. Using free software like RealAudio (http://www.realaudio.com) you can listen to stations all over the world, with FM-quality sound. Internet radio is quickly becoming a great new outlet for independent music to get heard. You can find a list of Internet radio sites on Yahoo!, and get information about submitting your music to them.

NET CHARTS

NET charts are compiled from a national sample of influential radio stations, club DJs and retail outlets

COLLEGE CHART

WC	LC	TC	Artist	Title	Label
1	2	1	**Helium**	*The Dirt Of Luck*	(Matador)
3	6	2	**Guided By Voices**	*Alien Lanes*	(Matador)
4	1	3	**The 6ths**	*Wasps' Nests*	(London)
2	9	4	**The Orb**	*Orbus Terrarum*	(Island)
4	13	5	**KMFDM**	*Nihil*	(Wax Traxl/TVT)
5	3	6	**Morphine**	*Yes*	(Rykodisc)
4	4	7	**Flying Saucer Attack**	*Further*	(Drag City)
4	5	8	**Spiritualized**	*Pure Phase*	(dedicated/Arista)
3	10	9	**Red House Painters**	*Ocean Beach*	(4AD)
1	20	10	**Yo La Tengo**	*Electr-O-Pura*	(Matador)
1	25	11	**Pavement**	*Wowee Zowee*	(Matador)
1	23	12	**The Muffs**	*Blonder And Blonder*	(Reprise)
3	12	13	**Sleeper**	*Smart*	(Arista)
2	16	14	**Half Japanese**	*Greatest Hits*	(Safe House)
2	42	15	**Tsunami**	*World Tour And Other Destinations*	(Simple Machines)
2	21	16	**Godhead Silo**	*Elephanititus Of The Night*	(Kill Rock Stars)
6	14	17	**Mike Watt**	*Ball-Hog Or Tugboat?*	(Columbia)
5	7	18	**Archers Of Loaf**	*Vee Vee*	(Alias)
9	11	19	**Negativeland**	*Fair Use*	(Seeland)
2	15	20	**Grifters**	*The Eureka EP*	(Shangri-La)
2	19	21	**Laika**	*Silver Apples Of The Moon*	(Too Pure/American)
1	30	22	**All**	*Pummel*	(Interscope)
4	8	23	**Elastica**	*Elastica*	(DGC)
3	28	24	**Squirrel Nut Zippers**	*The Inevitable*	(Mammoth)
7	22	25	**The Roots**	*Do You Want More?*	(DGC)
8	31	26	**Cub**	*Come Out Come Out*	(Mint)
-	-	27	**Various Artists**	*Oi! A Skampilation*	(Radical)
-	-	28	**Heartworms**	*Thanks For The Headache*	(Darla)
-	-	29	**Aphex Twin**	*I Care Because You Do*	(Sire/Elektra)
1	38	30	**Soundtrack**	*Tank Girl*	(Elektra)
3	33	31	**Barbara Manning**	*Sings With The Original Artists*	(Feel Good All Over)
3	27	32	**Ben Lee**	*Grandpaw Would*	(Grand Royal)
1	18	33	**Ned's Atomic Dustbin**	*BrainBloodVolume*	(Work)
8	17	34	**PJ Harvey**	*To Bring You My Love*	(Island)
1	46	35	**Wilco**	*AM*	(Sire/Reprise)
1	48	36	**Mudhoney**	*My Brother The Cow*	(Reprise)
8	34	37	**Mary Lou Lord**	*Mary Lou Lord*	(Kill Rock Stars)
-	-	38	**Mr. T Experience**	*...And The Women Who Love Them*	(Lookout)
-	-	39	**Home**	*IX*	(Relativity)
5	24	40	**Smog**	*Wild Love*	(Drag City)
10	RE	41	**Team Dresch**	*Personal Best*	(Chainsaw)
1	49	42	**Juliana Hatfield**	*Only Everything*	(Mammoth/Atlantic)
-	-	43	**Tad**	*Infrared Riding Hood*	(Elektra)
-	-	44	**Engine Kid**	*Angel Wings*	(Revelation)
-	-	45	**The Fall**	*Cerebral Caustic*	(Permanent)
-	-	46	**Radiohead**	*The Bends*	(Capitol)
-	-	47	**Hum**	*You'd Prefer An Astronaut*	(RCA)
1	44	48	**Masada w/ John Zorn**	*Alef*	(DIW)
1	36	49	**Goo Goo Dolls**	*A Boy Named Goo*	(Metal Blade)
6	RE	50	**Various Artists**	*Incredibly Strange Music, Vol.2*	(Asphodel/RESearch)

CLUB CHART

WC	LC	TC	Artist	Title	Label
3	8	1	**KMFDM**	"Juke Joint Jezebel"	(Wax Traxl/TVT)
3	3	2	**Dink**	"Get It On"	(Capitol)
5	9	3	**Nitzer Ebb**	"Kick It"	(Geffen)
9	4	4	**Moby**	"Everytime You Touch Me"	(Elektra)
1	26	5	**White Zombie**	"More Human Than Human"	(Geffen)
2	13	6	**Real McCoy**	"Run Away"	(Arista)
6	1	7	**Human League**	"Tell Me When"	(EastWest)
11	2	8	**Duran Duran**	"White Lines"	(Capitol)
5	5	9	**Elastica**	"Connection"	(Geffen)
14	7	10	**Traci Lords**	"Control"	(Radioactive)
2	24	11	**Prodigy**	"Poison"	(Mute)
4	10	12	**B-Tribe**	"Nadie Entiende"	(Atlantic)
10	6	13	**Waterliilies**	"Never Get Enough"	(Kinetik/Sire)
4	14	14	**Jimmy Somerville**	"Heartbeat"	(London)
12	11	15	**Billie Ray Martin**	"Your Loving Arms"	(EastWest)
4	16	16	**Technotronic**	"Move It"	(SBK)
12	12	17	**Wolf Gang Press**	"Going South"	(4AD/WB)
2	28	18	**Towa Tei**	"Technonova"	(Elektra)
1	32	19	**Nicki French**	"Total Eclipse Of The Heart"	(Critique)
1	27	20	**Freaky Chakra**	"March Of The Tangent Prone"	(Astralwerks)
1	28	21	**Ned's Atomic Dustbin**	"All I Ask Of Myself"	(Chaos)
2	19	22	**Angel Corpus Christi**	"Candy"	(Almo)
2	43	23	**Urban Dance Squad**	"Demagogue"	(Virgin)
-	-	24	**Senser**	"States Of Mind"	(Atlas)
4	20	25	**Holy Gang**	"Free Tyson Free"	(Roadrunner)
9	18	26	**Blondie**	"Atomic"	(Chrysalis)
2	25	27	**Professor Trance**	"Drumming Circle"	(Island)
1	39	28	**Foetus**	"Null" EP	(Columbia)
5	21	29	**Rednex**	"Cotton Eyed Joe"	(Battery)
1	30	30	**Madonna**	"Bedtime Stories"	(Maverick)
4	29	31	**Bush**	"Everything Zen"	(Trauma)
9	23	32	**Whigfield**	"Saturday"	(Curb)
2	33	33	**PJ Harvey**	"Down By The Water"	(Island)
12	22	34	**Die Warzau**	"Liberated/Material"	(Wax Traxl)
6	27	35	**U2**	"Melon"	(Island)
1	41	36	**Roman & Winnie Projekt**	"Taste Of Honey"	(Zoe Magic)
5	15	37	**Transglobal Underground**	"Temple Head"	(Epic)
2	47	38	**God Lives Underwater**	"No More Love"	(American)
24	34	39	**Dink**	"Green Mind"	(Capitol)
7	36	40	**Wink**	"Higher State Of Consciousness"	(Strictly Rhythm)
14	31	41	**Erasure**	"I Love Saturday"	(Mute/Elektra)
2	46	42	**Sugar Ray**	"Hold Your Eyes" EP	(Atlantic)
-	-	43	**Peter Scherer**	"Nerve Type No"	(MetroBlue)
-	-	44	**Aphex Twin**	"Ventolin"	(Sire)
7	37	45	**Fun-Da-Mental**	"Dog Tribe"	(Mammoth)
6	35	46	**Hunger**	"If"	(Gut)
4	45	47	**Fem 2 Fem**	"Where Did Love Go"	(Critique)
8	40	48	**Fini Tribe**	"Brand New"	(ffrr)
7	42	49	**Massive Attack**	"Protection"	(Virgin)
7	44	50	**Bad Religion**	"Infected"	(Atlantic)

TOP ADDS (College)
1. Aphex Twin
2. Rosa Mota
3. Clouds
4. Crowsdell
5. The Fall

GIANT STEPS (College)
1. Tsunami
2. Oi! A Skampilation
3. Heartworms
4. Aphex Twin
5. Mr. T Experience

COLLEGE DANCE

TOP ADDS (Club)
1. White Zombie
2. KMFDM
3. Real McCoy
4. Prodigy
5. Senser

GIANT STEPS (Club)
1. Frankie Knuckles
2. Senser
3. KMFDM
4. Prodigy
5. White Zombie

College Dance

WC	LC	TC	Artist	Title	Label
6	4	1	**Prodigy**	*Music for the Jilted Generation*	(Mute)
1	1	2	**Freaky Chakra**	*Lowdown Motivator*	(Astralwerks)
2	16	3	**Towa Tei**	"Technova"	(Elektra)
1	14	4	**B Tribe**	"Nadie Entiende"	(Atlantic)
4	10	5	**V/A**	*Harthouse Axis Of Vision*	(Onion)
-	-	6	**Baby Doc & The Dentist**	"Tales Of The Seraphin"	(Prolekult)
3	5	7	**V/A**	*Global Virus*	(Planet Earth)
8	2	8	**V/A**	*Trance Atlantic*	(Total/BMG)
5	7	9	**Dubtribe**	"Mother Earth" RMX	(Organico)
7	3	10	**Autechre**	*Amber*	(Wax Traxl/TVT)
1	12	11	**Orb**	*Orbus Terranium*	(Island)
11	18	12	**777**	*7.3 System 7*	(Astralwerks)
2	20	13	**Aphex Twin**	*I Care Because You Do*	(Sire)

Club Dance

WC	LC	TC	Artist	Title	Label
-	-	14	**Ultra Shock**	"Sound Of The E"	(Logic)
-	-	15	**Speedy J**	*G Spot*	(+8)
-	-	16	**Hazed**	"Bells"	(+8)
8	6	17	**Moby**	*Everything Is Wrong*	(Elektra)
-	-	18	**Peter Scherer**	"Nerve Type No"	(MetroBlue)
-	-	19	**V/A**	*The American Dream*	(Moonshine)
3	15	20	**Transglobal Underground**	"Temple Head"	(Epic)
-	-	21	**Prototype 909**	"Transistor Rhythm"	(Instinct)
-	-	22	**Professor Trance**	"Drumming Circle"	(Island)
8	9	23	**V/A**	*Logic Trance Vol 2*	(Logic)
8	8	24	**V/A**	*Trip Hop Test*	(Moonshine)
-	-	25	**Legion Of Green Men**	*Spatial Specific*	(+8)

Above: A sample radio chart.

Radio

There are three types of radio stations: Commercial, Public and College. Out of the three, you probably have a realistic chance of getting your music played on college and public radio, at least at first. People at these stations are generally more receptive to independently released, unknown records. These stations are looking for new music; they want to be the ones who "discover" a major new artist. Commercial radio tends to be more conservative when it comes to taking chances on new bands. They usually wait until a release proves itself in the college radio arena before they'll add it to their playlist. With this in mind, it make more sense to put your efforts into college and public radio first, and then worry about commercial radio.

The Importance of Radio Airplay

Almost every college in the U.S. has a student-run radio station. They range from one watt, carrier current stations which can only be heard on campus, to 100,000 watt stations with a range of over 100 miles. The one thing they have in common is that they will broadcast music from unknown, unproven bands and artists. Also, most college stations have dozens of different specialty shows that feature almost every style of music, and the people that listen to these shows are devoted music fans, and are probably your biggest potential audience.

In recent years, the major corporate labels have pumped millions of dollars of advertising and promotion into the college market in an attempt to influence what gets played. Take one look at today's college radio top ten and you'll realize that they've succeeded, to a degree. There are still hundreds of independent labels getting airplay all over the country, and some compete directly with the majors.

For the independent artist, getting college (or any) radio airplay is extremely important. Getting your music heard across the country will open up huge opportunities. If your goal is to get signed by a major label, these labels pay close attention to the college charts, and use them as a prospecting sheet for new bands. Playlists from the stations that played your record are also a good addition to your press kit, and are necessary to convince distributors to carry your music. If you want to do a nationwide tour or sell your records to stores in other parts of the country, you need to be getting some sort of radio airplay.

Get Copies of the Trades

There are several publications which keep track of what gets played on college radio. Among them are *College Music Journal (CMJ), Hits, Records & Radio, The Gavin Report* and *Billboard*. Stations report their top 20 or 30 songs to these magazines, which compile them into national college radio charts. They also accept advertising, and a call or letter to any of the above will get you a sample copy and ad rates (see Press list).

These are trade publications which get read by Music Directors, (they decide what music gets played) Program Directors, (they decide when and how often it gets played) DJs (they play their own personal choices along with a playlist determined by the MD and PD) and other record labels. Advertisements placed in these publications are different than ads in consumer magazines, and should be targeted directly at the radio station personnel. (e.g. "The new single from band X, on your desk now! Play it!") These ads should be timed to appear when your record arrives at the station and for several weeks or months after. This will help to distinguish your release from the dozens of others that stations receive each week. If it's a great ad, it can generate airplay and interest from stations, distributors, etc. These publications also print directories of bands and labels, so ask them for information on how to be included.

The Send Out

Directories of college, public and commercial stations are available from several of the radio trade magazines, and a huge list of them is in another book I wrote called *Getting Radio Airplay*. Get sample copies of as many trades as you can; examine each station's playlist to see if your style of music will fit in with their format. You'll also be able to find out which stations are currently reporting to the trades. Concentrate your promotional efforts on the reporting stations!

If you can afford it, send your release to all the stations that play your style of music. You probably can't, so send it to stations in your state, in surrounding states and to stations that report to the trade publications.

What Format To Send

In recent years, CDs have basically taken over as the format for radio, although many college stations still actively play vinyl. Cassettes, whether they are cassette singles or a full-length releases, are going to get substantially less airplay (like zero) than CDs and vinyl. You are dooming yourself to little or no exposure by sending a tape, unless you're sending it to a local music specialty show at a station in your hometown or something.

Once your CD gets there, it'd be nice if it actually got played rather than taken home by station personnel or sold to the local record store. If you're sending CDs, you may have to send several copies to the larger stations in order to ensure one makes it into the CD player.

CD Singles

Most large record labels send CD singles to radio stations. These are standard 5" CDs with one or two tracks on them (not those little 3" discs). CD singles usually are just a disc in a jewel case, with no fancy inner sleeves. Graphics, pictures and information are printed on the disc itself. These CD singles are good for radio, and should be viewed as a promotional expense. You'll have a tough time selling them to retail stores or distributors.

Every station has different specialty shows; the rap show, hardcore show, reggae, etc. I know some of you don't want to pigeon-hole your music by giving it a "label", but you'll have a better chance of getting airplay if your record gets to someone who likes your style of music. So on the outside of your package, write SPEEDMETAL, or whatever your style may be.

Above: Sample radio-specific ads.

Pick a "Stressed" Cut

Along with your record, include a letter to the music director. It's very important to identify the "single" or "stressed" track; the song that most deserves airplay; the song you feel is the strongest on your record. No music director is going to sit and listen to every song in its entirety, then decide which song the station should play. Typically, the MD will listen to the one song that you tell him or her to listen to. If they like it, they'll play it. If they don't, they won't. Also, ask to be put on the station's mailing list for playlists. This is very important. Say something to the effect that your label will send them all it's upcoming new releases if they send you playlists. Also, an 11"x17" poster, xeroxed or printed, should be included if possible. If you've ever been inside a radio station, you've seen these things plastered everywhere. Posters get other DJs and passers-by interested in your release.

Reply Cards

Another idea is to include a stamped postcard addressed back to you, which reads "If you'd like to receive more new releases from X Records, fill out this postcard and drop it in a mailbox." On the card, ask for the station name, address and phone number, the name of the person who opened your package, their position at the station, etc. Now you'll have the name and number of someone you can call to see how your record is doing. This is a good way of finding out exactly who gives a damn about your release, then follow it up with a phone call about clubs and stores in the area, if they liked the record, etc.

One thing you should always take into consideration when sending to college radio is that these are schools; many stations are closed down or run by a skeleton crew over the summer and winter vacations. Don't send your records during these months! The best times to send are usually September to November or February to May.

When You're In Town

Most college stations sponsor shows on campus or in their city. If a station is playing your record, chances are they'll want to help you put a show together in their town. Ask about doing an on-air interview. Interviews are free airtime and are great advertisements for your show (see the touring chapter). Many stations will give away copies of your release, so ask about it. For the cost of a few records, you'll be getting airplay, advertising your band or show and gaining a few more fans in that area.

Touring

Touring, in my opinion, is without a doubt the best way to promote your band. Besides being able to meet and play in front of people you've never seen before, touring gives you a captive audience to which you can sell your records, T-shirts and other band merchandise. You might even get paid for the gig!

Booking a Tour

How do you go about booking an independent tour? There are booking agents who specialize in arranging tours for new bands, but unless these people are approaching you, it's usually very hard to get them interested in a band no one's heard of. At the end of this chapter I've included the names and phone numbers of some of these booking agents. With some vocal creativity and persistence you may be able to get one of them to book you a tour.

Plan Ahead

Your best bet will probably be to book the tour yourself. It's important that you have some sort of college or community radio airplay or other notoriety so that you can interest clubs in your act, and you should begin planning the tour at least three or four months before you actually start touring. After you've done a radio send-out, concentrate on the stations that played your record. These stations are already fans of your music, they know everything about the music scene in their town, most of them sponsor or present shows on campus or in town, and they have the clout to get the shows booked.

Getting the support of individual college and public stations is the best way to plan a tour. At the least, they'll be able to tell you what clubs in their city cater to your style of music. Ask if they would like to sponsor a show. This usually includes announcing the show on the air, giving away tickets to the show and doing an on-air interview with your band. If they're interested, call the clubs and tell them that your band is in the Top 10 at K-whatever, and that the station will be involved in the show. There aren't too many clubs that will pass up a situation like that, but it depends on how much money you're trying to get the club to pay you.

The Money

Most clubs won't pay an out-of-town, independent band more than $100 or $200, tops. Many won't even give you a guarantee, they'll want to pay you a percentage of the money collected at the door. You should always try to get a flat guarantee or a combination of guarantee and percentage of the door. If the club doesn't promote the show, you might wind up with spare change, which won't pay for the gas to your next gig.

Get a Contract!

Once you've struck a deal with the club or promoter, send them a contract (see example). Do not agree to play unless you get a signed contract from the club. If they won't sign a contract, they're hiding something and chances are you'll get screwed over. Once you get the contract back, make a copy of it and bring copies of all the contracts on tour with you. This will help enlighten any club managers who have bad memories.

Local Press

Find out which newspapers or magazines cover music events in each town on your tour (ask the club). You should send these publications a press kit, which should include your release, a bio or one sheet, and an 8" x 10" picture. The picture is important for local press when you're touring, because the chances are much better that they'll actually print it if a new band is coming to town. The club bookers or promoters will probably also want to see your release and press kit; if they aren't familiar with your music, they'll want to see it before they book your show. The clubs will also need your picture for fliers and posters; a better plan is to send the club your own pre-made fliers.

Tour Publications

There are a few national publications which can help out touring bands. One is *Pollstar*, which lists bands' tour schedules, venues, booking agents, etc. It's pretty major label oriented, but it's a good way to find potential venues. Their number is 209-271-7900.

Another good source of touring information is the *Musician Magazine Guide to Touring & Promotion,* a special issue which comes out twice a year. You can obtain one by calling Musician at 212-536-5208. *MaximumRocknRoll* also publishes a special issue called *Book Your Own Fucking Life* that can help punk or alternative bands (see press list for address). Also check out *Book Your Own Tour* by Liz Garo (Rockpress), which contains a ton of booking information and advice for all styles of music.

PERFORMANCE AGREEMENT

This agreement is for the services of _____(herein called "artist") and _____(herein called "purchaser") for the engagement descibed below is made this day_____, 19___, between the undersigned artist and purchaser.

1. Place of Show _____
2. Date(s) of Show _____
3. Times: Load In _____ Sound Check _____ Start_____
4. Number and Length of Sets _____
5. Sound System _____
6. Compensation: Performance _____
                          Lodging _____
                          Meals _____
                          Transportation _____
                          Other _____
                          TOTAL_____
7. Payment is to be made in cash___or check___no later than _____
8. Sales of merchandise by artist will be on the following terms _____
_____
9. Other _____
_____

10. The recording, reproduction or transmission of Artist's performance is prohibited absent written consent of Artist. Artist's obligations under this contract are subject to detention or prevention by sickness, accident, riots, strikes, epidemics or any other Act of God which could endanger the health or safety of the Artist. If any of the Artist's compensation is based on door receipts, Purchaser agrees to provide the artist a statement of gross receipts within two hours of the conclusion of the performance if asked, and Artist shall have the right to have representation at the door or the box office at all times. Said representation shall have the right to examine box office records relating to the above performance only. In the event Purchaser fails to fulfill its obligation provided herein, Purchaser will be liable to Artist in addition to the compensation provided herein. Either party may cancel this agreement without obligation to other if notice is received 21 days in advance of show. In witness whereof, the parties sign this contract this _____ day of _____ 19___.

_____ Purchaser   _____ Artist

Above: A sample booking contract.

Booking Agents

Agency for The Performing Arts/LA
9000 Sunset Blvd. Ste. 1200
Los Angeles, CA 90069
310-273-0744
Fax: 310-275-9401

Agency for The Performing Arts/NY
888 Seventh Ave.
New York, NY 10106
212-582-1500
Fax: 212-245-1647

The Agency Group
1775 Broadway #433
New York, NY 10019
212-581-3100
Fax: 212-575-0567
Alternative, Hip-Hop, Rock

American Concert
P.O. Box 24599
Nashville, TN 37202
615-244-2290
Fax: 615-244-9570
Country

Artist Representation & Management, Inc.
1257 Arcade St.
Minneapolis, MN 55106
612-483-8754
Fax: 612-331-5091
Rock

American Talent Group
221 W 57th 8th Fl
New York, NY 10019
212-713-0050
Fax: 212-713-0062
Rock

Ashley Street Talent
312 S Ashley St
Ann Arbor, MI 48104
313-995-5777
Fax: 313-995-8884
ashleyt@concentric.net
Rock

Bennett Morgan & Associates, Ltd.
1282 Route 376
Wappingers Falls, NY 12590
914-227-6065
Jazz, R&B

Berkeley Agency
2608 9th St.
Berkeley, CA 94710
510-843-4902
Fax: 510-843-7271
E-mail: berkagency.com
Jazz, Latin, Blues

Big Beat Productions, Inc.
1515 University Dr.#108A
Coral Springs, FL 33071
305-755-7759
Fax: 305-755-8733
All Styles

Buddy Lee Attractions, Inc.
38 Music Square E Ste. 300
Nashville, TN 37203
615-244-4336
Country

BSA Inc.
PO Box 1516
Champaign, IL 61824
217-352-8700
Fax: 217-352-9227
All styles

California Talent Associates
P.O. Box 2596
Petaluma, CA 94953-2596
707-778-1727
Fax: 707-778-1768
E-mail: CalHardbod@aol.com
All Styles

Nancy Carlin Associates
411 Ferry St. Ste. 2
Martinez, CA 94553
510-372-4260
Fax: 510-372-3762
Acoustic, World, Folk
nancyc@well.com

Keith Case & Associates
59 Music Square W
Nashville, TN 37203
615-327-4646
kcase@ibm.net
Bluegrass, Acoustic, Country, Folk

Cellar Door Entertainment
305 Lynnhaven Pkwy #201
Virginia Beach, VA 23452
757-463-1940
www.cellardoor.com
All Styles

Concerted Efforts, Inc.
P.O. Box 99
Newtonville, MA 02160
617-969-0810
Fax: 617-969-6761
members.aol.com/concerted /home.htm
Blues, World Beat, Folk

Creative Artists Agency
9830 Wilshire Blvd.
Beverly Hills, CA 90212
310-288-4545
Fax: 310-288-4800
All styles

Creature
3411 St. Paul Ave
Minneapolis, MN 55416
612-925-6011
Fax: 612-925-5909
Alternative

DMR
The Galleries of Syracuse
Ste. 250
Syracuse, NY 13202
315-475-2500
Fax: 315-475-0752

Day and Night Prod.
3001 Granite Rd. Ste. 2
Woodstock, MD 21163
410-521-6416
Fax: 410-521-6420
Blues, R&B, Roots

East Coast Entertainment
P.O. Box 11283
Richmond, VA 23230
804-355-2178
Fax: 704-372-9436
www.ecoast.com

East Coast Entertainment
67 Peachtree Park Dr., #101
Atlanta, GA 30309
404-634-0016
Fax: 404-634-8481
All styles

Entertainment Artists
903 18th Ave. S
Nashville, TN 37212
615-320-7041
Fax: 615-320-0856
entartnash@aol.com
Country

Entertainment Connection.
P.O. Box 80801
Billings, MT 59108
406-656-9678
Fax: 406-652-1180
All Styles

Eternal Talent
1598 E. Shore Dr.
St. Paul, MN 55106
612-771-0107
Fax: 612-774-8319

Famous
250 W. 57th #821
New York, NY 10107
212-245-3939
Fax: 212-459-9065
Contemporary Pop

Fantasma Productions, Inc.
2000 S. Dixie Hwy.
W. Palm Beach, FL 33401
407-832-6397
Fax: 407-832-2043
fantasma@fantasma.com
All styles

Fast Lane Productions
4856 Haygood Rd. #200
Virginia Beach, VA 23455
757-497-2669
Fax: 757-481-9227
Reggae, World Beat
fastlane@fastline intl.com

Fat City Artists
1906 Jetatkins Pl. #502
Nashville, TN 37212
615-320-7678
Fax: 615-255-7085
Rock, Alt., R&B, Jazz, Country

Frontier Booking Int'l.
1560 Broadway Ste. 1110
NYC, NY 10036
212-221-1919
Alternative, Rock, Pop

Frontier Booking Int'l
900 Sunset Blvd. #515
Los Angeles, CA 90069
213-850-5373
hq4fbi@aol.com
Alternative, Pop, Metal

Full House Entertainment Agency
3268 Belmont St. 2nd Fl.
Bellaire, OH 43906
614-676-5259
Fax: 614-676-5921

G.G. Greg Artist
Management
1288 E. 168th St.
Cleveland, OH 44110
216-692-1193
Fax: 216-692-1197

Go Ahead Booking
P.O. Box 5068
Hoboken, NJ 07030
201-798-1639
Fax: 201-798-7406

Good Music Agency
111 3rd Ave. S. #130
Minneapolis, MN 55401
612-204-3040
Fax: 612-204-3044

Harmony Artist, Inc.
8833 Sunset Blvd. PH W
Los Angeles, CA 90069
310-659-9644
Fax: 310-659-9675

Headline Talent, Inc.
1650 Broadway Ste. 508
New York, NY 10019
212-581-6900
Fax: 212-581-6906

David Hickey Agency
P.O. Box 719
Aledo, TX 76008
817-441-5488
Fax: 817-441-5484
R&B, Texas Roadhouse

Abby Hoffer Enterprises
223 1/2 E. 48th St.
New York, NY 10017-1538
212-935-6350
Fax: 212-758-4987
ahoffer@ix.netcom.com
Jazz, R&B, Big Band

ICM
8942 Wilshire Bl.
Beverly Hills, CA 90211
310-550-4000
Fax: 310-550-4108

Jam - A Complete Entertainment Agency
2900 Bristol St. Ste. E-201
Costa Mesa, CA 92626
714-556-9505
All Styles

Jensen Crew Agency
PO Box 9532
Anaheim, CA 92812
714-534-8912

Ted Kurland Associates
173 Brighton Ave.
Boston, MA 02134
617-254-0007
Fax: 617-782-3577

Lobotomy Talent Group
106 Florentia St.
Seattle, WA 98109
206-270-9644
Alternative

M.T. Booking
PO Box 20702
Seattle, WA 98102
206-325-6246
Fax: 206-323-0635

Mainstage Management Int'l
P.O. Box 5517
Los Alamitos, CA
90721-5517
714-220-6707
Fax: 714-220-6747

Majestic International
297-101 Kinderkamack Rd.
Oradell, NJ 07649
201-265-8313
Fax: 201-265-0603

Maris Agency
17620 Sherman Way
Van Nuys, CA 91406
818-708-2493

Mary McFaul Booking Management
P.O. Box 30081
Seattle, WA 98103
206-545-7375
Fax: 206-633-1877

Mission Control
15030 Ventura Bl. #541
Sherman Oaks, CA 91403
818-905-6488
Fax: 818-907-9839
miscon@earthlink.net

Monterey Artists
901 18th Ave. S
Nashville, TN 37212
615-321-4444
Fax: 321-2446

Monterey Peninsula Artists
509 Hartnell St.
Monterey, CA 93940
408-375-4889
Fax: 408-375-2623

Dale Morris & Associates
818 19th Ave. S
Nashville, TN 37203
615-327-3400
Fax: 615-327-0312

Mt. High Entertainment
9356 La Mesa Dr.
Alta Loma, CA 91701
714-980-8900
Fax: 714-944-5018
All Styles

Music Man Productions
568 Snelling Ave. N.
St. Paul, MN 55104
612-646-6416
Fax: 612-645-2600

New Orleans Entertainment Agency
3530 Rue Delphine
New Orleans, LA 70131
504-391-9866
Fax: 504-392-2695

Scott O'Malley & Assoc.
P.O. Box 9188
Colorado Springs, CO 80932
719-635-7776
Fax: 719-635-9789
somagency@aol.com
All Styles

Overland Entertainment
257 W 52nd St.
New York, NY 10019
212-262-1270
Fax: 212-262-5229

Pacific Talent, Inc.
5410 SW Macadam St.# 280
Portland, OR 97201
503-228-3620
Fax: 503-228-0480
pacifictalent.com

Paradise Artists, Inc.
P.O. Box 1821
Ojai, CA 93024
805-646-8433
Fax: 805-646-3367
Jazz

Pegasus Productions
424 Pershing Dr.
Silver Springs, MD 20910
301-587-1135
Fax: 301-588-1952

John Penny Entertainment
484 Lexington St.
Waltham, MA 02154
617-891-7800
Country

Performers of the World
89001 Melrose Ave.
West Hollywood, CA 90069
310-205-0366
Fax: 310-205-0365
pow-stp@ix.netcom.com
All styles

Pinnacle Entertainment
83 Riverside Dr.
New York, NY 10024
212-580-1229
Fax: 212-595-0176

Premier Talent
3 East 54th Street 14th Fl
New York, NY 10022
212-758-4900
Fax: 212-755-3251

Pretty Polly Productions
P.O Box 938
Boston, MA 02117
617-965-1245
Fax:617-965-8630
ppollyprod@aol.com
All Styles

Prince/SF Productions
2674 24th Ave.
San Francisco, CA 94116
415-731-9977

Producers Incorporated
11806 N. 56th St. #B
Tampa, FL 33617
813-988-8333
Fax: 813-985-3293
All Styles

Proton Productions
7578 Market Place Drive
Eden Prarie, MN 55415
612-349-6606
Fax: 612-349-6584

Pure Focus/ Backstreeet Booking
5658 Kirby Ave.
Cincinnati, OH 45239
513-542-9544
Fax: 513-542-2341
djppfb@aol.com
Alt., AAA, Punk

Pyramid Entertainment
89 Fifth Ave. 7th Fl.
New York, NY 10003
212-242-7274
Fax: 212-242-6932
Dance, Rock, Alt., Urban
peg@pyramid-ent.com

QBQ Entertainment
341 Madison Ave. 14th FL
New York, NY 10017
212-949-6900
Fax: 212-949-6970
Hard Rock, Metal

Rajiworld Productions
4440 Ambrose Ave #116
Los Angeles, CA 90027
213-665-9314
Fax: 213-665-9304
e-mail: bliss1144@aol.com
All styles except metal

RAVE
3470 19th St.
San Francisco, CA 94110
415-282-5866
Fax: 415-282-6455
Alternative
troy@raveman.com

Jeff Roberts & Associates
206 Bluebird Dr.
Gloodlettsville, TN 37072
615-859-7040
Fax: 615-859-6504
Contemportary Christian

Rock of Ages Productions
517 N. Lake Bl #4
Palm Beach, FL 33408
561-848-1500
Fax: 561-848-2400
All Styles

Howard Rose Talent Agency
8900 Wilshire Blvd. #320
Beverly Hills, CA 90211
310-657-1215
Fax: 310-657-1216
Contemporary

The Rosebud Agency
P.O. Box 170429
San Francisco, CA 94117
415-386-3456
Fax: 415-386-0599
rosebudus@aol.com
Blues, Rock, Jazz, Folk

Elizabeth Rush Agency, Inc.
93 Harvey St.
Cambridge, MA 02140
617-893-8792

S.T.A.R.S. Productions
1 Professional Quadrangle
2nd Fl.
Sparta, NJ 07871
201-729-7242
Fax: 201-729-2979
info@stars-prod.com

Silver Star Prod./Gulf Artists
1800 Amberwood Dr.
Riverview, FL 33569
813-689-3944
Fax: 813-685-6899

The Brad Simon
Organization, Inc.
122 E. 57th St.
New York, NY 10022
212-980-5920
b445@aol.com
All Styles

The Talent Agency
1005-A Lavergne Cir.
Hendersonville, TN 37075
615-822-1143
Fax: 615-824-6846
Country

Tapestry
17337 Ventura Blvd. #208
Encino, CA 91316
818-906-0558
Fax: 818-906-0697
tapestry77@aol.com
All Styles

Top Billing Int'l
1222 16th Ave. S
Nashville, TN 37212
615-327-1133
Fax: 615-327-1199

Triangle Talent
10424 Watterson Trail
Louisville, KY 40299
502-267-5466
Fax: 502-267-8244
www.triangletalent.com

Twin Towers Touring
611 Broadway #730
New York, NY 10012
212-995-0649
Fax:212-979-1428
Alternative

Universal Attractions
225 W. 57 St 5th Fl.
New York, NY 10019
Fax: 212-582-7575
Fax: 212-333-4508
Rock & Roll

Variety
555 Choro St.
Santa Barbara, CA 93401
805-544-1444
Fax: 805-544-2444
All Styles

Vision International
P.O. Box 201
Highland, MD 20848
301-854-0888
All Styles
ajsvision.aol.com

William Morris Agency
151 El Camino Dr.
Beverly Hills, CA 90212
310-859-4000
Fax: 310-859-4462

William Morris Agency
1325 Ave. of Americas
15th Fl.
New York, NY 10019
212-586-5100
Fax: 212-246-3583

William Morris Agency
2100 W End Ave #1000
Nashville, TN 37203
615-963-3321
Fax: 615-963-3090

World Class Talent
707 18th Ave. S.
Nasville, TN 37203
615-327-3978

HAPPY
— GOES•MAD —
BOOKING

Contract #_____

This contract for the personal services of the musicians for the engagement
described below, is made this _____ day of _____, 19   between the
undersigned purchaser of music (herein called "Purchaser") and the undersigned
musicians (herein called "Artist").

1.　　Place of Engagement: _____

2.　　Artist: _____

3.　　Number of Musicians/Crew _____

4.　　Day and Date of Engagement _____

5.　　Club Capcity _____　Ticket Price _____

6.　　Gross Potential _____

7.　　Guest List _____

8.　　Compensation Agreed Upon _____

9.　　Purchaser Shall Make Payments as Follows _____

　　　_____

　　　_____

10.　All contract riders attached hereto are hereby made a part of this
　　　contract.

11.　A cancellation fee equal to 50% of the guarantee compensation shall be
　　　paid to Artist if show is cancelled by purchaser for reasons other than
　　　 riot, strike, epidemic, an act of God or other legitimate condition beyond
　　　Purchaser's control.

12.　No portion of the performance shall be recorded, reproduced or trans-
　　　mitted from the place of performenace, in any manner or by any means
　　　whatsoever, without specific written approval or Artist or Artist's
　　　representative.

13.　All claims and disputes which may arise between the Purchaser and the
　　　Artist regarding application or interpretation or any terms or conditions
　　　of this contract shall be referred exclusively to binding arbitration.

14. Signed contracts and rider must be received no later than _____

_____　　　　　_____
　　　PURCHASER　　　　　　　　　　　　　　ARTIST

_____　　　　　_____

_____　　　　　c/o   HAPPY*GOES*MAD booking
　　　　　　　　　　　　　　　　　　　　　　　　749 Tularosa Drive
　　　　　　　　　　　　　　　　　　　　　　　　LA,CA. 90026

Above: Another sample booking contract.

Record Label Directory

The following is a directory of major and independent labels. I put this in here so you can (A) See if your label name is already taken, and (B) Contact these labels to see if they're interested in licensing your record.

Why should you have someone else put your record out for you? Well, if the label you've started is successful (you're selling records, getting airplay and reviews, getting paid) you may not want to. But, if you want to let someone else deal with the details while you concentrate on your music, or you want the kind of mass coverage a larger, established label can provide, licensing may be for you.

Licensing

A licensing deal, or a P&D (production & distribution) deal usually works as follows: You pay for the recording and the artwork, they pay for manufacturing and release the album (with their logo, or yours and theirs). Who pays for advertising and promotion depends on the individual circumstances. I'm sure you've seen records with three or four different company's logos on them. Label A licensed it to Label B who has a P&D deal with Label C, etc. If you license your record (or someone licenses their record to you) you'll be receiving a royalty on each copy sold, as it you were a band signed to the label. Usually a licensing royalty is at a higher rate than a standard artist royalty, because the label that is licensing it from you does not have to pay recording costs. Licensing deals should always be entered into with a definite time limit, for example, a five year term.

Releasing Other Artists' Records

If you're planning on releasing records from other artists, you have several choices on how to structure a deal (these are really simplified).

1. You pay for the recording, artwork, production, everything. The band makes a percentage (11% to 15%, usually) of each record sold. They don't get paid on albums given away to radio stations, press, etc. As you're selling this band's record, you would compute their royalties, but the band would not be entitled to payment until the royalty figure has met the amount you spent on the recording of the album and artwork. You keep all royalties until you've been paid back for your up-front expenses, which should be agreed upon at the time of the deal. You have the rights to put out this record for a specified period of time (for most large labels this period is forever, or in perpetuity, but the term should be whatever both parties are comfortable with), as long as you abide by the contract and pay the band.

2. The band pays for the recording and artwork, you manufacture and market the records. You pay the band a percentage (11% to 25%) of every record sold. They do not have to wait until their royalties recoup your recording costs because they paid for the recording. Term: 2 to 5 years.

3. You or the band pays for the recording, you put out the record and give the band copies of the record (instead of royalties) that they can sell at shows, to friends, etc. If you pressed 1000 CDs, for example, you could give the band 200 and you sell the rest. This is a pretty informal deal, but it can work well if it's done right.

Compilation Records

You may also want to put out compilation records or split singles. Here's one way to do it: Let's say that you want to do a compilation CD of 12 different bands, one song each. Those 12 bands probably have an average of 4 members per band. If those 48 band members each pitch in $50, you've got $2400, easily enough to make 1000 CDs (not including recording, each band would have to furnish their own recording). The CDs are split between the 48 band members — about 20 CDs each. They then sell the CDs at shows and to friends for $10 a piece = $200. Now everyone's made money and the bands have the potential to gain exposure and new fans.

These are just a few examples of ways to release records. See the sample contracts section for a typical record contract; you can use this as a reference in writing your own agreements.

Record Label Directory

1/4 Stick
P.O. Box 25520
Chicago, IL 60625
312-463-8316
Fax: 312-463-8316
Alternative, Hardcore

12-Inch
PO Box 4083
Urbana, IL 61801
217-359-2418

1201
40 Cummings St.
Rochester, NY 14609
716-482-1080
Alternative

121 Street
22-18 121 St.
College Pt., NY 11356
718-359-4110
Fax: 718-359-4110

1-800-PRIME-CD
11 E 14th St., Ste. 300
New York, NY 10003
212-366-5982
Fax: 212-366-0615

21st Circuitry
PO Box 170100
San Francisco, CA 94117
415-2529578

333
333 W 52nd St., Ste 1003
New York, NY 10019
212-265-3740

37
7560 Garden Grove Blvd.
Westminster, CA 92683
714-891-0868
R&B, Rock, Alternative

37
701 Brook Hollow Road
Nashville, TN 37205
615-356-0094
Country, Alternative

415
150 Bellam Blvd Ste 255
San Rafael, CA 94901
415-485-5675
Rock, Alternative

4AD
8533 Melrose Ave Ste B
Los Angeles, CA 90069
310-289-8770
Fax: 310-289-8680
E-mail: john4ad@primenet.com
www.4ad.com
Alternative

4th & Broadway
825 Eighth Ave
New York, NY 10019
212-333-8000
Urban, Hip-Hop

40 Acres & A Mule
8 St. Felix St. First Fl.
Brooklyn, NY 11217
718-858-9634
All Styles

5th Beetle
29 Martin Park Rd
Wallaceburg, ONT,
CAN N8A 2J7
519-627-3111

50 Skidillion Watts
5721 SE Laguna Ave.
Stuart, FL 34997-7828
407-283-6195
Alternative

550
550 Madison Ave., 21st Fl
New York, NY 10022
212-833-8000
Fax: 212-833-5441
www.sony.com

57
3155 Roswell Rd., Ste. B
Atlanta, GA 30305
404-237-5757
Fax:404-237-5739

665
Terminal Market, Ste 145A
Bronx, NY 10474
718-589-8891

9-B South
Box 381 Station A
Vancouver, BC V6C 2N2
CANADA
604-683-9629

9 Winds
PO Box 10082
Beverly Hills, CA 90213
213-827-0126

A Major Label
PO Box 2510120
Little Rock, AR 72225
800-284-8784

A&M
1345 Denison St
Markham, ONT, CAN L3R5V2
905-415-1993
Fax: 905-415-0805

A&M
1416 N. LaBrea Ave.
Hollywood, CA 90028
213-469-2411
All Styles

A&M
825 8th Ave., 27th floor
New York, NY 10019
212-333-1328
All Styles

A.T.S.
5826 Fifth Ave #3-19
Pittsburgh, PA 15232
412-521-1370

A2Z
105 Duane St #52B
New York, NY 10007
212-346-0653

a&r/ENT
P. O . Box 22113
San Francisco, CA 94122
415-681-8876
Self-Released Titles

A&R
900 19th Ave. S Ste. 207
Nashville, TN 37212
615-329-9127

ABKCo
1700 Broadway 41st Fl.
New York, NY 10019
212-399-0300
All Styles

Abrasive
PO Box 565
Burbank, CA 91503
818-840-0660
Fax: 818-840-0660
AbrasiveR@aol.com

Accurate
117 Columbia St
Cambridge, MA 02139
617-354-4309
Jazz, Progressive

Ace
532 La Guardia Place, Ste 128
New York, NY 10012
718-403-0463
fax: 718-403-0018
www.superdude.com

Ace Beat/Anitra
376 6th Ave.
Newark, NJ 07107
201-482-7936
Fax: 201-485-0289
Dance

Ace Beat
6 Blossom Ct.
Daly City, CA 94104
415-991-0108
Hip-Hop, R&B

Ace Group
PO Box 661587
Los Angeles, CA 90066
310-822-2770
Fax: 310-301-3332

Ace of Hearts
P.O. Box 579
Kenmore Station
Boston, MA 02215
617-536-1770
Progressive

Acme Entertainment Inc.
P.O. Box 81491
Chicago, IL 60681
800-566-2263
Alternative

Acoustic Disk
PO Box 4143
San Rafael, CA 94913
800-221-3472
Acoustic

Action Box
PO Box 10423
Burbank, CA 91510
818-566-1278

Aim Records
P.O. Box 117
Ojai, CA 93024
805-646-9936
Country, Folk, Rock

Adelphi/ Genes
PO Box 7778
Silver Spring, MD 20907
301-434-6958
Fax: 301-434-3056

Adelphi/Sunsplash
P.O. Box 7688
Silver Spring, MD 20907
301-434-6958
Fax: 301-434-3056
Blues, Folk, Ethnic, Jazz, Rock

Adobe
P.O. Box W
Shallowater, TX 79363
806-873-3537

Adrian Belew Presents
2612 Erie Ave., PO Box 8385
Cincinnati, OH 45208
513-871-1500
Fax: 513-871-1510

Advanced Research Records
P.O. Box 3556
San Rafael, CA 94912
415-485-0313
Fax: 485-0313

Africassette
PO Box 24941
Detroit, MI 48224
313-881-4108

Aggressive
1301 Sixth Ave
New York, NY 10019
212-259-5500

Ajax
P.O. Box 805293
Chicago, IL 60680
312-772-4783
Indie Rock

AJK c/o K-Tel International
15535 Medina Rd.
Plymouth, MN 55447
612-559-6800

Alcazar
P.O. Box 429
Waterbury, VT 05676
802-244-5178
Fax: 802-244-6128
World Beat, Reggae, Blues, New
Age

Alchemy Records
1335 N La Brea, #2218
Hollywood, CA 90028
213-939-2703

Alert
41 Elmwood Ave
Buffalo, NY 14201
716-885-5200

Alert
41 Britain St., Ste 305
Toronto, ONT,CAN M5A1R7
416-364-4200
Fax: 416-364-8632

Alias Records
2815 W. Olive Ave
Burbank, CA 91505
818-566-1034
Fax: 818-566-6623
Alternative

Aliso Creek Productions
P.O. Box 8174
Van Nuys, CA 91409
818-787-3203

All American Music
808 Wilshire Blvd
Santa Monica, CA 90401
310-656-1100
Fax: 310-656-7430

All Ball
P.O. Box 9248
Berkeley, CA 94709
510-848-8234

Allied
PO Box 460683
San Francisco, CA 94146
415-431-5698

Alligator
P.O. Box 60234
Chicago, IL 60660
312-973-7736
Fax: 312-973-2088
Roots, Rock, Blues, R&B

Allisongs, Inc.
1603 Horton Ave.
Nashville, TN 37212
615-292-9899

All Points
138 Arena St., Ste A
Los Angeles, CA 90245
310-333-1733
Fax: 310-333-1732

Allseason's International Music
879 West 190th St.
4th Floor
Gardena, CA 90248
310-217-4077
Fax: 310-769-1785

Almo Sounds
360 N La Cienega
Los Angeles, CA 90048
310-289-3080
Fax: 310-289-8662

Almo Sounds
110 Greene St., Ste 801
New York, NY 10012
212-226-1000
Fax: 212-226-8385

ALP
5400 S W 63rd St
Miami, FL 33155
305-667-7477

Alpha International
212 N 12th St
Philadelphia, PA 19107
215-425-8682
Fax: 215-425-4376
All Styles

Altenburgh Records
990 River Rd, P.O. Box 154
Mosinee, WI 54455
715-693-2230
Jazz

Altered
PO Box 724677
Atlanta, GA 30339
770-419-1414
Fax: 770-419-1230
IchibanR@aol.com

Alterian
1107 S Mountain Ave
Monrovia, CA 91016
818-932-1488
Fax: 818-932-1494

Alternative Tentacles
P.O. Box 419092
San Francisco, CA 94141
415-282-9782
Fax: 415-282-9786
http://iuma.southern.com/virus/
Punk Rock

Amalgamated/Mighty
P.O. Box 1833
Los Angeles, CA 90078
213-465-8686

American Global Media
209 Natoma Ave
Santa Barbara, CA 93101
805-562-2551

American Recordings
3500 W. Olive Ave.
Ste. 1550
Burbank CA 91505
818- 973-4545
Fax: 818-973-4571
http://american.recordings .com/

American Gramaphone
9130 Mormon Bridge Road
Omaha, NE 68152
402-457-4341
Fax: 402-457-4332
Country, Pop, New Age

Amethyst Group Ltd.
273 Chippewa Dr.
Columbia, SC 29210-6508
803-750-5391

Amherst
1762 Main St.
Buffalo, NY 14208
716-883-9520
Fax: 716-884-1432

Amoeba
5337 La Cresta Court
Los Angeles, CA 90038
213-467-6671

Amok
243 Main St E., Ste 1550
Milton ONT
L9T 1P1 CANADA
905-876-3550
Fax: 905-876-3552

Amphetamine Reptile
2645 1st Ave. S
Minneapolis, MN 55408
612-874-7047
612-874-7058
Noisy, Alternative, Rock

Anansi
330 Spaulding Dr., # 104
Beverly Hills, CA 90212
310-552-0030

Angel
810 Seventh Ave
New York, NY 10019
212-603-4167

Anomaly
PO Box 260
Milton Mills, NH 03852
603-473-9700

Another Planet
740 Broadway
New York, NY 10013
212-529-2600
Fax: 212-420-8216
aplanet@aol.com

Antilles
825 Eighth Ave
New York, NY 10019
212-333-8000
Fax: 212-333-8194

Antithesis
273 Chippewa Dr.
Columbia, SC 29210-6508
803-750-5391

Antone's
500 San Marcos, Ste 200
Austin, TX 78702
512-322-0617
Blues

Aquarius
200-1445 Lambert Closse
Suite 200
Montreal, QUE H3H 1Z5
CANADA
514-939-3775

Arabellum Studios
654 Sand Creek Rd.
Albany, NY 12205
518-869-5935
All Styles

Arabesque
10 W 37th St
New York, NY 10018
212-279-1414

Ardent
2000 Madison Ave
Memphis, TN 38104
901-725-0855

Arf!Arf!
PO Box 465
Middleborough MA 02346
617-876-1646
60s Garage Rock, Alternative

Ardent Records
2000 Madison Ave.
Memphis, TN 38104
901-725-0855
Rock

Arhoolie
10341 San Pablo Ave.
El Cerrito, CA 94530
510-525-7471
Roots

Arista
8370 Wilshire Blvd
Beverly Hills, CA 90211
213-655-9222

Arista
7 Music Circle N
Nashville, TN 37203
615-780-9100

Artifact
1374 Francisco St
Berkeley, CA 94702
510-540-5539
Fax: 510-704-9881
info@artifact.com

Asphodel
PO Box 51, Chelsea Station
New York, NY 10113
212-965-0953
Fax: 212-965-0959
asphodel@interport.net

Astralwerks
114 W 26th St
New York, NY 10001
212-989-2929
Fax: 212-989-9791
astralwerks@cyberden.com

Atavistic
PO Box 578266
Chicago, IL 60657
312-384-9626
Fax: 312-384-9677
74552.44@compuserve.com

Atlantic/Atco
75 Rockefeller Plaza 12th Fl
New York, NY 10019
212-275-2500

Atlantic/Atco
9229 Sunset Blvd 9th Fl
Los Angeles, CA 90069
310-205-7420

Atomic
1813 E. Locust St. Ste. #2
Milwaukee, WI 53211
414-332-5551
Alternative, Techno

Atomic Theory
PO Box 1122
Minneapolis, MN 55440
612-378-3729

Attic
102 Atlantic Ave.
Toronto ONT M6K IX9
CANADA
416-532-4487

Attitude
2071 Emerson St. Unit 16
Jacksonville, FL 32207
904-396-7604
Rap, R&B

Audrey's Diary
1475 Latson Rd
Howell, MI 48843
517-546-1062

August
P.O. Box 7041
Watchung, NJ 07060
908-753-1601
Pop, Rock, Alternative, Jazz

Aural Gratification
P.O. Box 380
Bearsville, NY 12409
914-679-4728

Autonomous Records
1100 Spring St., Ste 104-A
Atlanta, GA 30309
404-733-5505
Fax: 404-724-0889

Avante-Disregarde
PO Box 75
Flicksville, PA 18050
215-588-7366

AVC Entertainment, Inc.
6201 Sunset Blvd. Ste. 200
Los Angeles, CA 90028
213-461-9001
Fax: 213-962-0352
Pop, Rock, Soul

Avenue Communications
11100 Santa Monica Blvd.,
Ste 2000
Los Angeles, CA 90025
310-312-0300
Fax: 310-312-8879

AVI
10390 Santa Monica Blvd.,
Ste 210
Los Angeles, CA 90025
310-556-7744

Aware
PO Box 5112
Evanston, IL 60204
847-491-0036

Ax/ction
PO Box 623, Kendall Square
Cambridge, MA 02142
617-938-1321
Fax: 617-935-7794

Axiom/Island
825 Eighth Ave
New York, NY 10019
212-333-8000

Axis
2341 Chestnut St. #103
San Francisco, CA 94123
415-922-6178

B&W
PO Box 578040
Chicago, IL 60657
312-880-5375

Baby Faze
45 Pearl St
San Francisco, CA 94103
415-495-5312

Back Door
PO Box 15449
Atlanta, GA 30333
404-329-9293
iweb.www.com/backdoor

Backyard
808 Wilshire Blvd
Santa Monica, CA 90401
310-656-1100
Fax: 310-656-7430

Bad Taste
PO Box 148428
Chicago, IL 60614
312-227-6050
Fax: 312-227-6051
fgao@interaccess.com

Bag of Hammers
PO Box 928
Seattle, WA 98111
206-935-1476
fax: 206-935-1476

Bar/None
PO Box 1704
Hoboken, NJ 07030
201-795 9424
Fax: 201-795-5048
Alternative

Barber's Itch
545 Louisiana St
Lawrence, KS 66044
913-865-3886
Fax: 913-865-1478
bbarrish@falcon.cc.ukans.edu

Batish
1310 Mission St
Santa Cruz, CA 95060
408-423-1699
Fax: 408-423-5172
batish@cruzio.com

Beachwood
4872 Topanga Canyon Blvd. Suite
223
Woodland Hills, CA 91364
818-888-3534

Bearsville
P.O. Box 135
Wittenberg Rd.
Bearsville, NY 12409
914-679-8900
All Styles

Beau Tie
942 Sullivan Lane
South Parks, NV 89431
702-826-5383

Bedazzled
PO Box 39195
Washington, DC 20016
301-405-3002

Beggars Banquet
580 Broadway
New York, NY 10012
212-343-7010
212-343-7030
beggars@beggars.com

Beloved
318 E 34th St
New York, NY 10016
212-889-4129
Fax: 212-889-4129
beloved@sonicnet.com

Benson
365 Great Circle Rd.
Nashville, TN 37228
615-742-6800
Fax: 615-742-6915

Better Days
1591 Bardstown Rd.
Louisville, KY 40205
502-456-2394
Alternative, Dance

Beyond Records Corp.
569 County Line Rd.
Ontario, NY 14519
716-265-0260
Fax: 716-265-4693
Pop, Alternative, R&B
beyondgfi@aol.com

Big Cat Records
67 Vestry St
New York, NY 10013
212-941-6060
Fax-212-941-8040

Big Deal
PO Box 2072, Stuyvesant Station
New York, NY 10009
212-477-8655
Fax: 212-475-8889

Big Life
225 Lafayette St #601
New York, NY 10012
212-941-1666
fax: 212-941-1785

Big Money
P.O. Box 2483 Loop Station
Minneapolis, MN 55402
612-379-2614
Fax: 612-379-8507

Big Noise
69 Governer St Ste 307
Providence, RI 02906-2062
401-274-2909
All Styles

Big Pop
P.O. Box 12870
Philadelphia, PA 19108
215-551-3191
Fax: 215 467-2048
Alternative, Rock, Pop

Big Round Records Inc.
1855 Elm St.
Manchester, NH 03104
603-622-4747
Fax: 603-622-6142

Big Top
955 Massachusetts Ave.
Suite. 115
Cambridge, MA 02139
617-491-8373

Biograph
16 River St.
Chatham, NY 12037
518-392-3400
Fax: 518-392-2666
Blues, Jazz, Folk, Ragtime,
Country, Gospel

Bionic
PO Box 464
Mount Freedom, NJ 07970
201-927-5097

Bittersweet
920 Broadway, Ste 1403
New York, NY 10010
212-475-5423
Fax: 212-254-2629
bittsweet@aol.com

Bizarre/Planet records
740 N. La Brea Ave. 2nd Fl.
Los Angeles, CA 90038
213-935-4444
Fax: 213-936-6354

Black & Blue
400D Putnam Pike Ste. 152
Smithfield, RI 02917
401-949-4887
Alternative, Underground

Black Boot Records
5503 Roosevelt Way NE
Seattle, WA 98105
206-524-1020
Fax: 206-524-1102
Country, Blues, Rock
www.niemusic.com

Black Dwarf Records
15155 Stagg St. Suite 1
Van Nuys, CA 91405
818-786-0975
Fax: 818-786-7453
Alternative, Rock, Metal, Thrash,
R&B, Pop

Black Fire
4409 Douglas St NE
Washington, DC 20019
202-397-3572
Fax: 202-397-3572

Black Pumpkin
PO Box 4377
River Edge, NJ 07661
201-342-4855
Fax: 201-342-1556
bigmeenie@carroll.com

Black Rose/One Hot Note
454 Main St, Box 214
Cold Spring Harbor, NY 11724
516-367-8544
Jazz, R&B, Techno, Pop

Black Saint
c/o Sphere,Cargo
Bldg.80,Room2A,JFKA
Jamaica, NY 11430
718-656-6220

Black Top
PO Box 56691
New Orleans, LA 70156
504-895-7239
Contemporary Blues, Soul, R&B

Black Vinyl
2269 Sheridan Rd.
Zion, IL 60099
708-746 3767
Alternative Pop

Blackbird
185 Franklin St Fl 4
New York, NY 10013
212-226-5379

Blackheart Records
155 East 55th St. Suite 6H
New York, NY 10022
212-644-8900
Fax; 212-688-1883

Blackjack
663 10th St
Oakland,CA 94607
510-763-7632

Blackout!
PO Box1575
New York, NY 10009
212-841-8064
Fax: 212-841-5124
punker01@aol.com

Bloodshot Records
912 W Addison, Ste 1
Chicago, IL 60613-4339
312-525-3934
Alternative Country

Blue Duck
P.O. Box 10247
Pittsburgh, PA 15232
412-344-7378

Blue Gorilla
825 Eighth Ave, 19th Fl
New York, NY 10019
212-603-3908
Fax: 212-603-7650

Blue Man From Uranus
8040 Okean Terrace
Los Angeles, CA 90046
213-654-2452

Blue Moose
715 Grove St
Bridgeport, PA 19405
610-279-5614

Blue Note
810 Seventh Ave, 4th Fl
New York, NY 10019
212-603-8900
Fax: 212-603-4143
Jazz

Blue Rhythm
PO Box 564
Santa Cruz, CA 95061
408-462-5542

Blue Rose
1904 3rd AveSte 1007
Seattle, WA 98109
206-467-8825
Fax: 206-467-8795
tom-hewson@bluerose.wa.com

Blue Thumb
555 W 57th St 10th Fl
New York, NY 10019
212-424-1000
Fax: 212-424-1007

Blunt
23 E Fourth St
New York, NY 10003
212-979-6410

BMG
1540 Broadway, 37th Fl
New York, NY 10036
212-930-4000

BMG
150 John St., 6th Fl
Toronto, ONT,CAN M5V3C3
416-586-0022
Fax: 416-586-0454

BNA
1 Music Circle N
Nashville, TN 37203
615-780-4400
Fax: 615-780-4464

Bomp!/Voxx
P.O. Box 7112
Bubank, CA 91510
213-227-4141
Psychadelic, Alternative

Boner
P.O. Box 2081
Berkeley, CA 94702
415-695-1154
Alternative

Bong Load Custom Records
P.O. Box 931538
Hollywood, CA 90093-1538
818-854-0332

Bonneville Worldwide
Broadcast House, 55N300 W.,
Ste 315
Salt Lake City, UT 84110
801-575-3680
Fax: 801-575-3699
www.bwwe.com

Boom Shot
5871 Jeanne-Mance
Montreal, PQ,CAN H2V 4K9
514-272-3466

Boy's Life
6831 1/2 DeLongpre Ave.
Hollywood, CA 90028
213-243-6622
Fax: 213-462-6969
E-mail: boyslife69@aol.com

Boy-O-Boy Records
1415 Parker Suite 958
Detriot, MI 48214
313-822-1124

Brake Out
234 Sixth Ave
Brooklyn, NY 11215
718-636-1100
Fax: 718-636-1164

Brass
6607 Sunset Blvd
Los Angeles, CA 90028
213-465-2700
Fax: 213-465-8926

Breakfast Communications Corp.
36 Oakwood Ln.
Phoenixville, PA 19460
610-783-5371

Brilliant
PO Box 17116
Richmond, VA 23226
804-288-3242

Brinkman
PO Box 441837
Somerville, MA 02144
617-628-5333
namknir@aol.com

Broken ReKids
P.O. Box 460402
San Francisco, CA 94146
415-431-0425
Fax: 415-431-0425

Brownstone
1217 W Medical Park Rd
Augusta, GA 30909
706-733-1052
Fax: 706-737-2614

Buckshot
520 N Michigan Ave, Ste 612
Chicago, IL 60611
219-271-1317

Bulletproof
1636 Queens Rd
Los Angeles, CA 90069
213-656-8278

Bulls Eye Blues
1 Camp St.
Cambridge, MA 02140
617-354-0700
Blues

Burnside
3158 E Burnside
Portland, OR 97214
503-231-8943

Burnt Sienna
207 Powhatan
Columbus, OH 43204
614-279-2016

Bus Stop
PO Box 3161
Iowa City, IA 52244
217-339-3960

Buzzsaw Records
P.O. Box 20253
New York, NY 10011
212-620-7311
Rock

BYO
PO Box 67A64
Los Angeles, CA 90067
310-390-7000

C&S/Adrenalin
166 Fifth Ave
New York, NY 10010
212-675-4038
Fax: 212-675-4826
cnsrecords@aol.com

C'est La Mort
PO Box 1351
Eugene, OR 97440
503-942-8843

C.I.M.P.
Cadence Bldg
Redwood, NY 13679
315-287-2852
Fax: 315-287-2860

C. Junquera Prod./NH
P.O. Box 393
Lomita, CA 90717
310-325-2881

C/Z
4756 University Place NE #469
Seattle, WA 98105
206-528-0481
Alternative
http://www.w2.com/cz.html

Cabana Boy
1260 N Kings Rd, #4
W Hollywood, CA 90069
213-650-4318

Cachet
13 Laight St., 6th Fl
New York, NY 10013
212-334-0284
Fax: 212-334-5207

Cadence
Cadence Bldg.
Redwood, NY 13670
315-287-2852
Jazz

Caffeine Disk
PO Box 3451
New Haven, CT 06515
203-562-0793

Cajual
1229 N Branch, #218
Chicago, IL 60622
312-642-8008

Candy Floss
130 Sutter St 5th Fl
San Francisco, CA 94104
415-397-0442, x242

Candy Ass
PO Box 42382
Portland, OR 97242
503-238-9708
Fax: 503-238-0380

Capitol
1750 N Vine St
Hollywood, CA 90028
213-462-6252

Capitol
304 Park Ave. South
New York, NY 10010
212-492-5300

Capricorn
2205 State St
Nashville, TN 37203
615-320-8470
Southern Rock

Capricorn
450 14th St. NW Ste. 201
Atlanta, GA 30318
404-873-3918
Southern Rock

Caprice Int'l./
American Radio
P.O. Box 808
Lititz, PA 17543
717-627-4800

Caravan of Dreams
312 Houston St.
Fort Worth, TX 76102
817-877-3000
Jazz, Blues, Rock & Roll, Gospel,
Country

Cargo
4901-906 Morena Bl.
San Diego, CA 92117
619-483-9292
info@cargorec.com
Alternative, Punk

Cargo /Canada
7036 Blvd. St. Laurent
Montreal, QUE H2S 3E2
CANADA
514-495-1212
Alternative, Hardcore, Punk,
Industrial

Carlyle
1217 16th Ave. S
Nashville, TN 37212
615-327-8129
Rock, Alternative

Caroline
114 W. 26th St.
New York, NY 10001
212-989-2929
Fax: 212-989-9791
www.caroline.com
Alternative

Caroline
6161 Santa Monica Blvd.
Ste. 208
Los Angeles, CA 90038
213-468-8626
Alternative

Carpe Diem
2703 Fondren, Ste 105
Dallas, TX 75206
214-987-9535

Carrot Top
2438 N Lincoln Ave, 3rd Fl
Chicago, IL 60614
312-929-9117

Cash Only
22355 Cardiff Dr
Santa Clarita, CA 91350
805-254-4675

Castle
352 Park Ave S., 10th Fl
New York, NY 10010
212-685-6303
Fax: 212-685-7184

Castle Von Buhler
16 Ashford St
Boston, MA 02134
617-783-2421

Catapult
215 "A" Street
Boston, MA 02210
617-464-2288
Fax: 617-464-4478
catapult@usa1.com

Catasonic
P.O. Box 2727
1615 N. Wilcox
Hollywood CA 90078
213-664-1404
Alternative
http://www.catasonic.com
/catasonic

Caulfield
5701 Randolph
Lincoln, NE 68510
402-475-3524

Caustic Fish
1236 Clarkson St
Denver, CO 80218
303-825-8230

Cavity Search
PO Box 42246
Portland, OR 97242
503-243-3662

CBGB& OMFUG
315 Bowery
New York, NY 10003
212-254-0983

Celestial Harmonics
PO Box 30122
Tuscon, AZ 85751
602-326-4400
Fax: 602-326-3333

Celluloid Records
180 Varick St. 14th Fl
New York, NY 10014
212-606-3748

Century Media
1453 A 14th St., Ste. 324
Santa Monica CA 90404
310-396-0094
Fax: 310-396-1455
mail@centurymedia.com
Alternative, Grind, Core,
Underground

Cerebral Records
1236 Laguna Dr.
Carlsbad, CA 92008
619-434-2497

Channel 83
900 W. Grandview Ave.
Roseville, MN 55113
612-484-4195
All Styles

Charnel Music
PO Box 170277
San Francisco, CA 94117
415-664-1829
Fax: 415-664-1829
mason@net.com.com

Cheetah
3208-C E Colonial Dr. #131
Orlando, FL 32803
407-236-9494

Chemical City
226 W State St
Baton Rouge, LA 70802
504-389-1066

Chemistry
117 W 26th St, 5th Fl
New York, NY 10001
212-741-0007
Fax: 212-243-2603

Cherry Disc
25 Huntington Ave, Ste 319
Boston, MA 02116
617-262-5547
Fax: 617-262-8154

Chesky Records
355 W 52 St, 6Fl
New York, NY 10019
212-586-7799
Fax: 212-262-0814
Jazz, Classical, Pop

Chess
c/o MCA
70 Universal City Plaza
Universal City, CA 91608
818-777-4000
www. mcarecords.com

Choke, Inc.
1376 W. Grand
Chicago IL 60622
Alternative
http://kzsu.stanford.edu/uwi/soun
ds/choke/choke.html

Chrome Frog
PO Box 02372
Colombus, OH 43202
614-457-4179

Chrysalis
1290 Ave of the Americas,
42nd Fl
New York, NY 10104
212-492-1200
Fax: 212-245-4115

Chrysalis
9255 Sunset Blvd.
Los Angeles, CA 90069
213-550-0171

Chunk
PO Box 244
Easthampton, MA 01027
413-586-6767

Cinema Disc
6855 Santa Monica Blvd, Ste 317
Los Angeles, CA 90038
213-465-6292

City Hall
25 Tiburon Rd
San Rafael, CA 94901
415-457-9080

City of Tribes
3025 17th St
San Francisco, CA 94110
415-621-1549

Clean Cuts
Box 16264
Roland Park Station
Baltimore, MD 21210
410-467-4231
Jazz

Cleopatra
8726 S Sepulveda Blvd, Ste D82
Los Angeles, CA 90045
310-305-0172
Fax: 310-821-4702
cleopatra@cyberden.com

CLR
1400 Aliceanna St
Baltimore, MD 21231
410-522-1001

CMC
106 W Horton St
Zebulon, NC 27597
919-269-5508
Fax: 919-269-7217

CMH
PO Box 39439
Los Angeles, CA 90039
213-663-8073

CMP
530 N Third St
Minneapolis, MN 55401
612-375-9188

Coconut Grove
2980 McFarlane Rd, Ste D82
Coconut Grove, Fl 33133
800-554-7683

Cognition Audioworks
Box 34104
Halifax NS B3J 1S1 Canada
902-422-7131
Gothic-Ambient, Techno

Cold Chillin'
1995 Broadway 18th Fl.
New York, NY 10023
212-691-0040
Rap

Colerick
3575 Cahuenga Blvd. W, Ste 500
Los Angeles, CA 90068
213-874-9889

Columbia
550 Madison Ave.
New York, NY 10022
212-833-8000
www.sony.com

Columbia
34 Music Square E
Nashville, TN 37203
615-742-4321

Com Four
7 Dunham Place
Brooklyn, NY 11211
718-599-0513
Fax: 718-599-1052
All Styles

Comcast Rocks
451 Ridge Rd
Lyndhurst, NJ 07071
201-460-1000
Fax: 201-939-3504

Communion
290-C Napoleon St
San Francisco, CA 94124
415-647-5667

Composite
12012 Taliesin Place, #13
Reston, VA 22090
703-904-9879

Concord Jazz
P.O. Box 845-J
Concord, CA 94522
415-682-6770
Jazz-Mainstream, Acousitc, Latin

Conquest
4195 S Camiami Trail, Box 180
Venice, FL 34293-5112
941-475-8287

Contemporary
2600 10th St.
Berkeley, CA 94710
510-549-2500
Fax:510-486-2015
Blues, Country, Roots Rock
www.fantasyjazz.com

Continuum
380 Ludlow Ave
Cranford, NJ 07016
908-709-0011
Fax: 908-709-0641

Conversion
PO Box 5213
Huntington Beach, CA 92615
714-444-4358
Fax: 714-444-4379

C.O.P. International
981 Alien St.
Oakland, CA 94608
Fax: 510-654-1505
Alternative, Punk, Metal

Core
1719 West End Ave, 11th Fl,
West Tower
Nashville, TN 37203
615-321-4001
Fax: 615-321-0206

Cosmic
129 Franklin St, Ste 205
Cambridge, MA 02139
617-621-1007

Cosmic Force
10777 S W 188th St
Miami, FL 33157
305-233-3535
Fax: 305-233-3434

Country Music Foundation
4 Music Square East
Nashville, TN 37203
615-256-1639
Country

Crackerbarrel
Entertainment
168 Shore Road
Clinton, CT 06413
860-669-6581

Crackpot
PO Box 577016
Chicago, IL 60657
312-348-1154

Crackpot
2217 Nicollet Ave S
Minneapolis, MN 55404
612-874-2440
Fax: 612-874-2430

Crane Mountain
108 Allston St
Boston, MA 02134
617-482-6800

Crank
1223 Wilshire Blvd, #173
Santa Monica, CA 90403
310-917-9162
Fax: 310-917-9162

Creativeman
1875 Century Park E., Ste 1165
Los Angeles, CA 90067
310-556-1325
Fax: 310-556-3045
CMDisc@ix.netcom.com

Crescendo
8400 Sunset Blvd. Ste. 4A
Los Angeles, CA 90069
213-656-2614
All Styles

Crisis
PO Box 5232
Huntington Beach, CA 92615
714-375-4264
Fax: 714-375-4266

Croaker
PO Box 2391
Covington, LA 70434
504-893-1137

Cross Talk
1557 Honore
Chicago, IL 60622
312-292-1335
Fax: 312-292-1333

Crucial Youth
P.O. Box 14124
Oakland, CA 94614
510-532-8215
Reggae

Crunch Melody
1904 3rd Ave, Ste1007
Seattle, WA 98109
206-467-8825
Fax: 206-467-8795
Tom-Hewson@bluerose.wa.com

Crustacean
PO Box 37384
Milwaukee, WI 53237
414-321-9465
clangkamp@qgraph.com

Cruz
P.O. Box 7756
Long Beach, CA 90807
310-430-2077
Fax: 310-430-7286
Punk

Crystal Clear Sound
4902 Don Dr
Dallas, TX 75247
214-630-2957
Fax: 214-630-5936
crstlclr@onramp.net

Cuneiform
PO Box 8427
Silver Spring, MD 20907
301-589-8894

Curb
47 Music Square East
Nashville, TN 37203
615-321-5080
Fax: 615-327-3003

Curb
3907 Alameda Blvd
Burbank, CA 91505
818-843-2872

Curve Of The Earth
1312 Boyston St
Boston, MA 02215
617-536-6822

Cutting
104 Vermilyea Ave. Ste. B2
New York, NY 10034
212-567-4900
Fax: 212-304-3470

Cypress
1523 Crossroads of the World
Los Angeles, CA 90028
213-465-2711

D-Tox
PO Box 5655
Greensboro, NC 27435
910-370-1573

da
PO Box 3
Little Silver, NJ 07739
908-530-6887
Fax:908-842-5041
damusic@aol.com

Dada
PO Box 112
New Brunswick, NJ 08903
908-846-7258

Daemon
PO Box 1207
Decatur, GA 30031
404-373-5733
Fax: 404-373-1660

Dakota Arts
15 Oak St
Needham, MA 02192
617-433-0003
Fax: 617-433-0004

Dalin
PO Box 402338
Miami Beach, FL 33140
305-673-2588

Damage
496 Adams St
Boston, MA 02122
617-287-2453
Fax: 617-287-2510

Dancecard
PO Box 1841
Portland, OR 97201
503-727-2678

Dancing Cat
Box 639
Santa Cruz, CA 95061
408-429-5085
Jazz, New Age
www.dancingcat.com

Dark Beloved Cloud
5-16 47th Rd, #36
Long Island City, NY 11101
718-784-7708

Darla
625 Scott St, #301
San Francisco, CA 94117
415-441-4577
agrenj@delphi.com

Datapanik
1992B N High St
Columbus, OH 43201
614-294-3833

DB
432 Moreland Ave. NE
Atlanta, GA 30307
404-296-2021
Fax: 404-659-2876
Alternative, Rock

Dead Game Records
P.O. Box 15689
Houston, TX 77220-5689
713-672-4687
Fax: 713-672-4688

Dead Reckoning
PO Box 22151
Nashville, TN 37202
800-442-3323

Death Row
10900 Wilshire Blvd, Ste 1240
Los Angeles, CA 90024
310-824-8844
Fax: 310-824-8855

Decoder Ring
3628 Park St, Ste33
Jacksonville, FL 32205
904-354-7736
Fax: 904-354-0222

Deconstruction
PO Box 18015
Encino, CA 91416
818-386-1140
Fax: 818-386-2035

Dedicated
580 Broadway, Ste 1002
New York, NY 10012
212-334-5959

Deep Elm
P.O. Box 1965
New York, NY 10156
212-532-DEEP

Deep South
PO Box 37644
Raleigh, NC 27627
919-676-2089
Fax: 919-878-0113
DpSouthRec@aol.com

Def Jam
160 Barrack St., 12th Fl.
New York, NY 10013
212-229-5225
212-229-5296
All Styles

Deja Disc
537 Lindsey St
San Marcos, TX 78666
512-392-6610
Fax: 512-754-6886

Del-Fi
PO Box 69188
Los Angeles, CA 90069
310-358-2555
Fax: 310-358-2561
Del-FiRec@aol.com

Delicious Vinyl
6607 Sunset Blvd.
Los Angeles, CA 90028
213-465-2700
Hip-Hop, Rap, Heavy Metal,
Rock, Punk, Reggae

Delirium Vinyl
6607 Sunset Blvd
Los Angeles, CA 90028
213-465-2700
Fax: 213-465-8926
www.dvinyl.com

Delmark
4121 N. Rockwell
Chicago, IL 60618
312-539-5001
Fax: 312-539-5004
Jazz, Blues

Delmore
2802 E Madison Ave, Ste 197
Seattle, WA 98112
206-329-1876
Fax: 206-328-1211
www.panix.com/delmore

Delta Music Inc.
1663 Sawtelle Blvd.
Los Angeles, CA 90025
310-453-9504
Fax: 310-268-1279
www.deltamusic.com

Den O'sin
1734 "D" Street, #3
Bakersfield, CA 93301
805-634-9362

Derivative
PO Box 42031
Montreal, PQ, CAN H2W 2T3
514-849-8361
derivative@babylon.montreal.
qc.ca

Desafinado
4780 Ashford Dunwoody Rd, Ste
A119
Atlanta, GA 30338
770-998-7303

DeSoto
PO Box 60335
Washington, DC 20039
301-589-3909

Detroit Municipal
PO Box 20879
Detroit, MI 48220
810-547-2722
Fax: 810-547-5477

Deutsche Grammophon
825 Eighth Ave
New York, NY 10019
212-333-8000
Fax: 212-333-8402

DGC
9130 Sunset Blvd.
Los Angeles, CA 90069
213-278-9010
www.geffen.com

Diesel Only
100 N Sixth St
Brooklyn, NY 11211
718-388-4370
Fax: 718-388-5859

Digging
PO Box 1011
Orland Park, IL 60462
708-349-9200

Dionysus
P.O. Box 1975
Burbank, CA 91507
818-953-4036
Fax: 818-953-4036
ddionysus@aol.com
Punk, Surf, Psychedelic, Rock

Direct Hit
PO Box 496946
Garland, TX 75049
214-279-0929
Fax: 214-279-0929
directhit2@aol.com

Dirt
PO Box 1053, Knickerbocker
Station
New York, NY 10002
212-226-1632
Fax: 212-226-0715
dirtrec@aol.com

Dischord
3819 Beecher St. N.W.
Washington, DC 20007
703-351-7491
Alternative

Discipline
351 Magnolia Ave
Long Beach, CA 90802
310-491-1945

Discovery Records
2052 Broadway
Santa Monica, CA 90403
310-828-1033
Alternative, Jazz, Pop

Dive
P O. Box 4218
Sunnyside, NY 11104
718-392-9248

DIW
c/o Sphere, Cargo Bldg, 80,
Room 2A, JFK A
Jamaica, NY 11430
718-656-6220

DJ International
727 Randolph St.
Chicago, IL 60606
312-559-1845
Dance

DMZ
500 San Marcos, Ste 200
Austin, TX 78702
512-322-0617
Fax: 512-477-2930
www.antones.com

Doghouse
P.O. Box 8946
Toledo, OH 43623
419-243-3220
Hardcore & Punk Rock
www.lumberjack/online.com/dog
house

Dolo
611 Broadway, Ste 209
New York, NY 10012
212-253-1177

Domo
245 S Spaulding Dr., Ste 105
Beverly Hills, CA 90212
310-557-2100

Don't
PO Box 11513
Milwaukee, WI 53211
414-264-6927

**Don't Get All Heavy &
Uncool**
360 E 72nd St, Ste A1602
New York, NY 10021
212-517-3927

Doolittle
11926 Meadowfire
Austin, TX 78758
512-339-9622

dos
500 San Marcos, Ste 200
Austin, TX 78702
512-322-0617
Fax: 512-477-2930

Dossier
7 Dunham Place
Brooklyn, NY 11211
718-599-2205

Double Play
41 Sutter St, #1337
San Francisco, CA 94104
415-267-4837

Downs
160 Bleeker St, #4HE
New York, NY 10012
212-473-6333

Dr. Dream
841 W Collins Ave
Orange, CA 92667
714-997-9387
Fax: 714-997-0184
Rock

Drag City
P.O. Box 476867
Chicago, IL 60647
312-455-1015
Fax: 312-455-1057
All Styles

Dragon Street
P.O. box 670714
Dallas, TX 75367-0714
214-750-4584
fax: 214-369-5972
Alternative, Rock, Modern
Dance

Dreamworks SKG
100 Universal Plaza,
Bungalow 477
Universal City, CA 91608
818-733-7000

Drill
70 E 55th St, 26th Fl
New York, NY 10022
212-539-8448

Drip Dry
P.O. Box 3873
N. New Hyde Park, NY 11040
718-347-2373

Drunken Fish
PO Box 460640
San Francisco, CA 94146
415-550-7551

Duke Street
121 Logan Ave
Toronto, ONT M4M 2M9
CANADA
416-406-4121
Country, Classical, Rock

Dwell
PO Box 39439
Los Angeles, CA 90039
213-663-8098
Fax: 213-669-1470

DWV
PO Box 180540
Boston, MA 02118
617-629-4929

E Pluribus Unum
8424A Santa Monica Blvd, #831
W Hollywood, CA 90069
310-854-3535
Fax: 310-854-0810
epluribus@aol.com

Earache
295 Lafayette St. Suite 915
New York, NY 10012
212-434-9090
FAX: 212-343-9244

Earth Beat!/Music for Little People
P.O. Box 1460
Redway, CA 95560
707-923-3991
World Music

Eastern Front Records
7 Curve St.
Medfield, MA 02052
508-359-8003
Folk, Rock, Acoustic

Earwarks Audio/Wax Puppy
5245 Cleveland St., Ste. 210
Virginia Beach, VA 23462
804-490-9322
All Styles
earwark@norfork@infi.com

Earwig Music Company
1818 West Pratt Blvd
Chicago, IL 60626
312-262-0278
Fax: 312-262-0285
World, Progressive

ECM
1540 Broadway, 40th Fl
New York, NY 10036
212-930-4000
Fax: 212-930-4278
Jazz

Ecstatic Peace!
PO Box 9102
Waltham, MA 02254
617-562-0507

Eggbert
PO Box 10022
Fullerton, CA 92635
714-990-5652
Fax: 714-671-1661
eggbertcd@aol.com

Eight Ball Records
105 E Ninth St
New York, NY 10003
212-337-1414

Eight One Nine Prod
190 Martha St., Ste. 1
San Jose, CA 95112
408-298-8520
Fax: 408-298-8584
Punk, Alternative Underground
sj819@sysus.com

Einstein
228 W Broadway
New York, NY 10013
212-219-8242
Fax: 212-219-8773
roulet@artswire.org

Electrobeat
PO Box 69-3761
Miami, FL 33269
305-653-6578
Fax: 305-652-6578
ebeat@aol.com

Elektra
75 Rockefeller Plaza
New York, NY 10019-6907
212-275-4000
www.elektra.com

Elektra
345 N Maple Dr. Ste. 123
Beverly Hills, CA 90210
310-288-3800

Elephant 6
PO Box 9935
Denver, CO 80209
303-722-9314

ellipsis arts...
20 Lumber Rd
Roslyn, NY 11576
800-788-6670
Fax: 516-621-2750

El Recordo
1916 Pike Place,#12-370
Seattle, WA 98101
206-467-6483
Fax: 206-443-3491
ponyshow@halcyon.com

EMI
1290 6th Ave. 35th Floor
New York NY 10104
212-492-1200

EMI
35 Music Square East
Nashville TN 37203
615-256-6610

EMI
3109 American Dr
Mississauga, ONT, CAN L4V 1B2
905-677-5050
Fax: 905-677-1651

Emigre
4475 D St.
Sacramento, CA 95819
916-451-4344
Fax: 916-451-4351
Alternative

Empty
P.O. Box 12034
Seattle WA 98102
206-325-3775

Endangered
206 S Brand Blvd
Glendale, CA 91204
818-500-9809

Enemy
234 6th Ave
Brooklyn, NY 11215
718-636-1100
Fax: 718-636-1164
Alternative, Noise Rock, Hard
Jazz

Energy Records
545 8th Ave
New York, NY 10018-4307
212-695-3000
Thrash, Heavy Metal, Hardcore

Engine
PO Box 1575, Stuyvesant Station
New York, NY 10009
212-505-6929

Enja/Mesa Blue Moon
9229 Sunset Blvd.
Los Angeles, CA 90069
310-205-7445
Jazz, Adult Contemporary, World
Music, New Age

Entangled
PO Box 9263
Portland, OR 97207
503-646-3168

Epic/Sony
550 Madison Ave
New York, NY 10022
212-333-8000
www.sony.com

Epic/Sony
2100 Colorado Ave.
Santa Monica, CA 90404
310-449-2100

Epic/Sony
34 Music Square E
Nashville, TN 37203
615-742-4321

Epiphany
910 S Hohokam Dr., #101
Tempe, AZ 85281
602-894-8550

Epitaph
2789Sunset Blvd. Ste. 111
Hollywood, CA 90026
213-413-7353
Fax: 213-413-9678
Alternative

Equal Vision
PO Box 14th St
Hudson, NY 12534
518-822-1818

Era c/o K-tel
2605 Fernbrook Lane N.
Plymouth, MN 55447
612-559-6800

ESD
530 N Third St
Minneapolis, MN 55401
612-375-0233
Fax: 612-375-0272

Estrus
P.O. Box 2125
Bellingham, WA 98225
206-637-1187

Esync
PO Box 380621
Miami, FL 33238
305-759-1331

**Eternal Talent/
The Advantage**
1598 E Shore Dr
St Paul, MN 55106
612-771-0107
Fax: 612-774-8319

Etiquette/Suspicious
5503 Roosevelt Way NE
Seattle, WA 98105
206-524-1020
Fax: 206-524-1102
nie@eskimo.com
Etiquitte: Rock, Reissues;
Suspicious: R&B, Blues

Euro Tec/Shilho
P.O. Box 3077
Ventura, CA 93006
805-658-2488

Everlasting
341 Lafayette St, Ste 760
New York, NY 10012
718-545-6467

Evidence
1100 E Hector St, Ste 392
Conshohocken, PA 19428
215-832-0844
Fax: 215-832-0807

Excellent
322 Eighth Ave., Ste 1602
New York, NY 10001
212-620-0320
Fax: 212-243-1089

Extra Fancy
PO Box 26480
Los Angeles, CA 90026
213-969-2530

Eye Q
8756 Holloway Dr
W Hollywood, CA 90069
310-657-7241

Fat Possum
PO Box 1923
Oxford, MS 38655
800-659-9794

Fat Wreck
PO Box 193690
San Francisco, CA 94119
415-284-1790
Fax: 415-284-1791

Feedback
524 Windy Point Dr
Glendale Heights, IL 60139
708-545-9100

Feel Good All Over
PO Box 148428
Chicago, IL 60614
312-227-6050
Fax: 312-227-6051
fgao@interaccess.com

Falsified
P.O. Box 1010
Birmingham, MI 48012
313-831-2585
Local Alternative, Rock

Fantasy
2600 10th St.
Berkeley, CA 94710
510-549-2500
Fax: 510-486-2015
Jazz, Soul, R&B

Fiction
1540 Broadway, Ste 505
New York, NY 10036
212-930-4910

Fifth Column
PO Box 787
Washington, DC 20044
202-783-0044
Fax: 202-783-0046
fifthcolumn@tunanet.com

Figurehead
1916 s. Orange Ave.
Orlando, FL 32806
407-872-1836
Alternative

Finer Arts Records Co.
2170 S. parker Rd. Suite 115
Denver, CO 80231
800-783-HITS
FAX: 303-755-2617

Fingerpaint
7510 Sunset Blvd, Ste 544
Los Angeles, CA 90046
213-469-3268

Fingerprint Productions
P.O. Box 197
Merrimac, MA 01860
508-346-4577
Fax: 508-346-7608
Folk, Rock
www.instantmag.com/fingerprint

Fire Ant
2009 Ashland Ave
Charlotte, NC 28205
704-335-1400

Firenze
1827 Haight St. #65
San Francisco, CA 94117
707-579-5756
Alternative, Rock, Blues, Soul

First Priority
89 5th Ave. Ste. 700
New York, NY 10003
212-243-0505
Rap, R&B

Fish Of Death
PO Box 93206
Los Angeles, CA 90093
213-462-3404
www.fishofdeath.com

Flat Town
PO Drawer 10
Ville Platte, LA 70586
318-363-2139

Fleece
PO Box 70012
Houston, TX 77270
713-524-1167
Fax: 713-524-9532

Flip
8773 Sunset Blvd., Ste 205
W Hollywood, CA 90069
310-360-8556

Flipside
PO Box 60790
Pasadena, CA 91116
818-585-0395

Flurry
PO Box 6425
Minneapolis, MN 55406
612-874-2418
Fax: 612-874-2430

Fly
231 Main St
Farmingdale, NY 11735
516-249-3313
Fax: 516-293-4641

Flydaddy
PO Box 4618
Seattle, WA 98104
206-622-3070
Fax: 206-622-3192
flydaddy@subpop.com

Flying Fish
1304 W. Schubert Ave.
Chicago, IL 60614
312-528-5455
Folk, World Music

Flying Heart
4026 NE 12th Ave.
Portland, OR 97212
503-287-8045
Rock, Jazz, Blues
www.teleport.com/~flyheart

Folk Era
705 S Washington
Naperville, IL 60540
630-637-2303
Fax: 630-416-7213
FolkEra@aol.com

Fontana
825 Eighth Ave
New York, NY 10019
212-333-8306

Forefront
201 Seaboard Lane
Franklin, TN 37067
615-771-2900

Forever And A Day
15 Northwood Circle
New Rochelle, NY 10804
914-235-5922

Fort Apache
2 Tyler Court, Ste B
Cambridge, MA 02140
617-868-2242
Fax: 617-868-8907

Four-Letter Words
533 Sycamore, #4
San Carlos, CA 94070
415-508-8325

Free World Music
105 W. 28th St., 3rd Floor
New York, NY 10001
212-239-9592
World

Freeze/After Dark
322 Eighth Ave, Ste 200
New York, NY 10001
212-294-2900
Fax: 212-294-7169

Fresh Sounds
P.O. Box 36
Lawrence, KS 66044
913-841-6772
Guitar Rock

Front Hall Enterprises, Inc.
Wormer Rd.
P.O. Box 307
Voorheesville, NY 12186
518-765-4193

Frontier
P.O. Box 22
Sun Valley, CA 91353-0022
818-506-6886
Fax: 818-506-0723
frontiermo@aol.com
Alternative, Rock

Fruit of the Tune
PO Box 440
Montclair, NJ 07042
201-746-9633
Fax: 201-746-6725
mikemango@aol.com

Fuel
8033 Sunset Blvd, Ste 392
Los Angeles, CA 90046
213-653-4269

Funk Boy
140 Frost St
Brooklyn, NY 11211
718-349-7751

Funkin' Do Me
1217 N Bethlehem Pike
Amber, PA 19002
215-646-2361
Fax: 800-917-3451
weare@unsignedband.com

Funky Mushroom
3712 Old Philadelphia Plaza
Bethlehem, PA 18017
610-868-3330
Fax: 610-868-3339

The Futurist Label
285 W Broadway, Ste 300
New York, NY 10013
212-226-7272
Fax: 212-941-9409

Gasoline Alley
9720 Wilshire Blvd., 4th Fl
Beverly Hills, CA 90212
310-275-3377
Fax: 310-275-8774

Gee Street
825 Eighth Ave
New York, NY 10019
212-333-8000

Geffen
9130 Sunset Blvd.
Los Angeles, CA 90069
310-278-9010
www.geffen.com

Geffen
1755 Broadway 6th Fl.
New York, NY 10019
212-841-8600
www.geffen.com

Generator
PO Box 581277
Minneapolis, MN 55458
612-379-7651

Generic
433 Limestone Rd.
Ridgefield, CT 06877
203-438-9811
Fax: 203-431-3204
Rock, Alternative, Top 40

Geo Synchronous Records
P.O. Box 540962
Merrit Island, FL
32954-0962
407-452-2910
Rock, Blues
www.pan.com/geosync

Gern Blandsten
PO Box 356
River Edge, NJ 07661
201-265-9025

Gertown
8359 Fig St
New Orleans, LA 70118
504-866-2863

Get Hip
P.O. Box 666
Canonsburg, PA 15317
412-231-4766
Garage Punk

Giant
8900 Wilshire Blvd.
Beverly Hills, CA 90211
310-289-5500

Gladiator
2565 Monroeville Blvd
Monroeville, PA 15146
412-373-7693
Fax: 412-373-6506

Global Village
245 W 29th St
New York, NY 10001
212-695-6020
Fax: 212-695-6025

GM
167 Dudley Rd
Newton Centre, MA 02159
617-332-6398

GNP Crescendo
8400 Sunset Blvd. Ste. 4A
Los Angeles, CA 90069
213-656-2614
Fax: 213-656-0693
Jazz, Blues, Rock

Godman
84 Pleasant St
Grafton, MA 01519
508-757-1551

Go-Kart
PO Box 20, Prince St Station
New York, NY 10012
212-673-3380

Gold Castle
3575 Cahuenga Blvd. W., Ste 470
Los Angeles, CA 90068
213-850-3321

Goldenrod
3770 Tansy St.
San Diego, CA 92075
619-558-3184
Alternative
www.tumyeto.com/

Gong Sounds
1075 S W 188th St
Miami, FL 33160
305-378-9243

Good Kitty
201A N. Davis Ave
Richmond, VA 23220
804-358-5946

GoodSin
215 "A" St, 5th Fl
Boston, MA 02210
617-269-9296
Fax: 617-269-9296
goodsin@aol.com

Gopaco
PO Box 87587
Carol Stream, IL 60188
708-858-7801
Fax: 708-858-7806

Gotham Records
1841 Broadway, Ste 1012
New York, NY 10023
212-265-3820
Fax: 212-265-3145
Alternative

Gracenote
PO Box 247
Laurel Hill, NC 28351
910-462-2016

Gramavision
Shetland Park
27 Congress St.
Salem, Mass 01970
508-744-7678
Fax: 508-741-4506
Funk, Jazz
www.rycodisc.com

Grand Royal
P.O. Box 26689
Los Angeles, CA 90026
213-660-0934
miwa@grandroyal.com

Grass Records
72 Madison Ave, Fl. 8
New York, NY 10016
212-843-8300

Grateful Dead
PO Box X
Novato, CA 94948
415-648-4832

Gravity
P.O. Box 81332
San Diego CA 92138
619-276-0264

Great Southern
P.O. Box 13977
New Orleans LA 70185
504-482-4211
New Orleans, Cajun

Green Linnet
43 Beaver Brook Rd.
Danbury, CT 06810
203-730-0333
Fax:203-730-0345
www.grnlinnet.com
Celtic, Folk

Greener Pastures
70 Route 202 N
Peterborough, NH 03458
800-677-8838
Fax: 609-924-8613

Griffin
PO Box 87587
Carol Stream, IL 60188
708-858-7801
Fax: 708-858-7806

Grindstone
447 S Robertson Blvd, #201
Beverly Hills, CA 90211
310-246-0779

Groovy Tuesday
473 Atlantic Ave
E Rockaway, NY 11518
516-599-0028
Fax: 516-791-2941

GRP
555 West 57th St.,10th Fl.
New York, NY 10019
212-424-1000
Jazz

Guardian
810 Seventh Ave, Fl 4
New York, NY 10019
212-603-8633

Guess I'll Have To Use My Brain
2460 N Lake, #105
Altadena, CA 91001
818-398-6500
Fax: 818-398-6500

Guitar Recordings &
Cherry Lane
10 Midland Ave.
Port Chester, NY 10573
914-935-5200
Fax: 914-937-0614
Guitar, Heavy Metal

H.O.L.A.
235 Park Ave, S, 10th Fl
New York, NY 10003
212-996-5700
Fax: 212-996-8374

Hammerhead Records
41 E. University Ave.
Champaign, IL 61820
217-355-9052
Fax: 217-355-9057

Harbinger
PO Box 1241m
Bayshore, NY 11706
516-951-3625

Hard Hat
519 N. Halifax Ave.
Daytona Beach, FL
32118-4017
904-252-0381
Pop, Rock, Country

Harp
PO Box 460465
San Francisco, CA 94146
415-626-2377
Fax: 415-626-2377

Harriet
PO Box 649
Cambridge, MA 02238
617-666-4007
alborn@fas.harvard.edu

Heartbeat
1 Camp St.
Cambridge, MA 02140
617-354-0700
Fax: 617-491-0970
info@rounder.com
Reggae

Hearts of Space
1 Harbor Dr., Ste 201
Sausalito, CA 94965
415-331-3200
Fax: 415-331-3280
www.hos.com

Hefty
2521 Ashbury Ave
Evanston, IL 60201
818-560-6040

Helion
859 N. Hollywood Way
Ste. 281
Burbank CA 91505
818-352-9174
Rock, R&B, Jazz, Metal, Rap,
Country

Hell Gate
PO Box 6053
Astoria, NY 11106
718-626-1654

Heyday
2325 3rd St. #339
San Francisco, CA 94107
415-252-5590
Alternative

Hi-Ball
PO Box 61-7522
Chicago, IL 60661
312-292-9566
Fax: 312-395-0081
logletter@aol.com

Hifi
580 Broadway, Ste 200
New York, NY 10012
212-226-4580

High Chief
404 S Harding Rd
Columbus, OH 43209
614-237-7454

High Street
PO Box 9388
Stanford, CA 94309
415-329-0647
Fax: 415-329-1512

High Water
Memphis State U. Music Dept.
Memphis, TN 38152
901-678-3317

Higher Octave Music
23715 W. Malibu Rd.
Malibu CA 90265
310-589-1515
Fax: 310-589-1525
New Age

Hightone
220 4th St. Ste. 101
Oakland, CA 94607
510-763-8500
Blues, Rock

Hightone
220 4th St. #101
Oakland, CA 94607
510-763-8500
Blues, Country, Roots Rock

Hit & Run
PO Box 44302
Cleveland, OH 44114
216-481-7002

HitIt!
232 E Ohio, Ste 300
Chicago, IL 60611
312-440-9012

Hollywood
500 S. Buena Vista St.
Animation Building
Burbank, CA 91521
818-560-6197

Home Cooking
P.O. Box 980454
Houston, TX 77098
713-666-0258
Blues-Contemporary, Traditional,
Reissues

Homestead/Rockville
150 W. 28th St., Ste. 501
New York, NY 10001
Alternative, Punk Rock, Avant
Garde

Honey Puller
51 MacDougal St, Ste 330
New York, NY 10012
212-777-8764
Fax: 212-260-1928
benhp@spacelab.net.com

Horse Latitudes
PO Box 2483, Loop Station
Minneapolis, MN 55402
612-871-3130

Hunter
PO Box 607
Glendora, CA 91740
818-335-6796

I Wanna
PO Box 166
Wright Bros. Station
Dayton, OH 45404
513-898-8203

Ice
110 Greene St., Ste 111
New York, NY 10012
212-431-5522

Ichiban
P.O. Box 724677
Atlanta, GA 31139-1677
404-419-1414
Fax: 404-419-1230
IchibanR@aol.com
Rock, Jazz, Contemporary Blues,
Dance, Alternative, Metal, Urban

Idlers
3528 Neptune Ave
Brooklyn, NY 11224
718-372-0783

Ignition
2 Bridge Ave, The Galleria,
Bldg3, 2nd Fl
Red Bank, NJ 07701
908-530-7575
Fax: 908-219-0172
igrecords@aol.com

Igor
PO Box 81517
Pittsburgh, PA 15217
412-683-9329

Iguana
30 Glenn St
White Plains, NY 10603
914-428-5100

Ikus
12245 SW 130St
Miami, FL 33186
305-378-4417
Fax: 305-378-9441

Iloki
P.O. Box 49593
Los Angeles, CA 90049
310-472-7637

Imaginary Road
c/o Polygram Classics & Jazz,
825 Eighth Ave
New York, NY 10019
212-603-7980
Fax: 212-333-8402

IMI
541 N Fairbanks, Ste 2040
Chicago, IL 60611
312-245-9334
Fax: 312-245-9327

Immortal
646 Robertson Blvd.
Los Angeles, CA 90069
310-657-9500
Fax: 310-657-0656
All Styles

Immune
9269 Mission Gorge Rd. #211
San Diego, CA 92071
619-448-3062
All Styles

Impact
6255 Sunset Blvd, 11th Fl
Hollywood, CA 90028
213-466-6900

Impulse
555 W 57th St, 10th Fl
New York, NY 10019
212-424-1000
Fax: 212-424-1007

In The Red
2627 E Strong Place
Anaheim, CA 92806
714-441-2356

Incandescent
P.O. Box 22098
San Francisco, CA 94122
415-665-2548
Fax: 415-665-4988
E-mail: IncanSF@aol.com

Indecision
PO Box 5213
Huntington Beach, CA 92615
714-444-4358
Fax: 714-444-4379

Independent Music Group
33 Great Neck Rd
Great Neck, NY 11021
516-829-8811

Independent Project
PO Box 1033
Sedona, AZ 86339
602-204-1332

India Archive
2170 Broadway, Ste 343
New York, NY 10024
212-740-1508

Inertia
1608 N Cahuenga, #1261
Hollywood, CA 90028
213-427-8411

Instinct
26 W 17th St, Ste 502
New York, NY 10011
212-727-1360
Fax: 212-366-5979
Acid Jazz, Ambient, Underground

Intense
660 Newport Center Dr,
Ste 780
Newport Beach, CA 92660
714-721-9500
Fax: 714-721-6933

Interplanetary Truckers Union
PO Box 648
New York, NY 10011
800-219-1114
Fax: 516-799-7982

Interscope
10900 Wilshire Blvd.
12th Floor
Los Angeles, CA 90024
310-208-6547
Fax: 310-208-7343

Intersound
PO Box 1724
Roswell, GA 3077
800-945-3059
Fax: 770-664-7316
promoten@aol.com

Interworld
139 Noriega St
San Francisco, CA 94122
415-242-9788

Intrepid
93 Hazelton Ave., 3rd Fl.
Toronto, ONT M6K 1Y3
CANADA
416-345-8058
Fax: 416-324-9835
Alternative, Rock

Intuition
636 Broadway, #1218
New York, NY 10012
212-473-6044
Fax: 212-473-6454

Invasion
114 Lexington Ave.
New York, NY 10016
212-532-1414
Fax: 212-684-0958
Alternative, Dance, Folk,
New Age

Inverted
575 Madison Ave, Ste 1006
New York, NY 10022
212-605-0470
Fax: 212-308-9834

Invisible
PO Box 16008
Chicago, IL 60616
312-808-0222
Fax: 312-808-1117

Iris
P.O. Box 422
Port Washington, NY 11050
516-944-7905
Jazz, Blues
iris.records.internetmca.com

Island
825 Eighth Ave, 24th Fl
New York, NY 10019
212-333-8000
Fax: 212-603-3970

Island
1345 Denison St
Markham, ONT, CAN L3R 5V2
905-415-1993
Fax: 905-415-0850

Issues
PO Box 1389
Lawndale, CA 90260
310-430-6838
Fax: 310-430-7286

JAM
3424 Wedgewood Dr.
Kalamazoo, MI 49008
616-349-2721
Progressive Pop Rock

Jellybean
235 Park Ave S 10th Fl
New York, NY 10003
212-996-5700
Fax: 212-996-8374

Jesus Christ
PO Box 4971
Chapel Hill, NC 27515
919-933-FUCK
cognac@vnet.net

Jewel/Paula
PO Box 1125
Shreveport, LA 71163
318-227-2228
Fax: 318-227-0304

Jiffy Boy
PO Box 255
New Brunswick, NJ 08903
908-249-5455

Jive
137-139 W 25th St.
8th Floor
New York, NY 10001
212-727-0016
Fax: 212-645-3783
Rap

Jive
700 N. Green, Ste. 200
Chicago, IL 60622
312-942-9700
Rap

Johann's Face
PO Box 479-164
Chicago, IL 60647
312-226-0957

Jonkey Enterprises
663 W. California Ave
Glendale, CA 91203
818-242-4034
World

June Appal
306 Madison St
Whitesburg, KY 41858
606-633-0108

Justice Records
P.O. Box 980369
Houston, TX 77098
713-520-6669
Fax: 713-525-4444
Electric

JVC
3800 Barham Blvd, Ste 305
Los Angeles, CA 90068
213-878-0101

K
Box 7154
Olympia, WA 98507
360-786-1594
Fax: 360-786-5024
Alternative
www.olywa.net/kpunk

K2B2
3112 Barry Ave.
Los Angeles, CA 90066
213-732-1602
Jazz

K-Tel International (USA)
2605 Fernbrook Lane N
Minneapolis, MN 55447
612-559-6800
Fax: 612-559-6803
www.k-tel.com

Kereshmeh
12021 Wilshire Blvd, #420
Los Angeles, CA 90025
310-451-3046
Fax: 310-260-3147

Kill Rock Stars
120 N. State St., #418
Olympia WA 98507
206-357-9732
Fax:360-357-6408
KRSPromo@aol.com

KLB
580 Broadway
New York, NY 10012
212-941-8123
Fax: 212-941-1982

KMH
PO Box 99577
Troy, MI 48099
810-228-2657

Knitting Factory
74 Leonard St
New York, NY 10013
212-219-3006
Fax: 212-219-3401
Jazz, Rock
www.knittingfactory.com

Koch International
2 Tri-Harbour Court
Port Washington, NY 11050
516-484-1000
Fax: 516-484-4746
koch@kochint.com

Kokopelli
PO Box 8200
Santa Fe, NM 87504
505-820-2110
Fax: 505-820-2124
www.koko.com

Komotion
PO Box 301
Redwood Estates, CA 95044
408-353-8597
Fax: 408-353-8527

Krane Pool
PO Box 7164, Capitol Station
Albany, NY 12224
518-426-8606

Kranky
PO Box 578743
Chicago, IL 60657
312-728-2935

La-Di-Da
PO Box 202, Stuyvesant Station
New York, NY 10014
212-673-8418

Laface
3350 Peachtree Rd
Atlanta, GA 30326
404-848-8070

Lame Ear
1224 Quincy St NE
Minneapolis, MN 55413
612-331-3487

Land of Fun
1525 E Nine Mile Rd
Ferndale, MI 48220
810-547-6863

Landmark
106 W 71st St
New York, NY 10023
212-873-2020
Fax: 212-877-0407

Last Beat
2819 Commerce St
Dallas, TX 75226
214-748-9201
Fax: 214-748-9160

Lava
75 Rockafeller Plaza
New York, NY 10019
212-265-3440

Lazy Eye Wreckords
PO Box 4636
Omaha, NE 68104
402-455-6842

LD
613 Ridge Rd.
Lewisberry, PA 17339
717-938-1351
All Styles

Lench Mob
16501 Ventura Blvd, Ste 303
Encino, CA 91436
818-386-6990
Fax: 818-386-6999

Leviathan
PO Box 745
Tyrone, GA 30290
404-463-8646

Life & Death
PO Box 3654
Hollywood, CA 90078
213-465-9622

Lime Skull/Limedisc
P.O. Box 12425
Venice, CA 90295-3425
310-823-8939
Alternative, Industrial, Dance,
Metal

Limestone City
10451 Bellagio St
Bel Air, CA 90077
310-827-6822

Limited Potential
P.O. Box 268586
Chicago, IL 60626
312-764-9636
Fax: 312-764-8727

Link
121 W. 27th St. #401
New York, NY 10001
212-924-2929
Fax: 212-929-6305
Linkrec@aol.com
Rock, Alternative

Liquid Meat
PO Box 460692
San Marcos, CA 92069
619-753-8734

Little Brother
PO Box 3324
Eugene, OR 97403
503-341-4900

Little Dog
223 W Alameda, Ste 101
Burbank, CA 91502
818-557-1595

Livin' Large
1995 Broadway, 18th Fl
New York, NY 10023
212-724-5500

LobeCandy Records
7514 Girard Ave., Ste.1-440
La Jolla, CA 92037
619-551-9571

Logic
2630 Medicine Ridge Rd
Plymouth, MN 55441
612-542-9125

Logic
270 Lafayette St, Ste 1402
New York, NY 10012
212-219-2040
Fax: 212-219-2050

London
825 8th Ave.
New York, NY 10019
212-333-8000
Fax: 212-333-8030

Long Play
PO Box 55233
Atlanta, GA 30308
404-681-4915
Fax: 404-577-2927
longplay22aol.com

Lookout
P.O. Box 11374
Berkeley CA 94701
510-849-8300
Fax: 510-849-0512
lkoutnews@aol.com

Loose Cannon
825 Eighth Ave
New York, NY 10019
212-333-8000

Loosegroove
417 Denny Way, Ste 200
Seattle, WA 98109
206-728-9781
Fax: 206-728-0336
loosegrv@aol.com

Love Is Sharing Pharmaceuticals
348 Lamont Dr
Decatur, GA 30030
404-378-8542

Lovely
10 Beach St
New York, NY 10013
212-941-8911

Low Blow
8205 Santa Monica Blvd, #1-202
W Hollywood, CA 90046
213-660-5946
Fax: 213-660-3648
www.lowblow.com

Luaka Bop
PO Box 652, Cooper Station
New York, NY 10276
212-255-2714
Fax: 212-255-3809
yaluaka@aol.com

Luke/Effect
8400 NE 2nd Ave.
Miami, FL 33138
305-757-1969
Fax: 305-757-3456
Rap, Dance, R&B

Lumberjack Records
2543 N 55th St
Omaha, NE 68104
402-280-3358
Rock

Luv n' Haight
PO Box 192104
San Francisco, CA 94119
415-979-0887

Lyrichord
141 Perry St
New York, NY 10014
212-929-8234

M.U.D.D.
PO Box 814
Brookfield, CT 06804
203-759-1488

Mafia Money
PO Box 8562
Madison, WI 53708
608-257-5804
Fax: 608-257-5804

Magnatone Records
PO Box 2576
El Segundo, CA 90245
213-934-7360

Maison De Soul
PO Drawer 10
Ville Platte, LA 70586
318-363-2139

Maitre'D
70 E. 10th St.
New York, NY 10003
212-228-1708
Fax: 212-979-0556

Making of Americans
PO Box 490, Cooper Station
New York, NY 10276
212-260-4990

Malaco
3023 W Northside Dr
Jackson, MS 39213
601-982-4522

Malicious Vinyl
6607 Sunset Blvd
Los Angeles, CA 90028
213-465-2700

Mammoth
101"B"St
Carrboro, NC 27510
919-932-1882
Fax: 919-932-2206
Alternative
www.nando.net/mammoth

Mango
825 Eighth St
New York, NY 10019
212-333-8000

Manifesto
5967 W Third St, Ste 301
Los Angeles, CA 90036
213-954-1555
Fax: 213-954-1116
manifest@manifesto.com

Mapleshade
2301 Crain Hwy
Upper Marlboro, MD 20774
301-627-0525
Fax: 301-627-4136

March
P.O. Box 578396
Chicago, IL 60657
Fax: 312-296-4321
Alternative, Cuddlecore
cuddlecore@aol.com

Mardi Gras
3331 St Charles Ave
New Orleans, LA 70115
504-895-0441

Margaritaville
66 Music Square W
Nashville, TN 37203
615-329-2899
Fax: 615-329-4006

Marilyn
PO Box 7112
Burbank, CA 91510
213-227-5433
orbit23@aol.com

Masquerade
695 North Ave NE
Atlanta, GA 30308
404-577-8178
Fax: 404-577-7460
masq@mindspring.com

Massive
PO Box 2088
Salem, MA 01970
617-643-9322

Matador
676 Broadway 4th Fl.
New York, NY 10012
212-995-5882
212-995-5883
www.matador.recs.com
Rock

Matt Label
P.O. Box 52707
Durham, NC 27717
Fax: 919-419-0808
Alternative

Mauroy Records
691 10th Ave.
San Francisco, CA 94118
415-386-6036
Fax: 415-386-6036

Mausoleum
18 E 53rd St, 11th Fl
New York, NY 10022
212-758-4636

Maverick Records
8000 Beverly Blvd.
Los Angeles, CA 90048
213-852-1177
Fax: 213-852-0500

Mayhem
285 W Broadway, Ste 300
New York, NY 10013
212-226-7272
Fax: 212-941-9409

Maza
31 Brookline Dr
Massapequa, NY 11758
516-579-7407

MCA
2450 Victoria Park Ave
Willowdale, ONT, CAN
M2J 4A2
416-491-3000
Fax: 416-490-8206
www.mca.com

MCA
70 Universal City Plaza
Universal City, CA 91608
818-777-4000

MCA
1755 Broadway 8th Fl.
New York, NY 10019
212-841-8000

MCA
60 Music Square East
Nashville, TN 37203
615-244-8944

Mechanic
285 W Broadway, Ste 300
New York, NY 10013
212-226-7272
Fax: 212-941-9409
Rock, Alternative, Pop, Funk
Rock

Medicine
75 Rockefeller Plaza, 21st Fl
New York, NY 10019
212-275-4666
Fax: 212-275-4670

Megaforce
PO Box 779
New Hope, PA 18938
908-591-1117
Fax: 908-591-1116

Megalithic
6798 Glacier Dr
West Bend, WI 53095
414-562-4744

Mekkatone
322 Eighth Ave, Ste 200
New York, NY 10001
212-294-2900
Fax: 212-294-7169

Melodie Makers
PO Box 163024
Miami, FL 33116
305-871-1879
Fax: 305-595-7925

Meltdown
PO Box 1389
Hollywood, CA 90078
Fax: 213-221-9833

Mercy Records
735 1/2 New Hampshire
Suite B
Lawerence, KS 66044
913-843-4141
Alternative

Mercury
Worldwide Plaza
825 8th Ave. 19th Fl
New York, NY 10019
212-333-8000
Fax: 212-603-7664

Mercury/Polydor
1345 Denison St
Markham, ONT, CAN L3R 5V2
416-415-9900
Fax: 905-415-0850

Merge
P.O. Box 1235
Chapel Hill, NC 27514
919-929-0711
Fax: 919-929-4291
Alternative

Meridian
1310 Clinton St, Ste 217
Nashville, TN 37203
615-327-9389

Merkin
310 E Biddle St
Baltimore, MD 21202
410-234-0048
Fax: 410-539-2835

Mesa/Blue Moon
209 E. Alameda Ave. #101
Burbank, CA 91502
818-841-8585
Fax: 818-841-8581
Jazz, Adult Contemporary, World
Music, New Age

Messenger
PO Box 1607
New York, NY 10113
212-560-2538
Fax: 212-675-6164
messrec@pipeline.com

Metal Blade
2345 Erringer Rd., Ste. 108
Simi Valley CA 93065
805-522-9111
805-522-9380
metal_blade@earthlink.net
Metal

Metropolis
739 N. Harvard Ave.
Villa Park, IL 60181
630-941-3571
Fax: 708-941-8763

Metropolitan
900 Passaic Ave.
East Newark, NJ 07029
201-483-8080
Pop

Midnight Fantasy
3810 Woodridge Ave
Wheaton, MD 20902
301-942-9200
Fax: 301-942-2826

Midnight International
P.O. Box 390
Old Chelsea Station
New York, NY 10011
212-675-2768
60's Garage Rock, Punk,
Psychedelic

Mighty
PO Box 1833
Los Angeles, CA 90078
213-465-8686

Mighty Mike Records
175 E. Delaware Place
Suite 8510
Chicago, IL 60611-1732
312-943-7777
R&B, Rock, Alternative

Milan
1540 Broadway, Ste 29D
New York, NY 10036
212-782-1086
fax: 212-782-1078
Soundtracks, World Music, Jazz

Milestone
2600 10th St.
Berkeley, CA 94710
510-549-2500
Jazz, Blues, Roots Rock
www.fantasyjazz.com

Mind Cure
PO Box 19438
Pittsburgh, PA 15213
412-621-3256

Mint
699-810 W Broadway
Vancouver, BC, CAN V5Z 4C9
604-669-6468

Minty Fresh
P.O. Box 577400
Chicago, IL 60657
312-665-0289
Fax: 312-665-0219
Alternative

Miramar Records
200 Second Ave. W
Seattle, Wa 98119
206-284-4700
New Age, Adult , Jazz
www.useattle.uspan.com/miramr

Mirror
645 Titus Ave.
Rochester, NY 14617
716-544-3500
All Styles

Mobile Fidelity Sound Lab
P.O. Box 1657
Sebastopol, CA 95473-1657
707-829-0134
www.mofi.com

Mode
PO Box 1026
New York, NY 10116
212-979-1027
Fax: 212-979-1027

Modern World Music
134 Ave. B, Ste. 5A
New York, NY 10009
212-529-5881
Fax: 212-529-5882
Classical, Jazz, Rock

Mojazz
5750 Wilshire Blvd, Ste 300
Los Angeles, CA 90036
213-634-3324

Mojo
1547 14th St
Santa Monica, CA 90404
310-260-3181

Monkey
3991 Royal Drive NW
Kennesaw, GA 30339
404-419-1414
Fax: 404-419-1230

Monkey Hill
804 Spain St
New Orleans, LA 70117
504-947-5166

Monolyth
P.O. Box 980, Prudential Center
Boston, MA 02199-0980
617-437-0117
Rock, Alternative

Monsterdisc
1333 N Kingsbury, Ste 203
Chicago, IL 60622
312-266-5770

MoodFood
1381 Kildaire Farms Rd, Ste 246
Cary, NC 27511
919-319-6358
Fax: 919-319-6785

Moon Ska
PO Box 1412, Cooper Station
New York, NY 10276
212-673-5538
Fax: 212-673-5571
moonska@pipeline.com

Moonshine
8525 Santa Monica Blvd
W Hollywood, CA 90069
310-652-8145
Fax: 310-652-8146
sheri@moonshine.com

Mordam
PO Box 988
San Francisco, CA 94101
415-243-8230

Morninglory
1014 State St
Santa Barbara, CA 93101
805-966-0266
Fax: 805-966-9675

Motel Records
210 E 49th St, 2nd Fl
New York, NY 10017
212-755-4328
212-755-6092

**Motor Jam Records/
Honcho Mogul**
77 Bleecker St. Suite C212
New York, NY 10012
212-473-7673
Fax: 212 473-6093
All Styles

Motown
11150 Santa Monica Blvd.,
Ste. 1000
Los Angeles, CA 90025
310-996-7200
R&B, Pop

Motown
1345 Denison St
Markham, ONT, CAN L3R 5V2
905-415-1993
Fax: 905-445-3353

Motown
825 8th Ave.
New York, NY 10019
212-424-200

Mule Dog
6260 E Riverside, Ste 111
Loves Park, IL 61111
815-962-4829

Multitone
PO Box 582891
Minneapolis, MN 55458
612-948-1478
multone@aol.com

murderecords
PO Box 2372, Halifax Central
Halifax, NS, CAN B3J 3E4
902-422-6114
Fax: 902-422-2194
murder@ra.isisnet.com

Muscle Car
PO Box 5857
Concord, CA 94524
510-933-8737
Fax: 510-933-8737

Muse
160 W. 71st St.
New York, NY 10023
212-873-2020
212-877-0407
Jazz

Music Castle
333 E Plumb Lane
Reno, NV 89502
702-787-2520

Music For Little People
PO Box 1460
Redwood, CA 95560
707-923-3991
Fax: 707-923-3241

Music Of The World
PO Box 3620
Chapel Hill, NC 27515
919-932-9600
Fax: 919-932-9700

Musicmasters
1710 Hwy 35
Ocean, NJ 07712
908-531-3375

Musidisc
143 Ave. B Ste. 5A
New York, NY 10009
212-529-5881
Classical, Jazz, Rock

Mute
140 W 22 St.
New York, NY 10011
212-255-7670
Alternative
http://www.mutelibtech.
com/mute/

Mute
3218 1/2 Glendale Blvd.
Los Angeles, CA 90039
213-666-5672
Alternative

Mutha
P.O. Box 416
West Long Branch, NJ 07764
908-571-3197
Hard Core Metal, Psychedelic,
Alternative

Narada
4650 N Port Washington Rd.
Milwaukee WI 53212
414-961-8350
New Age, Jazz, Contemporary,
Instrumental

Necessary
676 Broadway, Fl 3
New York, NY 10012
212-473-9497

Neko
30-78 36 St
Astoria, NY 11103
718-777-0913

Nemperor
P.O. Box 542
Lennox Hill Station
New York, NY 10021
212-249-0041
Pop

Nervous
1510 Broadway Ste. 900
New York, NY 10036
212-730-7160
House, Hip-Hop

Nettwerk
1250 W. 6th
Vancouver, BC V6H 1A5
CANADA
604-654-2929
Alternative
www.nettwerk.com

Nettwerk
632 Broadway, #301
New York, NY 10012
212-477-8198
Fax: 212-477-6874

Network Sound
PO Box 5213
Huntington Beach, CA 92615
714-444-4358
Fax: 714-444-4379

Neurodisc
450 N Park Rd, Ste 700
Hollywood Hills, FL 33021
305-963-0555
Fax: 305-964-1117

Nevermore
P.O. Box 170150
Brooklyn, NY 11217
718-625-4492

New Age
PO Box 5213
Huntington Beach, CA 92615
714-444-4358
Fax: 714-444-4379

New Albion
584 Castro #515
San Francisco, CA 94114
415-621-5757
Folk, Ethnic, Classical, Jazz

New Alliance
P.O. Box 1389
Lawndale, CA 90260
310-430-6838
Fax: 310-430-7286
Rock, Alternative, Spoken Word

New Breed
134 W 26th St, #770
New york, NY 10001
212-255-0672
Fax: 212-627-0208

New Clear
P.O. Box 559
Felton, CA 95018
408-338-7283

New Lav
222 Guideboard Rd, Ste104
Clifton Park, NY 12065
518-877-3037

New World
701 7th Ave.
New York, NY 10036
212-302-0460
Fax: 212-944-1922
American Composer, Jazz,
Classical, Folk, Ethnic

New World of Sound
PO Box 4634
Highland Park, NJ 08904
Fax: 201-656-7383

Next Plateau
536 Broadway
New York, NY 10012
212-274-7500
Fax: 212-941-0509
Rap, Dance

NG
622 Broadway, Room 4B
New York, NY 10012
212-505-5414
Fax: 212-505-6045
E-mail: THOWELL3@aol.com
All Styles

Nice
571 Grand Ave
St Paul, MN 55102
612-291-1919

Nighthawk
Box 15856
St. Louis, MO 63114
314-576-1569
Fax: 314-576-6960
Reggae, Blues

Nine Winds
PO Box 10082
Beverly Hills, CA 90213
213-858-8072

No Blow
900 N. 73rd St. #106
Seattle, WA 98103
206-706-7655
Guitar Oriented Rock

Nocturnal
P.O. Box 399
Royal Oak, MI 48068
313-542-NITE

Noise
8721 Sunset Blvd, Ste P6/P7
W Hollywood, CA 90069
310-289-2515
Fax: 310-659-0767

No Life
7209 Santa Monica Blvd
W Hollywood, CA 90046
213-845-1200
Fax: 213-845-4164

Noiseville
P.O. Box 124
Yonkers, NY 10710
914-793-5122
Underground

Nomad
PO Box 3620
Chapel Hill, NC 27515
919-932-9600
www.rootsworld.com/rw/motw

No Name
16133 Ventura Blvd, Ste 535
Encino, CA 91436
818-783-1077

Nonesuch
75 Rockefeller Plaza, 8th Fl
New York, NY 10019
212-275-4910
Fax: 212-315-1124
Alternative, Classical, World
Music, Roots

None Of The Above
2530 Middle Country Rd
Centereach, NY 11720
Fax: 516-737-3867

Nonsequitur
PO Box 344
Albuquerque, NM 87103
505-224-9483

No Other
1992 N High St
Columbus, OH 43201
614-299-7621

Noo Trybe
338 N Foothill Rd
Beverly Hils, CA 90210
310-288-1464
Fax: 310-288-2470

Northeastern
P.O. Box 3589
Soxonville, MA 01701
508-820-4440
Fax: 508-820-7769

Norton
P.O. Box 646
Cooper Station
New York, NY 10003
718-789-4438
Rock & Roll

Notting Hill
3143 Willow Lane
Bronx, NY 10461
718-828-3488

Nova
1730 Olympic Blvd.
Santa Monica, CA 90404
310-392-7445
Contemporary Jazz, Urban, Jazz
Pop, Classcial

NovaMute
140 W 22nd St, 10th Fl
New York, NY 10011
212-255-7670
fax: 212-255-6056
mute@mute.com

Novus
1540 Broadway, 35th Fl
New York, NY 10036
212-930-4257
Fax: 212-930-4779
Jazz

Nowsville
PO Box 3611
Myrtle Beach, SC 29578
803-626-7579

Nuclear Blast America
PO Box 251
Millersville, PA 17551
717-872-6315

NYC
275 W 10th St
New York, NY 10014
212-627-9426

O.O.
261 Grovers Ave
Black Rock, CT 06605
203-367-7917
Fax: 203-333-0603
celli005@aol.com

Oarfin
216 Third Ave N
Minneapolis, MN 55401
612-673-0508

Oblivion
1660 E Herndon, Ste 135
Fresno, CA 93720
209-432-7329
fax: 209-434-3472
oblivion@cybergate.com

Ocean Music
1600 Falmouth Rd, Ste 150
Centerville, MA 02632
508-477-1626
Fax:508-539-2181
Rock, Roots, Pop, Singer-
Songwriter

October
800 Washington Ave N
Minneapolis, MN 55401
612-339-0690

Octopus
PO Box 1310
Mill Valley, CA 94942
415-383-8886
Fax: 512-383-8488
www.obsolete.com/waveform

Oglio
901A N. Pacific Coast Hwy,
Ste 200
Redondo Beach, CA 90277
310-798-2252
Fax: 310-798-3728

Oh Boy
33 Music Square W, Ste 102A
Nashville, TN 37203
615-742-1250
Fax: 615-742-1360

Okra
1992 2B N. High St.
Columbus, OH 43201
614-294-3833
Country, Rock, Progressive

Old School
179 Prospect Ave.
Wood Dale, IL 60619I-2727
708-616-8471
Fax:708-616-0341
E-mail: oldschtrc@aol.com
Alternative

Omnium
PO Box 7367
Minneapolis, MN 55407
612-379-0405
Fax: 612-379-0354
www.omnium.com/pub/omnium

One Dimensional
PO Box 1926, Harvard Square
Station
Cambridge, MA 02238
617-492-5398
fax: 617-492-6074

Only New Age Music
8033 Sunset Blvd. Suite 472
Los Angeles, CA 90046
213-851-3355
Fax: 213-851-7981
New Age/NAC

Onset
PO Box 1918
Garden Grove, CA 92642
714-638-7106
Fax: 714-638-7106

Openeye
151 University Ave
Palo Alto, CA 94301
415-326-1674
Fax: 415-326-1669
openeye@openeyerecords.com

Or
PO Box 30310
Indianapolis, IN 46230
317-466-1967
Fax: 317-466-0042

Orchard
41B Duesenberg Dr
Thousand Oaks, CA 91362
805-494-9021

Orchard Lane
10400 Yellow Circle Dr
Minnetonka, MN 55343
612-931-8455

Original
418 Lasher Rd
Tivoli, NY 12583
914-756-2767

Original Sound
7120 Sunset Blvd.
Hollywood, CA 90046
213-851-2500
Oldies But Goodies

Orleans
828 Royal St, #536
New Orleans, LA 70116
504-837-5042

Outpost
8932 Keith Ave
Los Angeles, CA 90069
310-285-7373

Outpunk
PO Box 170501
San Francisco, CA 94117
415-923-9113

Overture
47551 Iroquis Court
Novi, MI 48374
810-349-0115
Fax: 910-349-9140
www.overturemusic.com
Hard Rock, New Age

Pablo
2600 10th St.
Berkeley, CA 94710
510-549-2500
Jazz, Blues, Roots Rock
www.fantasyjazz.com

Pacific Arts
11858 La Grange Ave
Los Angeles, CA 90025
310-820-0991
Fax: 310-826-4779

Paisley Park
7801 Audubon Rd
Chanhassen, MN 55317
612-474-8555
Fax: 612-474-4849

Pallas
915 Broadway
New York, NY 10010
212-387-7575

Pandisc
6157 NW 167th St. Ste. F-11
Miami, Fl 33015
305-557-1914
Dance, Rap, Blues

Parc
1101 N. Lake Destiny Rd.
Ste. 450
Maitland, FL 32751
407-660-1665
Rock, Pop

Pasta
PO Box 295, Stuyvesant Station
New York, NY 10009
212-995-5494

Pavement
17 W 703A Butterfield Rd
Oakbrook, IL 60521
708-916-1155

Pcl
711 Eighth Ave
San Diego, CA 92101
619-236-1080

PCP
PO Box 1689, Grand Central Station
New York, NY 10009
212-982-4018

Pendulum
1290 Sixth Ave, 9th Fl
New York, NY 10019
212-397-2244
Fax: 212-397-2240

Pentacle Records
P.O. Box 5055
Laguna Beach, Ca 92652
714-494-3572
Fax: 714-494-3572
Melodic Rock, Alternative

Performance
2 Oak St
New Brunswick, NJ 08903
908-545-3004
Fax: 908-545-6054

Permanent
PO Box 628
Chapel Hill, NC 27514
919-932-3512
Fax: 919-932-3512

Philadelphia International
309 S. Broad St.
Philadelphia, PA 19107
215-985-0900
All Styles

Philips
825 Eighth Ave
New York, NY 10019
212-333-8000
Fax: 212-333-8402

Philo
One Camp St.
Cambridge, MA 02140
617-354-0700
Fax: 617-491-1970
id@rounder.com
Singer/Songwriter, Folk

Pinecastle/Webco
5108 S Orange Ave
Orlando, FL 32809
407-856-0245
Fax: 407-858-0007
pinecast@nebula.ispace.com

Pipeline
119 Engineers Dr
Hicksville, NY 11801
516-681-2125

Playback Records
2241 NE 201 St.
Miami, FL 33180
305-935-4880
Fax: 305-933-4007

Plump
30 W 21st St, 7th Fl
New York, NY 10010
212-366-6633
Fax: 212-366-0465
Plumprec@aol.com

PM Records
23481 Geneva
Oakpark, MI 48237
810-544-0189
Fax: 810-546-0376
All Styles

Poindexter
127-5 S College Rd
Wilmington, NC 28403
919-313-0076

Point
825 Eighth Ave, 26th Fl
New York, NY 10019
212-333-8000
Fax: 212-333-8402

Point Music
632 Broadway 9th Floor
New York, NY 10012
212-333-8345
Fax: 212-533-1776
All Styles

Polydor
Worldwide Plaza
825 Eighth Ave.
New York, NY 10019
212-333-8000

Polydor/Atlas
1416 N La Brea Ave
Hollywood, CA 90028
213-856-6600
Fax: 213-856-6610

PolyGram
Worldwide Plaza
825 Eighth Ave.
New York, NY 10019
212-333-8000

PolyGram
11150 Santa Monica Blvd.
Ste. 1100
Los Angeles, CA 90025
310-996-7200

PolyGram/Mercury Records
66 Music Square Wesr
Nashville, TN 37203
615-320-0110

Pop Bus
5891 Darlington Rd
Pittsburgh, PA 15217
412-422-6743

PopLlama
P.O. Box 95364
Seattle, WA 98145-2364
206-527-8816
Fax:206-527-0316
Alternative

Pop Narcotic
1085 Commonwealth Ave #339
Boston MA 02215
617-762-9073
Fax: 617-762-7108
Alternative
www.webcom.com/~popnarc/

Postcards
225 Lafayette St, Ste 604
New York, NY 10012
212-966-6083
Fax: 212-966-7457
info@postcds.com

Post Mortem
P.O. Box 358
New Milford, NJ 07646
201-262-7558

Pound
450 N Park Rd, Ste 700
Hollywood Hills, FL 33021
305-963-0555
Fax: 305-964-1117

Pow Wow
1776 Broadway, Ste 1206
New York, NY 10019
212-245-3010
Fax: 212-956-2326

Powderfinger
PO Box 382644
Cambridge, MA 02238
617-623-3824

PRA Records
1543 7th St
Santa Monica, CA 90401
310-393-8283
Fax: 310-393-9053
All Styles
pra@prarecords.com

Pravda
3823 N. Southport
Chicago, IL 60613
312-549-3776
Fax: 312-549-3411
pravdausa@aol.com
Alternative

Primitech
PO Box 210330
San Francisco, Ca 94121
415-824-8186
Fax: 415-824-8185

Priority
6430 Sunset Blvd. Ste. 900
Hollywood, CA 90028
213-467-0151
Rap, Rock

Prison Planet
PO Box 112666
Anchorage, AK 99511
907-345-5206
907-277-3300

Private Music
9014 Melrose Ave.
Los Angeles, CA 90069
213-859-9200
Alternative, Jazz

Private
8750 Wilshire Blvd
Beverly Hills, CA 90211
310-358-4500
Fax: 310-358-4501

Profile
740 Broadway 7th Fl.
New York, NY 10003
212-529-2600
Fax: 212-420-8216
Rap, Dance

Project-A-Bomb
2012 Garfield, Ste 21
Minneapolis, MN 55405
612-872-9773

Projekt
P.O. Box 1591
Garden Grove, CA 92642
213-344-0589
Fax: 213-344-0889
Gothic-Ambient

Prospective
P.O. Box 6425
Minneapolis, MN 55406
612-874-2418
Fax: 612-874-2430
Rock & Roll

Propulsion
176 Madison Ave, 4th Fl
New York, NY 10016
212-779-3265
Fax: 212-779-3255
proprex@aol.com

Proteen
P.O. Box 60363
Harrisburg, PA 17106-0363
717-737-2176
Alternative

Psonik
PO Box 2727
Lehigh Valley, PA 18002
215-435-1669

Punk In My Vitamins?
120 State St, #241
Olympia, WA 98501
360-705-1315

Putamayo
627 Broadway
New York, NY 10012
212-995-9400

Qbadisc
322 8th Ave, Ste 200
New York, NY 10001
212-294-2900
Fax: 212-294-7169

Quality
3500 W Olive Ave, Ste 650
Burbank, CA 91505
818-955-7020

Quango
9744 Wilshire Blvd, #305
Beverly Hills, CA 90212
310-278-8877

Quark
PO Box 7320, FDR Station
New York, NY 10150
212-838-6775
Fax: 212-8338-6775
New Age

Quicksilver/Increase
6860 Canby Ave. Ste. 118
Reseda, CA 91335
818-342-2880
Fax: 818-342-4029
Gospel, Oldies, Jazz, Rock

Queenie
PO Box 2621, Stuyvesant Station
New York, NY 10014
212-780-0092

Quixotic
GPO Box 7296
New York, NY 10116
212-979-6938

Qwest
3800 Barham Blvd.
Ste. 503
Los Angeles, CA 90068
213-874-2829
Fax: 213-874-5049
R&B, Dance, Jazz, Rock, Techno

R.E.X.
1207 17th Ave S, #103
Brentwood, TN 37212
615-370-8813
Fax: 615-370-8793

Rabbid Rabbit
1723 Aliceanna St
Baltimore, MD 21231
410-563-0351
fax: 410-327-5872

Racer
2443 Fillmore St, #202
San Francisco, CA 94115
415-931-1614
racer@racerrecords.com

Radial
PO Box 10566
Chicago, IL 60610
312-943-3486
Fax: 312-280-1606

Radical
77 Bleeker St, Ste C221
New York, NY 10012
212-475-1111
Fax: 212-475-3676

Radikal Records
1119 N. Wilson Ave.
Teaneck, NJ 07666
201-836-5116
Fax: 201-836-0661

Radioactive
156 W 56th St, 5th Fl
New York, NY 10019
212-462-4820
Fax: 212-262-0043
radioactive@radioactive.net

Rage
309 Ave. C, Ste 3C
New York, NY 10009
212-260-1779

Rage-n-Records
212 North 12th St.
Philadelphia, PA 19107
215-977-9777
Fax: 215-496-9321
All Styles

Rainforest Records Inc.
PO Box 1218
Wilsonville, OR 97070
503-682-3944
Fax: 503-682-7899

RAL/defJam
160 Varick St, 12th Fl
New York, NY 10013
212-229-5200
Fax: 212-229-5299

Rap-A-Lot
12337 Jones Rd. Ste. L221
Houston, TX 77070
713-890-5402
Rap

RAS
2447 Linden Lane
Silver Spring, MD
20910
310-588-9641
Reggae

Rattlesnake Venom Records
8833 Sunset Blvd, PHW
Los Angeles, CA 90069
310-659-9644
Rock

Rave Records
13400 W Seven Mile Rd
Detroit, MI 48325
810-540-RAVE
Fax: 810-338-0739
rave_rec@ix.netcom.com

Rawkus
65 Reade St, Ste 2B
New York, NY 10007
212-566-3160
Fax: 212-566-5866

Razor & Tie Music
214 Sullivan St, 4th Fl
New York, NY 10012
212-473-9173
Fax: 212-473-9174
razntie@aol.com
Rock, R&B

RCA
1540 Broadway
New York, NY 10036
212-930-4000
Fax: 212-930-4546

RCA
8750 Wilshire Blvd.
Beverly Hills, CA 90211
310-358-4000

RCA
1 Music Circle N.
Nashville, TN 37203
615-664-1200

React
9157 Sunset Blvd, #210
W Hollywood, CA 90069
310-550-0233
Fax: 310-550-0235
reactr@aol.com

Real
7218 1/2 Beverly Blvd
Los Angeles, CA 90036
213-933-5586

Real Music
85 Libertyship Way, #207
Sausalito, CA 94965
415-331-8273
Fax: 415-331-8278

Real World
114 W 26th St
New York, NY 10001
212-989-2929
Fax: 212-989-9791
caroline@sonicnet.com

Rebel
PO Box 3057
Roanoke, VA 24015
703-343-5355

Reckless
1401 Haight St.
San Francisco, CA 94117
415-431-8435
Fax: 415-431-2920
Psychedelic

Reckless Freak
21 VanDam St, #1
New York, NY 10013
212-229-2798

Red Boots Tunes
5503 Roosevelt Way NE
Seattle, WA 98105
206-524-1020
Fax: 415-206-524-1102
Country

Red Decibel
2217 Nicollet Ave S
Minneapolis, MN 55404
612-874-2410
Fax: 612-874-2430
reddecibel@aol.com

Red Handed
8055 Lankershim Blvd, Deck #4
N Hollywood, CA 90068
818-771-0336
Fax: 818-504-2054

Red House
PO Box 4044
St Paul, MN 55104
800-695-4687
Fax: 612-379-0945
Acoustic, Singer/Songwriter

Red Light
880 Lee St. Ste. 208
Des Plaines, IL 60016
708-297-6538
Fax: 708-297-5849
Rock, Metal

Red Rocket Records, USA
213 12th Ave E
Seattle, WA 98102
206-322-2154
Pop, Dance, techno, Progressive
Rock, Industrial

Refined
2105 Maryland Ave
Baltimore, MD 21218
301-685-8500

Relapse
P.O. Box 251
Millersville, PA 17551
717-397-9221
Fax: 717-397-9381
promo@relapse.com
Metal, Industrial, ambient &
experimental noise

Relativity
20525 Manhattan Pl.
Torrance, CA 90501
310-212-0801
Rock, Alternative

Relentless
615 Sixth Ave
Asbury Park, NJ 07712
908-528-8585

Relix
P.O. Box 92
Brooklyn, NY 11229
718-258-0009
Psychedelic, Classic Rock

Rephi
8605 Windward Cir.
Eden Prairie, MN 55344
612-941-0639
Alternative Rock
www.reynold.com

Reprise
3300 Warner Blvd
Burbank, CA 91505
818-846-9090
Fax: 818-846-8474
www.RepriseRec.com

Resist
2408 Penmar Ave
Venice, CA 90290
310-252-3911

Restless
1616 Vista Del Mar
Hollywood CA 90028
213-957-4357 x237
Fax: 213-957-4355
Alternative

Reunion
2908 Poston Ave
Nashville, TN 37202
615-320-9200

Revelation Records
P.O. Box 5232
Huntington Beach, CA 92615
714-375-4264
Fax: 714-375-4266
Alternative
www.RevHQ.com

Revolution
8900 Wilshire Blvd, Ste 200
Beverly Hills, CA 90211
310-289-5500
Fax: 310-289-5501

Rhino
10635 Santa Monica Blvd
Los Angeles, CA 90025
310-474-4778
Fax: 310-441-6575

Rif Raf Records
417 W 2nd St
Salida, CO 81202
719-539-5457
Electric

Righteous Babe
PO Box 95, Ellicott Station
Buffalo, NY 14209
716-852-8020

Ring Of Four
7043 Runnymede Dr
Montgomery, AL 36117
334-244-8974

Ringing Ear
9 Maplecrest
Newmarket, NH 03857
603-659-7516
Fax: 603-862-3563

Riot
3210 21st St
San Francisco, CA 94110
415-282-3600
Fax: 415-282-1476

Ripe & Ready
575 Bloomfield Ave
Montclair, NJ 07042
201-746-6681
Fax: 201-746-6725

Ripsaw
4545 Connecticut Ave. NW
Ste. 805
Washington DC 20008
202-362-2286
Rock & Roll, Roots, Rockabilly,
Blues

Rise
2116 Guadalupe, #210
Austin, TX 78705
512-478-7420

Rising Son
4 Van Duesenville Rd,
PO Box 657
Housatonic, MA 01236
413-528-1953
Fax: 413-528-1958
rsrhq@aol.com

Rivera
P.O. Box 1848
Orange, CA 92668
714-639-0400
Blues

River Road
60 S Dain St, 14050 Dain Plaza
Minneapolis, MN 55402
612-661-4056

Road Cone
Box 8732
Portland, OR 97207
503-238-5587

Roadrunner
536 Broadway, 4th Fl
New York, NY 10012
212-219-0077
fax: 212-219-0301
Heavy Metal, Underground,
Industrial

Robbins
30 W 21st St, 11th Fl
New York, NY 10010
212-675-4321
Fax: 212-675-4441
info@robbinsent.com

Rock Dog Records
P.O. Box 3687
Hollywood, CA 90078
213-661-0259
Rock, Alternative

Rocket
825 Eighth Ave
New York, NY 10019
212-333-8000
Fax: 212-333-6783

Rockfish
591 Manhattan Ave
Brooklyn, NY 11222
718-383-0616

Rockville
45 West 34th St., Ste. 1001
New York, NY 10001
212-630-0700

Rode Dog
2908 Poston Ave
Nashville, TN 37203
615-329-2611

ROIR
611 Broadway Ste. 411
New York, NY 10012
212-477-0563
Fax: 212-505-9908
Rock, Reggae, Blues,
Alternative

Rotten
P.O. Box 2157
Montclair, CA 91763-0657
909-624-2332
Fax: 909-624-2392
Rock, Alternative

Rounder
1 Camp St.
Cambridge, MA 02140
617-354-0700
Fax: 617-491-1970
id@rounder.com
Folk, Blues, Roots, World Music,
Bluegrass, Country

Rowdy
75 Marietta St
Atlanta, GA 30303
404-521-3277
Fax: 404-525-4480

Royalty
176 Madison Ave, 4th Fl
New York, NY 10016
212-779-0101
Fax: 212-779-3255

RRR
151 Paige St.
Lowell, MA 01852
508-454-8002
Electronic, Avant-Garde,
Experimental

Ruffhouse
129 Fayette St
Conshohocken, PA 19428
610-940-9533
Fax: 610-940-6667
Rap, Alternative

Ruling Factor
375 S. Winooski Ave. #1
Burlington, VT 05401
802-658-7458
New Acoustic, Psychedelic Pop

Running Dog
PO Box 1438
Kingson, RI 02881
401-783-8062

Ruthless Records
21860 Burbank Blvd.
Suite 100
Woodland Hills, CA 91367
818-710-0060
Fax: 818-710-1009
Rap

Rykodisc
Shetland Park, 27 Congress St
Salem, MA 01970
508-744-7678
Fax: 508-741-4506
into@rykodisc.com

Safe House
PO Box 349
W Lebanon, NH 03784
802-295-1269
Fax: 802-295-4930

**Salmon Eye/
Lethal Gospel**
P. O. Box 410099
San Francisco, CA
94141-0099
415-647-3714
Hard Rock

Saturn
1 Dormant Square
Pittsburgh, PA 15216
412-343-5222
Fax: 412-341-8164

Scat
4349 Westminister Pl
St Louis, MO 63108
314-533-3280
Fax: 314-533-1193
Alternative

Schoolkids
523 E Liberty
Ann Arbor, MI 48104
313-994-8031

Scorpio
P.O. Box A
Trenton, NJ 08691
800-782-7769
All Styles
scorpiomus@aol.com

Scotti Bros
808 Wilshire Blvd
Santa Monica, CA 90401
310-656-1100
Fax: 310-656-7430
Dance, Rock, Top 40

Scratch
317A Cambie St.
Vancouver, BC V6B 2N4
CANADA
604-687-6355
Alternative Rock

Scream
175 Homestead Dr.
Youngstown, OH 44512
216-782-3500
All Styles

Sdr
11427-48 Ave
Edmonton, AB T6H 0C9
403-437-4822

Sector 2
2116 Guadalupe, Ste 812
Austin, TX 78705
512-476-9988

Select
16 W. 22nd St., 10th Fl.
New York, NY 10010
212-691-1200
Fax: 212-691-3375
House, Rap, R&B

Setanta
PO Box 245
Hoboken, NJ 07030
201-659-7333

Seventh Heaven
PO Box 28190
Bellingham, WA 98228
206-398-2846

Shanachie
37 E. Clinton St.
Newton, NJ 07860
201-579-7763
Reggae, World Beat

Sh-Mow
PO Box 1306
Boulder, CO 80306
303-443-7703
Fax: 303-415-1624
shmowbco@aol.com

Shake
598 Victoria CP 36587
Saint Lambert, PQ, CAN
J4P 3S8
514-465-2389

Shanachie
13 Laight St, 6th Fl
New York, NY 10013
212-334-0284
Fax: 212-334-5207

Shang-Hai Killa
918 Emmet St, 1st Fl
Schenectady, NY 12307
518-347-1604

Shangri-La
1916 Madison Ave
Memphis, TN 38104
901-274-1916

RELEASING AN INDEPENDENT RECORD

Shaolin
PO Box 58547
Salt Lake City, UT 84158
801-595-1123
Fax: 801-328-2060

Shimmy Disc/Koko Pop
JAF Box 1187
New York, NY 10116
212-675-0922
Hardcore, Avant Garde,
Alternative

Shotput
3155 Roswell Rd, Ste 330
Atlanta, GA 30305
404-237-5757
Fax: 404-237-5739
shotputrec@aol.com

Shrapnel
PO Box P
Novato, CA 94948
415-898-5046

Shredder
75 Plum St Ln Ste. 3
San Rafael, CA 94901
415-243-0599
Punk, alternative

Skene! Records
P.O. Box 4522
St. Paul, MN 55104
612-824-2270
Rock, Punk

Signet
322 Eighth Ave, Ste 200
New York, NY 10001
212-294-2900
Fax: 212-294-7169

Silas
70 Universal City Plaza
Universal City, CA 91608
818-777-4504

Silent Records
340 Bryant St, 3rd Fl E
San Francisco, CA 94107
415-957-1320
Fax: 415-957-0779
www.silent.org

Silva Screen
1600 Broadway, Ste 910
New York, NY 10019
212-757-1616

Silvergirl
PO Box 161024
San Diego, CA 92176
619-282-9843

Silvertone
137-139 W. 25th St.
New York, NY 10001
212-727-0016
Fax: 212-645-3783
Alternative, Blues Reissues, Pop

Silver Wave
P.O. Box 7943
Boulder, CO 80306
303-443-5617
Fax: 303-443-0877
New Age, Contemporary, Jazz,
World
www.silverwave.com

Simple Machines
PO Box 10290
Arlington, VA 22210
703-276-0680
Fax: 703-276-2618
www.southern.com/SMR/

Sin Klub
PO Box 2507
Toledo, OH 43606
419-475-1189

Sire
75 Rockefeller Plaza, 21st Fl.
New York, NY 10019
212-275-4560
Fax: 212-581-6416

Skillet
PO Box 8291
Ann Arbor, MI 48107
313-994-9339

Skin Graft
PO Box 257546
Chicago, IL 60625
312-989-9865
Fax: 312-989-9202

Skinnie Girl
120 NE State, Ste 1200
Olympia, WA 98501
360-709-9445
Fax: 360-709-9446
jbutter24@aol.com

Skoda
15 Ninth St NE
Washington, DC 20002
202-547-8006

The Skull Duggery Label
77 Scituate Ave.
Scituate, MA 02066
617-545-1533

Skunk Entertainment
2116 Williamsbridge Rd, Ste 110
Bronx, NY 10461
212-576-8876

Sky
3991 Royal Drive NW
Kennesaw, GA 30339
404-419-1414
Fax: 404-419-1230
Alternative

Slash
PO Box 48888
Los Angeles, CA 90048
213-937-4660
213-937-7277
askslash@aol.com
Alternative, Zydeco

Slot
915 Cole St, Box 308
San Francisco, CA 94117
415-864-8540
Fax: 415-552-6193

Slumberland
PO Box 14731
Berkeley, CA 94712
510-654-6124

smae
740 Broadway
New York, NY 10003
212-529-2600

Smart
PO Box 48914, #390
Los Angeles, CA 90048
213-655-2750
Fax: 213-655-2750

Smashing
PO Box 87618
Carol Steam, IL 60188
708-545-2220

Smithsonian/Folkways
Office Of Folklife Programs
955 L'Enfant Plaza
Ste. 2600
Washington, DC 20560
202-287-3251
All Styles

The SOAR Corporations
5200 Constitution Ave. NE
Albuquerque, NM 87110
505-268-6110
Fax: 505-268-0237

Soh/Brave
Entertainment Group
37 Courrier Pl.
Rutherford, NJ 07070
201-783-9224

Solar
5152 Sepulveda Blvd., Ste. 197
Sherman Oaks, CA 91401
213-461-0390
R&B, Rap

Soleilmoon
Box 83296
Portland, OR 97283
503-335-0706
soleilmoon@aol.com
Ambient, Electronic

Songhai Empire
PO Box 4236, Rockefeller
Center Station
New York, NY 10001
718-365-6105

Sonic Records
136 Oakwood Drive, #H
Winston-Salem, NC 27103
910-773-0083
Fax: 910-773-0510
Rock
www.sonicrecords.com

Sonic
26 W 17th St, Ste 502
New York, NY 10011
212-727-1360

Sonic
PO Box 1029
Lake Arrowhead, CA 92352
909-337-7442

**Sonic Atmospheres/
Sonic Edge**
4620 W. Magnolia Blvd.
Burbank, CA 91505
818-558-6236
New Age, Jazz
www.enterprisestudio.com

Sonic Bubblegum
PO Box 35504
Brighton, MA 02135
617-782-1527
mhibarge@chipcom.com

Sonic Images Records
P.O. Box 691626
W Hollywood, CA 90069
213-650-1000
Fax: 213-650-1016
Adult Alternative
www.sonicimages.com

Sonic Underground
11526 Burbank Blvd
N Hollywood, CA 91601
800-34 SONIC

Sony
1121 Leslie St
North York, ONT, CAN
M3C 2J9
416-391-3311
Fax: 416-447-6973

Sony
550 Madison Ave, 31st Fl
New York, NY 10022
212-833-8000
Fax: 212-833-5780
www.sony.com

Sound Of Music
320 Brook Rd
Richmond, VA 23220
804-788-0607

Southern Studios
3900 N Claremont Ave, 3rd Fl
Chicago, IL 60618
312-463-3797
Fax: 312-463-3246

Spanish Fly
2217 Nicollet Ave S
Minneapolis, MN 55404
612-874-2400
Fax: 612-874-2430

Spenguy
PO Box 311147
Jamaica, NY 11431
718-341-0286
Fax: 718-481-7734

spinArt
P.O. Box 1798
New York, NY 10156-1798
212-343-9644
Fax: 212-343-1970
spinartrec@aol.com

Spirit
PO Box 170195
San Francisco, CA 94117
415-252-1139

Spirit of Orr
186 Lincoln St
Boston, MA 02111
617-542-2929
Fax: 617-524-2421

Spongebath
101 N Maple St
Murfreesboro, TN 37130
615-896-0770

Spotted Dog
PO Box 40-0041
Brooklyn, NY 11240
718-390-7951
spottedtom2aol.com

Spotty Boy
PO Box 4231
Richmond, VA 23220
804-233-9315

Square
P.O. Box 1926
Harvard Sq. Station
Cambridge, MA 02238
617-492-5398
Fax: 617-492-6074
R&B, Jazz, Ska, Dance, Industrial

Squid Hell
21 Union Ave #1
Boston, MA 02130
617-522-8814
Fax: 617-552-8814

SST
P.O. Box 1
Lawndale, CA 90260
310-430-7687
Fax: 310-430-7286
Alternative

St Francis
PO Box 95587
Seattle, WA 98145
206-634-1707
Fax: 206-634-3740

Stardog
825 Eighth Ave
New York, NY 10019
212-333-8000
Fax: 212-603-7654

Stash
140 W. 22nd St., 12th Fl.
New York, NY 10011
212-243-4321
Jazz, Blues

Steam
741 Piedmont Ave, Ste 300
Atlanta, GA 30308
404-873-4894

Step One
1300 Division St, Ste 304
Nashville, TN 37203
615-255-3009

StepSun
16 W 22nd St, Fl 10
New York, NY 10011
212-353-2900
Fax: 212-353-0201

Stern's
598 Broadway
New York, NY 10012
212-925-1648
Fax: 212-925-1689

Stickshift
63 Pitt St, #5R
New York, NY 10002
212-260-3389
Fax: 212-260-3424

Stony Plain
PO Box 861
Edmonton, ALB, CAN T5J 2L2
403-468-6423

Streetlife
808 Wilshire Blvd
Santa Monica, CA 90401
310-656-1100
Fax: 310-656-7430

Strictly Hype
9209 Ivanhoe St
Schiller Park, IL 60176
708-678-1271
Fax: 708-678-1272

Strictly Rhythm
920 Broadway, Ste 1403
New York, NY 10010
212-254-2400

Strugglebaby
2612 Erie Ave, PO Box 8385
Cincinnati, OH 45208
513-871-1500
Fax: 513-871-1510

Subharmonic
180 Varick St, Ste 1400
New York, NY 10014
212-675-7168

Sub Pop
1932 1st Ave. #1103
Seattle, WA 98101
206-441-8441
Alternative, Hard Rock,
Underground
http://www.subpop.com/

Subterranean
P.O. Box 2530
Berkeley, CA 94702
415-821-5880
Strange

Suburbian Dance Music
PO Box 47
West Creek, NJ 08092
609-294-2527
Fax: 609-296-1805

Sugar Free
PO Box 14166
Chicago, IL 60614
312-528-7080
voneggers@aol.com

Sugar Hill
P.O. Box 55300
Duke Station
Durham, NC 27717
919-489-4349
Fax: 919-489-6080
Bluegrass, Folk,
Singer/Songwriter

Sugar Hill
96 West St.
Englewood, NJ 07631
201-569-5170
Rap, R&B, Funk

Sumertone
P.O. Box 22184
San Francisco, CA 94122
415-759-8100
Jazz, Blues
www.merlsaunders.com

Summershine
PO Box 23392
Seattle, WA 98102
206-322-9119
Fax: 206-322-9119
summershine@subpop.com

Summerville
PO Box 2225, Stuyvesant Station
New York, NY 10009
212-780-9821
Fax: 212-780-9821

Sun
3106 Belmont Blvd
Nashville, TN 37212
615-385-1960

Sun Red Sun
PO Box 323
Dobbs Ferry, NY 10522
914-693-8543

Sundazed
PO Box 85
Coxsackie, NY 12051
518-731-6262

Sunsplash
PO Box 7778
Silver Spring, MD 20907
301-434-6958
Fax: 301-434-3056

Superjazzfunkandfolk
1338 Lexington Ave
North Tonawanda, NY 14120
716-694-0979

Surf
1427 N County Rd 900 E
Indianapolis, IN 46234
317-271-0767

Susstone
PO Box 6425
Minneapolis, MN 55406
612-874-2418
Fax: 612-874-2430

Swallow
PO Drawer 10
Ville Platte, LA 70586
318-363-2139

Sweet Pea
PO Box 408967
Chicago, IL 60640
312-275-4464

Swizzle
PO Box 684586
Austin, TX 78768
512-444-2202
swankrec@aol.com

T.E.C. Tones
PO Box 1477
Hoboken, NJ 07030
201-420-0238
Fax:201-420-6494
Alternative, Esoteric

T.O.N.
6201 Sunset Blvd, #77
Hollywood, CA 90028
213-467-7995
Fax: 213-467-7737

T.S.M.B.
11 Church Road
Owings Mills, MD 21117
800-987-8762
All Styles

Taang!
706 Pismo Court
San Diego, CA 92109
619-488-5950
Fax: 619-488-5156

TAG
14 E. 60th St, 8th Fl.
New York, NY 10022
212-508-5450
Fax: 212-593-7663

Taliesin
12918 Burbank Blvd, #1
Sherman Oaks, CA 91401
818-781-5701

Tangible
1745 Merrick Ave,#4
Merrick, NY 11566
516-379-5820

Tattoo
365 Great Circle Rd
Nashville, TN 37228
615-742-6993

Technique Records
P.O. Box 20034
Waco, TX 76702
817-751-7797
R&B

Teen Beat
PO Box 3265
Arlington, VA 20003
703-358-9382
Fax: 703-358-9044
www.erols.com/teenbeat

Teen Rebel
8625 NW Eighth St, Ste 402
Miami, FL 33126
305-460-8055

Telarc
23307 Commerce Park Rd.
Cleveland, OH 44122
216-464-2313
Fax: 212-360-9663
Jazz

Tellus
596 Broadway, Ste 602
New York, NY 10012
212-431-1130

Telstar
PO Box 1123
Hoboken, NJ 07030
201-659-2461
Fax: 201-653-9189

Texas Hotel
PO Box 72449
Davis, CA 95617
916-756-8959
Fax: 916-756-9624

Theologian
PO Box 1070
Hermosa Beach, CA 90254
310-379-3137
Fax: 310-798-4697

Thick
1013 W Webster ,#7
Chicago, IL 60614
312-244-0044

Thick Freshie
PO Box 465
Vestal, NY 13851
607-729-5487

Third Eye
1653 McLendon Ave
Atlanta, GA 30307
404-377-1919
thirdeye@atlanta.com

Third Gear
PO Box 1886
Royal Oak, MI 48068
810-548-8683
Fax: 810-398-5890
herv@rust.net

Thirsty Ear
274 Madison Ave., Ste. 804
New York NY 10016
212-889-9595
Fax: 212-889-3641
thirstye@aol.com
Alternative

Threshold
PO Box 451232
Miami, FL 33245
305-285-7793
envelope@aol.com

Thrill Jockey
P.O. Box 1527,
Peter Stuyvesant Station
New York, NY 10009
212-254-0355
Rock

Thump
3101 Pomona Blvd
Pomona, CA 91768
909-595-2144

Tim/Kerr
P.O. Box 42423
Portland, OR 97242
503-236-5428
Fax: 503-236-1056
tkrec@teleport.com
Alternative

Time Bomb
31652 Second Ave
Laguna Beach, CA 92677
714-376-2651

Tommy Boy
902 Broadway, 13th Fl.
New York, NY 10010
212-388-8300
Fax: 212-388-8400
tboy@tommyboy.mhs.
compuserve.com
Rap, Dance

Tone Casualties
1258 N Highland Ave
Los Angeles, CA 90038
213-463-0145
Fax: 213-463-0804

Tone-Cool
129 Parker St
Newton, MA 02159
617-956-1718

Too Damn Talented
353 Main St, Fl 2
Ridgefield Park, NJ 07660
201-641-8899

Tooth And Nail
PO Box 12698
Seattle, WA 98111
206-382-4910
Fax: 206-382-4909
toothlnail@aol.com

Topless
150 W 28th St, Ste 1103A
New York, NY 10001
212-807-7683

TopNotch
PO Box 1515
Sanibel Island, FL 33957
941-982-1515
Fax: 941-472-5033

Touch And Go
P.O. Box 25520
Chicago, IL 60625
312-388-8888
Fax: 312-388-3888
Alternative, Hardcore,
Underground

Touchwood
1650 Broadway, Ste 1210
New York, NY 10019
212-977-7800
Fax: 212-977-7963

Tourmaline Music
894 Mayville Rd
Bethel, ME 04217
207-824-3246
Alternative, Avant garde

Trance Syndicate
P.O. Box 49771
Austin, TX 78765
512-454-3265
Fax: 512-454-3287
Alternative

Trauma Records
15206 Ventura Blvd.
Suite 200
Sherman Oaks, CA 91403
818-382-2515
Fax: 818-990-2038

Treat & Release
1234 Mariposa Ave
San Francisco, CA 94107
415-487-3606
Fax: 415-487-3612
Alternative

TRG/Twin Tone
2217 Nicollet Ave S
Minneapolis, MN 55404
612-874-2400
Fax: 612-874-2430
www.tt.net/trg

Triad
7578 Market Place Dr
Eden Prairie, MN 55344
612-942-5775

Tried & True
PO Box 39
Austin, TX 78767
512-477-0036
Fax: 512-477-0095
jerryjeff@jerryjeff.com

Triloka

306 Catron
Santa Fe, NM 87510
505-820-2833
Fax: 505-820-2834
Jazz, World Beat

Trip
79 Franklin St, 3rd Fl
New York, NY 10013
212-274-0738

Triple XXX
P.O. Box 862529
Los Angeles, CA 90086-2529
213-221-2204
Fax: 213-221-2778
Alternative, Rock

Trippy
31 Oxford Lane
Harriman, NY 10926
201-646-4492

Tristar
79 Fifth Ave
New York, NY 10003
212-337-5400
Fax: 212-337-5433

Trix
106 W 71st St
New York, NY 10023
212-873-2020
Fax: 212-877-0407

Trixie
PO Box 379373
Chicago, IL 60637
312-496-6716

True North
151 John St. Ste. 508
Toronto, ONT M5V 2T2
CANADA
416-596-8696
Rock
trunorth@inforamp.com

Trumpeter
5660 E Virginia Beach Blvd,
Ste 103
Norfolk, VA 23502
804-455-8454

Tuff City
200 W 72nd St, Ste 56
New York, NY 10023
212-721-7215

Turdurcken
518 Bordeaux
New Orleans, LA 70115
504-895-3494
Fax: 504-895-3072

Turquoise Records Inc.
Hwy 931 P.O. Box 947
Whitesburg, KY 41858
Fax: 606-633-0485
Bluegrass, Folk

TVT
23 E. 4th St.
New York, NY 10003
212-979-6410
212-979-6489
Alternative

Tyscot
3532 N. Keystone Ave
Indianapolis, IN 46218
317-926-6271
Gospel

UltraModern
PO Box 6425
Minneapolis, MN 55406
612-874-2418
Fax: 612-874-2430

Unclean Records
P.O. Box 49737
Austin, TX 78765
512-452-9044
Fax: 512-452-9364
Alternative

Under Cover
622 Broadway, #3B
New York, NY 10012
212-777-2661

The Union Label
P.O. Box 370
Nevada City, CA 95959
800-869-0658
Jazz, Experimental

Unite
PO Box 191
Bronx, NY 10470
718-994-0329

Unity
207 Ashland Ave
Santa Monica, CA 90405
310-581-2700

Universal
1755 Broadway
New York, NY 10019
212-373-0600
Fax: 212-373-0660

Unkulunkie
834B Vallejo St
San Francisco, CA 91433
415-397-4957

Up
PO Box 21328
Seattle, WA 98111
206-441-8277

Upside Out
14755 Ventura Blvd, Ste 1-607
Sherman Oaks, CA 91403
818-990-3586

Upstart
1 Camp St
Cambridge, MA 02140
617-354-0700
Fax: 617-491-1970
id@rounder.com

Upstart
700 Rockmead Dr, Ste 246
Kingwood, TX 77339
713-359-2044

Urge
208 S W First Ave, Ste 220
Portland, OR 97204
503-226-8196
Fax: 503-227-3953

Us
535 Fifth Ave, Fl 35
New York, NY 10017
212-682-8403

Valley Vue
555 Commercial Rd, Ste 10
Palm Springs, CA 92262
619-778-6510

Vanguard
1299 Ocean Ave. Ste. 800
Santa Monica, CA 90401
310-451-5727
Fax: 310-394-4148
vangardrec@aol.com
Folk, Blues, Jazz

Varese Sarabande
11846 Ventura Blvd, Ste 130
Studio City, CA 91604
818-753-4143

Varrick
1 Camp St.
Cambridge, MA 02140
617-354-0700
Blues
www.rounder.com

VAR International
Box 2392
Woburn, MA 01888
617-935-5386

Venture Beyond Records
P.O. Box 3662
Santa Rosa, CA 95402-3662
707-528-8695
Fax: 707-528-8694
Alternative

Verve
825 Eighth Ave
New York, NY 10019
212-333-8000
Fax: 212-888-8194

Viceroy Records Music
547 W 27 St, 6Fl
New York, NY 10001
212-465-2357
Blues, Roots Rock

Victo
C.P. 460
Victoriaville, PQ, CAN G6P 6T3
819-752-7912
Fax: 819-758-4370

Victory Music
8455 Beverly Blvd. 6th Fl.
Los Angeles, CA 90048
213-655-6844
Fax: 213-655-6814

Victory
PO Box 146546
Chicago, IL 60614
312-666-8661
Fax: 312-666-8665
victoryrex@aol.com

Vinyl Communications
P.O. Box 8623
Chula Vista, CA 91912
619-476-0909
www.vinylcomm.com

Vinyl Solution USA
P.O. Box 6601
San Mateo, CA 94403
415-571-0440
Fax: 415-571-0492
All Styles

Vinylmania
60 Carmine St.
New York, NY 10014
212-924-7223
House

Virgin
30 W. 21st St., 11th Fl.
New York NY 10010
212-463-0980

Virgin
338 N. Foote Hill Rd.
Beverly Hills, CA 90210
213-278-1181
Fax: 310-278-6231

Virgin
514 Jarvis St
Toronto, ONT, CAN M4Y 2H6
416-961-8863
Fax: 416-961-8950

Vision Records
13385 West Dixie Highway
North Miami, FL 33161
305-893-9191
All Styles

Vital
PO Box 20247
New York, NY 10023
212-691-4041

Voiceprint
P.O. Box 32827
Kansas City, MO 64111
816-561-0723
Old-Style Progressive, No Heavy
Metal or Thrash

Void Ware
3023 N Clark St, PO Box 719
Chicago, IL 60657
312-935-7534

VP
89-05 138th St
Jamaica, NY 11435
718-291-7058

W.A.R.
2401 Broadway
Boulder, CO 80304
303-440-0666
Fax: 303-447-2484
warinfo@war.com

Wagon Train
3712 Old Philadelphia Plaza
Bethlehem, PA 18017
610-868-3330
Fax: 610-868-3339

Waldoxy
2023 W Northside Dr
Jackson, MS 39213
601-982-4522
Fax: 601-982-4528

Walk Away
462 Broadway, Ste 530
New York, NY 10013
212-274-0761
Fax: 212-274-0876
lodchet@aol.com

Walt
89 Fairview Ave
Port Washington, NY 11050
516-944-3345

Warhead
1417 Oak St
Kingsport, TN 37660
423-245-7101
Fax: 423-245-4545
warhead@ilinkgn.net

Warlock
122 E 25th St, Fl 6
New York, NY 10010
212-673-2700
Fax: 212-677-4443
Rap, Dance, R&B, Hip-Hop

Warner Bros./Reprise
3300 Warner Blvd.
Burbank, CA 91505
818-846-9090
Fax: 818-846-8474

Warner Bros.
75 Rockefeller Plaza
New York, NY 10019
212-275-4938
Fax: 212-315-1947

Warner Bros.
1815 Division St.
Nashville, TN 37203
615-748-8000

Warner
1810 Birchmount Rd
Scarborough, ONT, CAN
M1P 2H7
416-291-2515
Fax: 416-291-6044

Wasteland
156 W 56th St, 5th Fl
New York, NY 10019
212-462-4820
Fax: 212-262-0043

Water Lily Acoustics
PO Box 91448
Santa Barbara, CA 93190
805-968-8188

Waterbug
PO Box 6605
Evanston, IL 60204
708-332-1583

Watermelon
PO Box 402088
Austin, TX 78704
512-472-6192
Fax: 512-472-6249

Waveform
PO Box 1310
Mill Valley, CA 94942
415-383-8886
Fax: 512-383-8488
www.obsolete.com/waveform

Way Cool Music
16501 Pacific Coast Hwy, Ste100
Sunset Beach, CA 90742
310-592-6157
Fax: 310-592-6160

Way To Go
6671 Sunset Blvd
Hollywood, CA 90028
213-466-1661

Weasel Disc
1459 18th St, #140
San Francisco, CA 94107
415-621-3981

Weg
3635 Blanding Blvd
Jacksonville, FL 32210
904-779-2887

Whirligig
2111 University Blvd
Tuscaloosa, AL 35401
205-758-0690

Whr
111 Edgewood Blvd, #2
Lansing, MI 48911
517-393-9777

Wicked Disc
38 Everett St
Allston, MA 02134
617-254-1666
Fax: 617-254-1085
staff@wickeddisc.com

Widely Distributed
1412 W. Touhy
Chicago, IL 60626
312-465-2558
Fax: 312-465-2558

Wifflefist
PO Box 33561
Raleigh, NC 27636
919-821-0498
Fax: 919-833-8536
michaelp@alienskin.com

Wild Pitch
291 W 29th St 8th Floor
New York, NY 10001
212-594-5050
Fax: 212-268-4968
Rap, Rock

Wild West
8127 Melrose Ave, Ste 2
Los Angeles, CA 90046
213-651-9384
Fax: 213-651-1459

Wildchild
2301 Crain Hwy
Upper Marlboro, MD 20774
301-627-0525
Fax: 301-627-4136

Will
1202 E Pike, Ste 511
Seattle, WA 98122
206-329-5396
Fax: 206-329-5397

Windham Hill
P.O. Box 9388
Stanford, CA 94309
415-329-0647
Fax: 415-329-1512
New Age, Folk

Windmark
4924 Shell Rd
Virginia Beach, VA 23455
804-464-4924
Fax: 804-464-1773

Winner
PO Box 151095
San Rafael, CA 94915
415-453-5134

Winter Harvest
PO Box 60884
Nashville, TN 37206
615-227-7770

WMO
PO Box 322
Alta Loma, CA 91701
909-989-3628
Fax: 909-989-3628
wm@interserv.com

WORK
2100 Colorado Ave
Los Angeles, CA 90404
310-449-2666
Fax: 310-449-2095

World Of Hurt
6 Greene St. 2nd Fl.
New York, NY 10013
212-226-9194
Alternative, Hard Rock

World Domination
3575 Cahuenga Blvd. W.
Ste. 450
Los Angeles CA 90068
213-850-0254
Fax: 213-874-6246
Alternative
dominate@netvoyage.com

World One
18315 W. McNichols
Detroit, MI 48219
313-534-7070

Worry Bird Disk
PO Box 95485
Atlanta, GA 30347
770-270-5513
userwww.service.emory.edu/
jkraft/woe.html

WTG
2100 Colorado Ave.
Santa Monica, CA 90404
310-449-2100
All Styles

Xemu
45 Rockefeller Plaza, Ste 900
New York, NY 10111
212-787-5698
Fax: 212-841-5788

Xenofile
43 Beaver Brook Rd
Danbury, CT 06810
203-730-0333
Fax: 203-730-0345
www.grnlinnet.com

Y
PO Box 20241
Seattle, WA 98102
206-324-1710
fax: 206-324-3285
y.records@prostar.com

Yabyum
8255 Beverly Blvd
Los Angeles, CA 90048
213-655-6400

Yazoo
13 Laight St, 6th Fl
New York, NY 10013
212-334-0284
Fax: 212-334-5207

Yesha
PO Box 31725
Charlotte, NC 28231
704-377-6500
Fax: 704-377-6500

Yum
318 E 34St, Fl 6
New York, NY 10016
212-889-3656

Zero Hour
14 W 23rd St., 4th Fl
New York, NY 10010
212-337-3200
Fax: 212-337-3701
www.zerohour.com

Zimbob
PO Box 2421
Champaign, IL 61825
217-344-6878

Zulu
1869 W. 4th Ave.
Vancouver, BC V6J 1M4
CANADA
604-738-3232
Blues, Dance, Hardcore

Sample Contracts

Here are a few sample contracts that you can use as a reference source. These are only for reference! Don't just fill in the blanks and sign your friend's band to long-term deal. Always check with an attorney before entering into any music-related contract.

Recording Contract

The first is a standard, short-form (?!) recording contract, the type you'd get from a large independent label. Royalties in deals such as these could range anywhere from 11% to 15%, depending on the band's past history or how badly the label wants the band. Any money that is given to the band up front for recording purposes must be recouped before the band gets paid any royalties. In a deal such as this, the label gets the rights to the records in perpetuity, forever. This is not applicable to many record deals, including licensing, where a specific time period is agreed upon (the label may get to release the record for ten years, for example). At the independent level, in many cases a band may already have a record recorded and is looking for someone (your label) to put it out. It is not appropriate to take the rights to their recording forever simply because you're paying to manufacture it. There should be a definite time limit agreed upon, at which point all rights in the recording would revert back to the band. Check out some of the language and terms in this contract; this is just for your reference, do not use it sign your neighbor's band to a long-term record deal! You should always consult a music attorney before signing any contracts. The small amount of money you pay the lawyer to look at your agreement may save you a lot of money and headaches in the long term.

Management Contract

The second contract is a basic artist management agreement. Percentages in a management deal range between 15% and 25%, depending on the success of the band at the time of the agreement and the stature of the manager. Normally, the bigger the band is, the lower the manager's cut, because the manager is taking less of a risk. The manager knows he or she will make money. If the band is unknown and unproven, a manager may ask for a larger share of the earnings, because there is a big chance that he or she won't see a dime. Again, this is just for your reference, don't use this actual contract. Get an attorney.

BLISTERLIP RECORDS
1234 Scummyside Street
Hollywood, California 90036

Dated: _____

Contract Number: _____

Mr. Mick
Mr. Keith
Mr. William
Mr. Charlie
collectively p/k/a "Rolling Stones"
c/o Big Boy Mgmnt.
Gower Street
London

Gentlemen:

The following shall constitute your and our agreement with respect to your exclusively recording for us during the term of this contract master recordings embodying your performances. As used herein, the term "Master" shall refer to any master recording embodying your performances recorded during the Term (hereinafter defined).

1. (a) As used herein, the "Term" shall refer collectively to the first Contract Period, which shall commence as of the date hereof and continue until terminated as provided hereinbelow, and, at our election, all renewal Contract Periods as hereinafter provided. Notwithstanding anything to the contrary contained in this agreement, the Term shall expire no later than six (6) months after you fulfill your Recording Commitment (as such term is defined paragraph 2(a) hereof) for the last Contract Period provided for herein.

(b) You hereby grant us six (6) separate options, each to renew the Term for additional Contract Periods, with all such additional Contract Periods to be upon the same terms and conditions as are applicable to the first Contract Period, except as provided for in paragraph 19 below. Each such renewal Contract Periods shall sometimes hereinafter be called a "renewal" Contract Period. The renewal Contract Periods shall run consecutively and begin at the expiration of the previous Contract Period.

(c) Each Contract Period shall not expire until the Option Date for such Contract Period. The "Option Date" for a particular Contract Period shall be the later of (a) its scheduled anniversary date (i.e., twelve [12] months); or (b) the date six (6) months following the date of our initial release in the United States of the Required LP to be delivered by you in fulfillment of your recording commitment for such Contract Period. We shall have until the Option Date of the applicable Contract Period to exercise our option hereunder, or refrain therefrom. We shall notify you of our intention to exercise by specific written notice to you. In the event that we do not, prior to the Option Date of the current Contract Period, exercise our option, the Term shall continue regardless. However, notwithstanding the foregoing, you, at any time after such Option Date, shall have the right to send us written notice of your desire to terminate the Term (such notice shall hereinafter be called the "Renewal Request"). If we do not exercise our option in writing within fourteen (14) days after our receipt of a Renewal Request, the Term shall expire.

(d) The territory covered by this agreement shall be the world (the "Territory" herein).

page 1 of 13

2. (a) During the first Contract Period hereof, you shall record and deliver to us one (1) LP. The Masters which you are required to record hereunder during the first Contract Period, in accordance with the foregoing, are hereinafter sometimes referred to as your "Recording Commitment" for the first Contract Period. Your Recording Commitment for the first Contract Period shall be fulfilled at such time as all Masters comprising your Recording Commitment for the first Contract Period shall have been recorded, mastered and delivered to us in all respects in accordance with the provisions hereinbelow.

(b) Masters shall not be deemed to be delivered hereunder unless and until such time as the following items have been delivered to and have been accepted by one (1) of our authorized employees at the address for purposes of serving notices on us or at such other location as we may advise you from time to time: (1) fully mixed, equalized, edited and sequenced Master(s), technically and commercially satisfactory to us, in our reasonable business judgement, for our manufacture and sale of Records, clearly marked to identify you as the recording artist, the title(s) of the composition(s), recording date(s) and all original and duplicate Masters of the material recorded; (2) all elements necessary for us to have complete "label copy" information, typewritten in a form satisfactory to us, listing the title, timing, composer(s), publisher(s), administrator(s), and performing rights society(ies) of each Master; (3) all "liner notes," approved artwork and technical and artistic credits; (4) all "sideman" and any other third party clearances; and (5) the lyrics for each composition embodied in a Master, if any.

(c) Notwithstanding anything to the contrary contained herein, no later than four (4) months after the date of the commencement of the first Contract Period, you shall deliver to us the Required LP to be recorded and delivered by you during the first Contract Period hereof. Each Master shall embody your performance as the sole featured artist of a single selection previously unrecorded by you and shall be recorded in its entirety at a recording studio or studios. Each LP produced hereunder shall embody no less than eight (8) musical compositions (subject to the maximum mechanical royalties payable pursuant to paragraph 8 below) mutually designated by you and us. Recording sessions for the Masters hereunder shall be conducted by you at such recording studios as shall be mutually designated by you and us. The individual producer of the Masters shall also be mutually designated by you and us.

(d) Each Master shall be subject to our approval as technically satisfactory and commercially satisfactory for the manufacture and sale of phonograph records. Any master recording which is not produced, recorded or delivered in all respects in compliance with the terms and provisions hereof shall not, unless we otherwise consent in writing or commercially release such master recording, apply toward the fulfillment of your Recording Commitment and, upon our request, you shall record or re-record any such master recording until it is in such compliance.

(e) Notwithstanding anything to the contrary contained herein, we shall have the option, at our sole discretion, to require you to record Masters to be embodied on an album at live concerts or other live performances (hereinafter referred to as a "Live LP") any time, during the Term. In the event we shall so require you to record such Live LP, then (a) such Live LP shall be recorded and delivered to us hereunder no later than one hundred eighty (180) days after our request therefor; (b) the Live LP shall be in addition to and shall not apply toward the fulfillment of your recording commitment hereunder; (c) the recording fund in respect of the Live LP shall be an amount equal to two-thirds (2/3) of the amount of the recording fund specified in paragraph 3(b), below, in respect of the Required LP recorded and delivered by you hereunder immediately prior to our request that you record the Live LP; and (d) the royalty payable to you in connection with the Live LP and the Masters embodied thereon shall be reduced, computed and paid in accordance with the provisions of paragraph 6 below.

(f) (i) Nowithstanding anything to the contrary contained herein, during the term hereof, we shall have the right, but not the obligation, to request you to deliver to us and you shall deliver to us not less than two (2) Masters featuring Artist's performances (each of such Masters is hereinafter referred to individually as a "New Greatest Hits Master" and collectively as the "New Greatest Hits Masters") to be included in a "New Greatest Hits LP" (hereinafter defined). As used herein, the term "New Greatest Hits LP" shall refer to a Greatest Hits LP containing one or both of the New Greatest Hits Masters. Each New Greatest Hits Master shall (A) embody Artist's performances of a musical composition not theretofore recorded by Artist; (B) subject to Artist's prior professional commitments, be delivered to us no later than ninety (90) days after our request therefor; and (C) be in addition to and, accordingly, shall not be deemed delivered in any manner in satisfaction of your Delivery Commitment hereunder.

(ii) We shall pay for the costs of recording each New Greatest Hits Master an amount (the "New Greatest Hits Masters Fund") equal to fifteen percent (15%) of the royalty advance (specified in Schedule 3(b)(ii) below) applicable to the last LP delivered by you hereunder. All of the provisions hereof which apply to the administration of recording funds for Required LPs shall also apply to the New Greatest Hits Masters Fund.

3. (a) No recording sessions shall be commenced hereunder nor shall any commitments be made or costs incurred in connection therewith unless and until a proposed recording budget for the Masters to be recorded at such sessions shall have been submitted by you in writing and approved in writing by one of our authorized employees. We shall pay the Recording Costs of the Masters recorded at recording sessions conducted hereunder in accordance with the terms and provisions hereof, in an amount not in excess of the approved recording budget therefor. All Recording Costs shall be fully recoupable from any royalties at any time payable to you or your respective affiliates, as shall any monies for any reason paid by us to or on your behalf. You agree that such Recording Costs shall not for any reason exceed the amount of the applicable Recording Fund set forth below. In the event we shall pay or incur Recording Costs in excess of the Recording Fund, we shall deduct the amount thereof from any monies payable to you hereunder. In the event that the amount so paid or incurred by us in excess of the Recording Fund shall exceed the amount of monies otherwise payable to you hereunder or in the event we shall not so deduct any such amounts paid or incurred by us, you shall, upon our demand, promptly reimburse us for such payments. In the event you shall fail so to reimburse us or we shall fail to make such demand, we shall, in addition to all of our other rights or remedies which we may have in such event, have the right to deduct an amount equal to such payments from any and all monies payable by us to you or your respective affiliates hereunder.

(b) (i) We hereby allocate, for Masters sufficient to constitute the Required LP to be recorded during the first Contract Period an aggregate Recording Fund equal to five thousand dollars ($3,000.00).

(ii) We hereby allocate for Masters sufficient to constitute each Required LP hereunder in the renewal Contract Periods, an aggregate Recording Fund equal to sixty-five percent (65%) of the royalties earned by you in respect of USNRC Sales of records embodying the immediately preceding Required LP, as reported on the most recent accounting statement to you, subject to the minimums and maximums set forth below:

CONTRACT PERIOD	PRODUCT	RECORDING FUND MINIMUM	MAXIMUM
second	One (1) LP	$ 4,000	$20,000
third	One (1) LP	$ 5,000	$25,000
fourth	One (1) LP	$ 6,000	$30,000
fifth	One (1) LP	$ 7,000	$45,000
sixth	One (1) LP	$ 8,000	$60,000

page 3 of 13

---

4.   All master recordings recorded by you hereunder during the Term, from the inception of the recording thereof, and all phonograph records and other reproductions made therefrom, together with the performances embodied therein and all copyrights therein and thereto, and all renewals and extensions thereof, shall be our sole property in perpetuity throughout the Territory, free of any claims whatsoever by you or any other person, firm or corporation. In this regard, you and all other persons rendering services in connection with such master recordings shall be our employees for hire. Without limiting the foregoing, we and our designees shall have the perpetual and exclusive right throughout the Territory to manufacture, distribute, exploit and publicly perform Records, AV Devices, or other reproductions embodying all or any part of any of the Masters by any method or manner now or hereafter known, and to sell, lease, license, exploit, transfer or otherwise deal in or alter the same under any trademarks, trade names and labels.

5.   We and/or our designees shall have the right in perpetuity throughout the Territory, exclusively during the Term and non-exclusively thereafter, to use and/or publish your name(s), trademark(s), service mark(s) and logo(s) (both legal and professional, whether heretofore or hereafter adopted), and your likenesses, photographs, caricatures, voices, sound effects and any other aspects (including, without limitation, your signature[s] or any facsimile[s] thereof or any descriptive, biographical or other materials of any kind from any source) concerning you or any reproductions or simulations of any of the foregoing, for purposes of advertising, promotion, trade and otherwise without restriction, in connection with any Masters, any Records at any time derived from the Masters, and any of our and our affiliates' music-related business and products. Nothing contained herein shall be construed so as to grant us any so-called "merchandising rights." We and/or our designees shall also have the exclusive right in the Territory during the Term to refer to you as our exclusive recording artist, and you shall during the Term in any of your activities in the entertainment field use your best efforts to cause same to be billed and advertised as such.

6.   You shall be paid in respect of sales by us or our licensees of Records embodying the Masters recorded hereunder and in respect of any other exploitation by us or our licensees of such Masters, the following royalties upon the terms and conditions set forth below.

(a)   In respect of USNRC Sales of records hereunder, we shall pay a royalty at the rate specified in the U.S. Schedule below, based on the SRLP from time to time of the applicable records:

U.S. SCHEDULE

	Record Format	Royalty Rate
(i)	LP	11.0%
(ii)	Single Record and EP	7.0%

(b)   (i)   In respect of net sales of records through normal distribution channels outside the United States, we shall pay you a royalty at the rate specified in the Foreign Schedule below:

FOREIGN SCHEDULE

Country	LP Rate	Single Record and EP Rate
(A) Australia, Canada, France, Germany,		

page 4 of 13

	Japan, and United Kingdom	8.0%	6.0%
(B)	Rest of World	6.0%	4.0%

(ii)   The foregoing royalties shall be based upon the SRLP from time to time of the applicable records in the country of manufacture, the country of sale, the country of import, or the country of export, as we shall be paid; provided, however, if our licensees shall compute our royalties on a base price other than the SRLP, then, for the purposes of computing your royalties hereunder, the base price used by our licensees in accounting to us shall be deemed the SRLPs of such records.

(iii)   Notwithstanding the foregoing and with regard only to sales of royalty-bearing Records by our Licensees in Bulgaria, The People's Republic of China, Czechoslovakia, Hungary, India, Poland, Romania, the Soviet Union, Yugoslavia or other countries whose currencies are not readily convertible into United States dollars ("Soft Currency Countries"), your royalties hereunder with regard to such sales shall be limited to fifty percent (50%) of our actual net hard currency receipts. If we engage in so-called "countertrade" to convert royalty payments from such Soft Currency Countries into hard currency, "actual net hard currency receipts" shall be determined after the deduction of all applicable out-of-pocket expenses, taxes, commissions and/or other costs borne by us in connection with such countertrade.

(iv)   We shall not be obligated to pay royalties on any "Ex Fee Record" (as such term is hereinafter defined) until same is sold by our licensee(s) and we receive accounting and payment for such sales. For royalty computation purposes hereunder the sale of such an Ex Fee Record shall be deemed made at the time when and in the country where the licensee made its sale. The sale or other transfer to a licensee of an Ex Fee Record which embodies any Controlled Composition shall not obligate us to pay United States copyright royalty, but such Ex Fee Record shall be subject to the payment of mechanical royalties by the licensee at the rate applicable in the country of sale or, at our election, in the United States, when and if the licensee sells the applicable Ex Fee Record. As used herein, the term "Ex Fee Record" shall mean a record embodying a Master or Masters hereunder which is sold by us to a licensee, but on which sale we do not collect a royalty, pressing or other license fee (other than a reasonable reimbursement for our's costs) until such licensee sells such record.

(c)   (i)   The royalty in respect of a record sold in the following manner shall be at three-fourths (3/4) of the otherwise applicable rate: (A) In the United States, for export outside the United States; and (B) on a mid-price record line.

(ii)   The royalty in respect of a record sold in the following manner shall be at one-half (1/2) of the otherwise applicable rate: (A) budget record line or low-price record line; (B) by us through any direct mail or mail order distribution method; (C) as a premium or in connection with the sale or promotion of any other product; (D) to the United States government, its subdivisions, departments or agencies (including records sold for resale through military facilities) — the sales to which the foregoing provisions of this subparagraph 6(c)(ii)(D) refers are sometimes referred to herein as "PX Sales"; (E) to educational institutions or libraries; and (F) any other method or manner not specifically covered by other provisions of this agreement.

(iii) The foregoing royalties set forth in this paragraph 6(c) shall be based on the SRLP from time to time of the applicable record, with the provisions of subparagraph 6(b)(ii) applicable thereto if the record is sold or exploited outside the United States. Notwithstanding any of the foregoing, royalties for PX Sales, irrespective of where the initial transaction occurs, shall be based upon the published PX selling price for PX Sales in the United States.

(d)   In respect of any Master licensed by us for (A) record club distribution; (B) phonograph record use on a flat-fee or cent-rate royalty basis; (C) to the extent not covered by clause (B), phonograph record use on a so-called "original soundtrack album" or a compilation album sold through retail stores in conjunction with special radio or television advertisements (such as records of the type distributed by K-Tel); and (D) all other types of use (other than phonograph record use) on a flat-fee basis or a cent-rate or other royalty basis, your royalty shall be at a rate of fifty percent (50%), based on the net flat fee or net royalty (including any advances solely attributable to the Masters hereunder), as the case may be, received by us in respect of each such use.

(e)   Notwithstanding any of the foregoing:

(i) No royalties shall be payable on the following: (A) any record furnished as a free or bonus record to members, applicants, or other participants in any record club or other direct mail distribution method; (B) any record distributed for promotional purposes to radio stations, television stations or networks, record reviewers, or other customary recipients of promotional records; (C) any so-called "promotional sampler" record; (D) any record sold as scrap, overstock or as a "cut-out"; (E) any record furnished on a so-called "no-charge" basis to our "Customers," i.e., distributors, subdistributors, or dealers, whether or not affiliated with us; and (F) any record sold to our Customers at not more than fifty percent (50%) of the regular wholesale price of such record sold on a full-priced record line.

(ii) Royalties in respect of records sold at a discount in lieu of records furnished on a so-called "no-charge" basis to our Customers shall (except for records sold at not more than fifty percent (50%) of their regular wholesale price, for which no royalties shall be payable hereunder) be reduced in the same proportion as the regular wholesale price of such records is reduced on such sales. For convenience, those records sold as a sales inducement at a discount in lieu of records furnished on such a "no-charge" basis (definitionally determined herein as the percentage amount of such discount multiplied by the number of records sold at such discount) and records furnished as a sales inducement on such a "no-charge" basis are collectively sometimes referred to herein as "Free Goods." No royalties shall be payable in respect of Free Goods. References in this contract to "records for which no royalties are payable hereunder," or words of similar connotation, shall include, without limitation, all Free Goods. However, except as provided in subparagraph 6(e)(iii) below, we shall not ship LPs as Free Goods; provided, however, that in the event we shall do so, our sole obligation to you in connection therewith shall be to pay you royalties in respect thereof as if such records had been sold hereunder.

(iii)   (A) From time to time, we may conduct special programs of limited duration with respect to the marketing and merchandising of recordings of various artists, which may include you, or special "impact" programs of limited duration concerning the marketing and merchandising of your records hereunder, and all of said special programs (sometimes referred to herein as "Special Programs") may involve the distribution of Free Goods; (B) all such Free Goods shipped pursuant to any Special Programs are referred to herein as "Special Free Goods"; (C) we shall have the right, at our sole discretion, to ship hereunder Special Free Goods; and (D) no royalties shall be payable on any Special Free Goods shipped hereunder.

(f)   Notwithstanding any of the foregoing:

(i) In computing royalties hereunder, we shall deduct from the SRLP of a particular phonograph record hereunder (or other applicable price, if any, upon which royalties are calculated), an amount equal to any excise, sales, value added, or comparable or similar taxes included in such price.

(ii) In computing royalties hereunder, we shall deduct from the SRLP of a particular record hereunder (or other applicable price, if any, upon which royalties are calculated) a "packaging deduction" in an amount equal to the applicable following percentage of such price:

page 6 of 13

(A) twelve and one-half percent (12.5%) for Single Records packaged in color or other special printed sleeves and for long-playing records and EPs in disc form packaged in our standard no-fold, single pocket album jackets without any special elements (such as inserts or lyric sheets, attachments, specially printed inner sleeves or special ink or embossing); (B) twenty percent (20%) for all long-playing records and EPs in disc form not heretofore specified in this subparagraph 6(f)(ii); (C) twenty percent (20%) for reel-to-reel tapes, cartridges, and cassettes; and (D) twenty-five percent (25%) for compact discs, digital tapes or other recorded devices not heretofore specified in this subparagraph 6(f)(ii).

(iii)   (A) The SRLP of any Single Record shall be deemed to be the then-current SRLP of a seven-inch black vinyl disc record, and the SRLP of an EP in compact disc form ("CD EP" herein), Picture Disc EP, Picture Disc LP, or digital audio tape ("DAT" herein) shall be deemed to be the then-current SRLP of the equivalent record in black vinyl disc form.

(B) The SRLP of any LP in a compact disc configuration (a "CD LP" herein) shall be deemed to be one hundred fifty percent (150%) of our wholesale price to our distributors for such CD LP. In the event that such CD LP is sold through a major record label distributor (defined as WEA, CEMA, MCA, Sony Music, BMG, or PGD), the "wholesale price to our distributors" in the previous sentence shall be replaced by "post-distribution fee net per unit price."

(iv) Royalties hereunder shall be computed and paid only upon Net Sales for which payment has been received by us.

(g)   The royalty payable to you hereunder with respect to any phonograph record embodying Masters hereunder coupled together with other master recordings shall be computed by multiplying the otherwise applicable royalty rate by a fraction, the numerator of which shall be the number of selections contained on the Masters hereunder which are embodied on such phonograph record and the denominator of which shall be the total number of royalty-bearing selections embodied on such phonograph record.

7.   (a)   We shall send you royalty accountings along with payment of royalties due, if any, by September 30th for the first calendar half-year, and by March 31st for the second calendar half-year. For accounting purposes, sales of Records by our licensees (including, without limitation, our foreign subsidiaries and affiliates), if any, shall be considered to have occurred in the semi-annual accounting period in which we receive accounting statements and payment (in the United States and in United States currency) for such sales. If a licensee (including, without limitation, our foreign subsidiaries and affiliates) deducts or withholds taxes of any kind from its royalty payments to us or if such royalties are subject to currency conversion, bank or transfer charges, we shall deduct a pro rata share from your royalties. This agreement along with all royalty agreements heretofore or hereafter entered into between you and us and/or your respective affiliates shall be considered a single accounting unit. Each payment from us to you under this agreement may be made by a single company check payable to "ROLLING STONES" sent by regular mail to your address above (unless we have received a formal notice of your change of address).

(b)   We shall retain a reserve against all payable royalties as is reasonable in our best business judgment. Each such reserve shall be completely liquidated within four (4) semi-annual periods subsequent to the period for which it was established.

(c)   You or a Certified Public Accountant working on your behalf, at your sole expense, shall have the right to audit our books of account regarding solely the sale, distribution and exploitation of Records manufactured by us pursuant to this agreement for two (2) years after a specific statement is rendered. Such audit may only be conducted after at least thirty (30) days

page 7 of 13

written notice, during our normal business hours, and at our normal place of business. We shall have no obligation to make available any books of account more than once with respect to each royalty statement, or more than once during any calendar year. No suit or other action may be commenced with respect to any accounting statement (or the period to which it relates) unless objection is made in writing to us with respect thereto within two (2) years following the date upon which such statement is rendered and unless suit is commenced in a court of jurisdiction within one (1) year following the delivery of such objection; after such period, such suit or action shall be forever barred.

8.   You hereby grant us and our licensees an irrevocable license under copyright to reproduce each Controlled Composition or portion thereof in any media where all or any part of any or all of the Masters are utilized. In the United States and Canada, the Controlled Composition mechanical royalty rate for use of any Master (regardless of length) or portion thereof on any record shall be seventy-five percent (75%) of the then-current minimum statutory mechanical royalty rate for phonograph records as of the initial release date of the Master on which such Controlled Composition is initially embodied, paid on the basis of Net Sales. The cumulative mechanical royalty rate for all compositions embodied on any record, however, shall not exceed: (a) two (2) times the Controlled Composition mechanical royalty rate for any Single Record; (b) five (5) times such rate for any EP; or (c) ten (10) times such rate for any other record or reproduction. In the event the actual aggregate copyright royalty rate which we shall be required to pay in respect of any record hereunder exceeds the applicable maximum aggregate copyright royalty rate hereinabove specified, then we shall have the right, at our sole discretion, to deduct from any monies payable to you hereunder (whether in respect of Controlled Compositions or otherwise) an amount equal to the additional payments required to made by us as a result hereof. Notwithstanding the foregoing, if a particular selection recorded hereunder is embodied more than once in a particular record, we shall pay mechanical royalties in connection therewith as though the selection were embodied therein only once. For the purposes of this paragraph, different versions of a selection, including without limitation, vocal versions, instrumental versions, remixed, re-edited, and/or re-arranged versions, and versions of different durations shall nevertheless be deemed to be the same selection.

9.   You warrant and represent that: (a) you have the full right and authority to grant us all of the rights set forth in this agreement free and clear of any claims, rights and obligations; (b) you have not granted nor shall at any time grant to any third parties any rights which are inconsistent with the rights granted to us in this agreement; (c) the Masters and material embodied in the Masters are not and shall not be imitations or copies, and shall not infringe upon any common law, statutory law or other rights of any person, firm or corporation; (d) the group name "ROLLING STONES" has been and shall throughout the Term continue to be your sole property for all purposes, does not now and shall not at any time hereafter infringe upon any copyright, trademark, right of privacy or publicity, does not and shall not at any time constitute a libel, slander or defamation of any party and shall during the Term be used solely by us and/or our licensees; (e) you shall have the mechanical right to record the Masters; and (f) we shall not be required to make any payments in connection with the acquisition, exercise or exploitation of our rights pursuant to this agreement except as specifically provided for in this agreement.

10.   You shall not until at least five (5) years after the end of the Term for any purpose record or manufacture copies of or authorize or permit the recording or manufacturing of copies of the performance by you in whole or in part of any of the materials embodied in whole or in part in any of the Masters.

11.   You indemnify and hold us, our assignees, licensees, etc., harmless from any damages, liabilities, costs, losses and expenses (including legal costs and reasonable attorneys' fees) arising out of or connected with any claim, demand or action by a third party which is inconsistent with any of the warranties, representations or covenants made by you in this agreement. You agree to reimburse us on demand for any payment made by us at any time with

page 8 of 13

respect to any claim, demand or action to which the foregoing indemnity applies to the extent payment is made pursuant to a judgment or judicial order of any kind or pursuant to a settlement or compromise and same has been approved or consented to by you in writing. Pending the determination of any such claim, demand or action we shall have the right to withhold payment of any sums payable to you in an amount reasonably related to our estimated exposure in connection with such claim, demand or action (including our estimated attorneys' fees and estimated legal costs in connection with such claim, demand or action).

12.   We shall present to you at a later date a more formal and detailed agreement which shall contain the terms set forth in this agreement along with other provisions customarily contained in our exclusive recording agreements (including, but not limited to, complete "suspension," "further documents" and "group" clauses), and we shall negotiate with you in good faith regarding any changes in the "boilerplate" provisions thereof which are promptly requested by you in writing. Pending such presentation, this memorandum agreement shall be a binding agreement between you and us unless and except to the extent that such agreement should contradict the express terms of this agreement (and subject to any revisions thereof as provided above).

13.   (a)   In the event we approve the production of a Video, the cost of such Video shall be limited to specifically pre-approved sums necessary to make the applicable Video. All costs of each such Video shall be recoupable from Video Royalties. In addition, to the extent not recouped from Video Royalties, fifty percent (50%) of the costs of each such Video shall also be recoupable from record royalties payable to you hereunder with respect to the Masters. You acknowledge that we are under no obligation to produce a Video at any time.

(b)   We shall cause you to be paid a royalty in connection with sales of royalty-bearing AV Devices to the extent such AV Devices embody Videos hereunder ("Video Royalties"). Notwithstanding anything to the contrary contained in this agreement, with regard to sales of AV Devices manufactured by us in the United States, your Video Royalties shall be computed in all respects as if such AV Devices were LPs hereunder, with the following exceptions: (a) the basic royalty rate shall be fifteen percent (15%); and (b) the SRLP shall be equal to ninety percent (90%) of our "sub-distributor" price. With regard to sales of AV Devices licensed by us for manufacture and sale anywhere in the Territory, we shall credit your royalty account with fifty percent (50%) of our actual net receipts which are solely allocable to the Video(s) embodied therein. You hereby grant to us at no cost: (i) worldwide, perpetual synchronization licenses; and (ii) perpetual licenses for public performance in the United States (to the extent that ASCAP and BMI are unable to issue same), for the use of all Controlled Compositions in Videos. We shall be the sole owner of all rights in and to each Video (including the copyrights therein and thereto) in the Territory to the same extent that we own the Masters hereunder.

14.   We or our assignees shall have the right to assign the then existing Masters and all rights pertinent thereto and/or all of our rights under the remainder of the Term to any parent, subsidiary or affiliate corporation, or to any entity acquiring substantially all of the assignor's stock or assets, or to any corporation with or from which the assignor merges, consolidates or spins off.

15.   We shall have thirty (30) days from receipt of notice within which to cure any breach of this agreement. You will have a similar period, except with regard to a breach of your obligation to record under this agreement, for which we may immediately obtain injunctive relief. Notices to either party shall be sent to the applicable address on Page 1 of this agreement (unless formal notice of a new address has been received), postage prepaid, by registered or certified mail with return receipt requested. Further, notices to us shall be made to the attention of the Business Affairs Department. With respect to any matter hereunder which requires mutual designation or agreement, the parties agree to exercise their rights in a reasonable manner. With respect to any matter which requires the approval or consent of a party hereto, such approval shall not be unreasonably withheld.

page 9 of 13

16.　(a)　This memorandum agreement sets forth the entire agreement between you and us with respect to the subject matter of this agreement, any and all prior or contemporaneous negotiations, understandings, agreements, representations, warranties, inducements or the like heretofore made being superseded by and merged into this memorandum agreement. No modification, amendment, waiver, termination or discharge of this memorandum agreement or of any provision hereof shall be binding upon any party hereto unless confirmed by a written instrument signed by such party or its authorized representative. No waiver of any provision of this memorandum agreement or of any default hereunder shall affect any party's rights thereafter to enforce such provision or to exercise any right or remedy in the event of any other default, whether or not similar.

(b)　If any provision of this agreement is held void, invalid, illegal or inoperative, no other provision of this agreement shall be affected as a result, and, accordingly, the remaining provisions shall remain in full force and effect as though the void, invalid, illegal or inoperative provision had not been contained herein.

(c)　You and we shall each have the status of independent contractors under this agreement and nothing in this agreement constitutes a partnership or joint venture, nor are you our agent or employee. No party is intended to be or shall be a third party beneficiary of this agreement.

(d)　This agreement has been entered into in the State of California, and its validity, construction, interpretation and legal effect shall be governed by the laws of the State of California applicable to contracts entered into and performed entirely within the State of California, with venue solely in Los Angeles County.

17.　Definitions: (a) "LP": an aggregation of Masters embodying at least eight (8) selections with a cumulative playing time of at least thirty-five (35) minutes; (b) "EP": an aggregation of Masters embodying more than (3) selections with a cumulative playing time of at least twenty (20) minutes, but which is not an LP; (c) "Single Record": an aggregation of Masters embodying up to three (3) selections; (d) "selection": a single musical composition, medley, poem, story or similar work; (e) "Controlled Composition": a selection embodied in a Master which is at any time written or composed by you, in whole or in part, alone or in collaboration with other persons, or which is at any time owned or controlled, in whole or in part, directly or indirectly, by you, or any person, firm or corporation in which you have a direct or indirect interest; (f) "master recording": any original recording of sound, whether embodying sound alone or sound synchronized with or accompanied by visual images, which may be used in the recording, production and/or manufacture of phonograph records, together with any derivatives thereof (other than a phonograph record); (g) "record": any form of reproduction of sound, whether now known or hereafter devised, including but not limited to audio-only records (including, without limitation, phonograph records, audiocassettes, compact discs and digital audio tape [DAT]) and CD-Vs; (h) "AV Devices": all forms of "audio-visual" or "sight and sound" devices, whether now known or hereafter devised, including, but not limited to, videocassettes in the 8mm, Beta, VHS and V-2000 formats, and all types of videodiscs [excluding CD-Vs]); (i) "Video": an audio-visual reproduction, the soundtrack of which shall substantially consist of the performance of a particular Master hereunder or a selection embodied thereon; (j) "Recording Costs": all costs paid or incurred by us in connection with the Masters (including, but not limited to any monies paid or payable to anyone participating in any way in the creation of such Masters), up to approval by you or your designee of the final tape Masters (including, but not limited to sequencing, equalization, reference lacquer[s], compact disc mastering and pre-mastering); (k) "Required Master [or LP]" shall mean a Master [or LP] produced and recorded in fulfillment of your recording commitment hereunder; (l) "Sales": gross sales less returns and credits of any nature; (m) "Net Sales": eighty-five percent (85%) of Sales; (n) "USNRC Sales": Net Sales through normal retail channels in the United

States; (o) "mid-price record line": a record line or label the records of which bear a SRLP in the country and at the time in question which is in excess of seventy five percent (75%) and less than eighty five percent (85%) of the mode SRLP in such country at which our top-line records containing the same number of discs as the records in question are initially released in such country; (p) "budget record line" or "low-priced record line": a record line or label the records of which bear a SRLP in the country and at the time in question which is seventy five percent (75%) or less of the mode SRLP in such country at which our top-line records containing the same number of discs as the records in question are initially released in such country; and (q) "full-priced record line": a record line or label the records of which bear a SRLP in the country and at the time in question in excess of eighty five percent (85%) of the mode SRLP in such country at which our top-line records containing the same number of discs as the records in question are initially released in such country.

18.   You shall be solely responsible for and shall pay any and all royalties or other sums which may be payable to any producer of any of the Masters in respect of any exploitation thereof. In the event we shall account to or pay any producer directly, we shall have the right to approve any agreement with such producer (including, without limitation, any amounts payable to such producer), and we shall have the right to deduct from any monies payable to you hereunder any monies payable by us to any such producer.

19.   (paragraph intentionally deleted.)

20.   The word "you" as used in this contract refers individually and collectively to the members of the Group (whether presently or hereafter signatories to or otherwise bound by the terms and provisions of this contract) professionally known as "ROLLING STONES," and consisting, as of the date of the execution hereof, of the following individuals: (i) Mick; (ii) Keith; (iii) William; and (iv) Charlie. All of the terms, conditions, warranties, representations, and obligations applicable to you contained in this contract shall apply jointly and severally to each individual member of the Group.

21.   We shall pay to you, as advances recoupable by us from any and all royalties payable by us to you hereunder, the following sums, at the times and on the conditions hereinafter set forth:

        (a)   Within thirty (30) days after your satisfactory delivery to us of Masters sufficient to constitute the applicable Required LP, we shall pay to you, as advances recoupable by us from any and all royalties payable by us to you hereunder, the amount, if any, by which the applicable recording fund for such Required LP (as determined in accordance with the provisions of paragraph 3(b), above) exceeds the aggregate sum of the recording costs, producer's advances or fees and any other advances or costs which are paid or incurred by us with respect to the Masters for such Required LP.

22.   (Paragraph intentionally deleted.)

23.   (Paragraph intentionally deleted.)

24.   In the event we approve any tour subsidy, such subsidy shall be limited to specifically pre-approved sums actually necessary to do the applicable tour and shall be fully recoupable from any royalties at any time payable to any or all of the individuals comprising you or your respective affiliates. You acknowledge that we are under no obligation to provide a tour subsidy at any time.

25.   All artwork elements (i.e., photographs, logos, illustrations, etc.) provided by you to be embodied in record packaging, advertising and other promotional materials shall be free of

charge, unless otherwise consented to in advance in writing by our Art Director. We shall have the unrestricted and unlimited right to utilize all artwork elements provided by you in connection with the manufacture, sale and promotion of records embodying the Masters.

26.   You expressly acknowledge that your individual and collective services hereunder are of a special, unique, extraordinary and intellectual character, the loss of which would cause us irreparable injury and which cannot be reasonably or adequately compensated by damages. We agree that, in the event that each of Mick, Keith, William and Charlie shall not have each received the sum of six thousand dollars ($6,000.00) (excluding any advances payable to any producer or Masters hereunder and any recording costs hereunder) during any one (1) year period during the Term hereof, we shall pay to each of Mick, Keith, William and Charlie as a nonreturnable advance recoupable from any and all monies payable to you hereunder the amount by which six thousand dollars ($6,000.00) exceeds such sums theretofore received by each of you during such one (1) year period. In the event we shall for any reason fail to pay the aforesaid amount, you shall notify us in writing at any time prior to thirty (30) days after the expiration of any such one (1) year period of our such failure, and upon receipt of your such notice we shall pay to each of Mick, Keith, William and Charlie any portion of the aforesaid amount not theretofore paid by us to each of Mick, Keith, William and Charlie. You acknowledge and confirm that our such agreement is intended to preserve our right to seek injunctive relief to prevent the breach of this contract by you, and accordingly, it is your and our mutual intention that our such agreement be interpreted and construed in such a manner as to comply with the provisions of California Civil Code Section 3423 (Fifth) concerning the availability of injunctive relief to prevent the breach of a contract in writing for the rendition of personal services. If California law is hereafter amended to provide for a different minimum compensation requirement than six thousand dollars ($6,000.00) per annum as a requisite for injunctive relief, we shall have the right to elect (but not the obligation), upon our written notification to you, that the aforesaid references to six thousand dollars ($6,000.00) be deemed amended to such new figure as of the effective date of such law.

27.   (Paragraph intentionally deleted)

28.   We shall have the right to include two (2) Masters each Contract Period hereof on our series of compilation records ("Samplers"), e.g.,   , which we may release from time to time. These Samplers are sold at reduced SRLP and are intended to promote sales of records by artists whose masters are embodied thereon. No royalties of any kind (including mechanical royalties for Controlled Compositions) shall be payable to you or any third party in respect of sales of such Samplers. You also agree to grant us and our licensees an irrevocable mechanical license under copyright to reproduce each Master which is a Controlled Composition on such Samplers.

If the foregoing correctly reflects your understanding and agreement with us, please so indicate by signing below.

Very truly yours,

RECORDS

By _____

page 12 of 13

AGREED TO AND ACCEPTED:

_____
Mick
social security no. _____

_____
Keith
social security no. _____

_____
William
social security no. _____

_____
Charlie
social security no. _____

**IMPORTANT LEGAL DOCUMENT
PLEASE CONSULT YOUR OWN
ATTORNEY BEFORE SIGNING**

ARTIST MANAGEMENT AGREEMENT

AGREEMENT executed this   th day of   , 19   between   (herein referred to as MAN-
AGER) and   doing business as
(herein referred to as ARTIST).

1. TERM
Manager is hereby engaged as Artist's exclusive personal manager and advisor. The agreement shall
continue for three (3) years (hereinafter the "initial term") from the date thereof, and shall be renewed for one
(1) year periods (hereinafter "renewal period(s)") automatically unless either party shall give written notice of
termination to the other not later than thirty (30) days prior to the expiration of the initial term or the then
current renewal period, as applicable, subject to the terms and conditions hereof.

2. SERVICES
(a) Manager agrees during the term thereof, to advise, counsel and assist Artist in connection with all matters
relating to Artist's career in all branches of the music industry, including, without limitation, the following:

(1) with respect to matters pertaining to publicity, promotion, public relations and advertising;

(2) with respect to the proper formats for the presentation of Artist's artistic talents and in determination of the proper style, mood, setting, business and characterization in keeping with Artist's talents;

(3) with respect to such matters as Manager may have knowledge concerning compensation and
privileges extended for similar artistic values;

(4) with respect to agreements, documents and contracts for Artist's services, talents, and / or artistic,
literary and musical materials, or otherwise;

(5) with respect to the selection, supervision and coordination of those persons, firms and corporations who may counsel, advise, procure employment, or otherwise render services to on behalf of Artist, such
as accountants, attorneys, business managers, publicists and talent agencies.

(b) Manager shall be required only to render reasonable services which are called for by this Agreement as
and when reasonably requested by Artist. Manager shall not be required to travel or meet with Artist at any
particular place or places, except in Manager's discretion and following arrangements for cost and expenses
of such travel, such arrangements to be mutually agreed upon by Artist and Manager.

3. AUTHORITY OF MANAGER
Manager is hereby appointed Artist's exclusive, true and lawful attorney-in-fact, to do any or all of the following, for or on behalf of Artist, during the term of this Agreement:

(a) approve and authorize any and all publicity and advertising, subject to Artist's previous approval;

(b) approve and authorize the use of Artist's name, photograph, likeness, voice, sound effects, caricatures,
and literary, artistic and musical materials for the purpose of advertising any and all products and services,
subject to Artist's previous approval;

(c) execute in Artist's name, American Federation of Musicians contracts for Artist's personal appearances as
a live entertainer, subject to Artist's previous consent to the material terms thereof; and

(d) without in any way limiting the foregoing, generally do, execute and perform any other act, deed, matter or
thing whatsoever, that ought to be done on behalf of the Artist by a personal manager.

4. COMMISSIONS
(a) Since the nature and extent of the success or failure of Artist's career cannot be predetermined, it is the
desire of the parties hereto that Manager's compensation shall be determined in such a manner as will permit

Manager to accept the risk of failure as well as the benefit of Artist's success. Therefore, as compensation for Manager's services, Artist shall pay Manager throughout the full term hereof, as when received by Artist, the following percentages of Artist's gross earnings (hereinafter referred to as the "Commission"):

(1) Twenty percent (20%) of Artist's gross earnings or received in connection with Artist providing their services as a recording artist for the recording of master recordings to be manufactured and marketed as phonograph records, tapes and CDs during the term hereof. Manager shall receive said Commission in perpetuity on the sale of those master recordings recorded during the term hereof. In no event shall the term "gross earnings" be deemed to include payments to third parties, (which are now owned or controlled substantially or entirely by Artist), in connection with the recordings of master recordings prior to or during the term hereof;

(2) Twenty percent (20%) of the Artist's gross earnings from live performances;

(3) Twenty percent (20%) of the Artist's gross earnings derived from any and all of Artist's activities in connection with music publishing, or the licensing or assignment of any compositions composed by Artist alone or in collaboration with others (it being understood that no commissions shall be taken with respect to any compositions that are the subject of any separate music publishing agreement between Artist and Manager).

(b) The term "gross earnings" as used herein shall mean and include any and all gross monies or other consideration which Artist may receive, acquire, become entitled to, or which may be payable to Artist, directly or indirectly (without any exclusion or deduction) as a result of Artist's activities in the music industry, whether as a performer, writer, singer, musician, composer, publisher, or artist.

(c) Manager shall be entitled to receive his full commission as provided herein in perpetuity on Artist's gross earnings derived from any agreements entered into during the term of this agreement, notwithstanding the prior termination of this agreement for any reason. Artist also agrees to pay Manager the commission following the term hereof upon and with respect to all of Artist's gross earnings received after the expiration of the term hereof but derived from any and all employments, engagements, contracts, agreements and activities, negotiated, entered into, commenced or performed during the term hereof relating to any of the foregoing, and upon any and all extensions, renewals and substitutions thereof and therefore, and upon any resumptions of such employments, engagements, contracts, agreements and activities which may have been discontinued during the term hereof and resumed within one (1) year thereafter;

(d) The term "gross monies or other considerations" as used herein shall include, without limitation, salaries, earnings, fees, royalties, gifts, bonuses, share of profit and other participations, shares of stock, partnership interests, percentages music related income, earned or received directly or indirectly by Artist or Artist's heirs, executors, administrators or assigns, or by any other person, firm or corporation on Artist's behalf. Should Artist be required to make any payment for such interest, Manager will pay Manager's percentage share of such payment, unless Manager elects not to acquire Manager's percentage thereof.

5. NONEXCLUSIVITY
Manager's services hereunder are not exclusive. Manager shall at all times be free to perform the same or similar services for others, as well as to engage in any and all other business activities.

6. ARTIST'S CAREER
Artist agrees at all times to pursue Artist's career in a manner consistent with Artist's values, goals, philosophy and disposition and to do all things necessary and desirable to promote such career and earnings therefrom. Artist shall consult with Manager regarding all offers of employment inquiries concerning Artist's services. Artist shall not, without Manager's prior written approval, engage any other person, firm or corporation to render any services of the kind required of Manager hereunder or which Manager is permitted to perform hereunder.

7. ADVERTISING
During the term hereof, Manager shall have the exclusive right to advertise and publicize Manager as Artist's personal manager and representative with respect to the music industry.

8. ENTIRE AGREEMENT

This constitutes the entire agreement between Artist and Manager relating to the subject matter hereof. This agreement shall be subject to and construed in accordance with the laws of the State of California applicable to agreements entered into and fully performed therein. A waiver by either party hereto or a breach of any provision herein shall not be deemed a waiver of any subsequent breach, nor a permanent modification of such provision. Each party acknowledges that no statement, promise or inducement has been made to such party, except as expressly provided for herein. This agreement may not be changed or modified, or any covenant or provision hereof waived, except by an agreement in writing, signed by the party against whom enforcement of the change, modification or waiver is sought.

9. LEGALITY

Nothing contained in this agreement shall be construed to require the commission of any act contrary to law. Whenever there is any conflict between any provision of this agreement and any material law, contrary to which the parties have no legal right to contract, the latter shall prevail, but in such extent necessary to bring them within such legal requirements, and only during the time such conflict exists.

10. CONFLICTING INTEREST

From time to time during the term of this agreement, acting alone or in association with others, Manager may package an entertainment program in which the Artist is employed as an artist, or Manager may act as the entrepreneur or promoter of an entertainment program in which Artist is employed by Manager or Manager may employ Artist in connection with the production of phonograph records, or as a songwriter, composer or arranger. Such activity on Manager's part shall not be deemed to be a breach of this agreement or of Manager's obligations and duties to Artist. However, Manager shall not be entitled to the commission in connection with any gross earnings derived by Artist from any employment or agreement whereunder Artist is employed by Manager, or by the firm, person, or corporation represented by Manager as the package agent for the entertainment program in which Artist is so employed; and Manager shall not be entitled to the commission in connection with any gross earnings derived by Artist from the sale, license or grant of any literary rights to Manager or any person, firm or corporation owned or controlled by Manager. Nothing in this agreement shall be construed to excuse Artist from the payment of the commission upon gross earnings derived by Artist from Artist's employment or sale, license or grant of rights in connections with any entertainment program, phonograph record, or other matter, merely because Manager is also employed in connections therewith as a producer, director, conductor or in some other management or supervisory capacity, but not as Artist's employer, grantee or licensee.

11. SCOPE

This agreement shall not be construed to create a partnership between the parties. Each party is acting hereunder as an independent contractor. Manager may appoint or engage any other persons, firms or corporations, throughout the world, in Manager's discretion, to perform any of the services which Manager has agreed to perform hereunder except that Manager may delegate all of his duties only with Artist's written consent. Manager's services hereunder are not exclusive to Artist and Manager shall at all times be free to perform the same or similar services for others as well as to engage in any and all other business activities. Manager shall only be required to render reasonable services which are provided for herein as and when reasonably requested by Artist. Manager shall not be deemed to be in breach of this agreement unless and until Artist shall first have given Manager written notice describing the exact service which Artist requires on Manager's part and then only if Manager is in fact required to render such services hereunder, and if Manager shall thereafter have failed for a period of thirty (30) consecutive days to commence the rendition of the particular service required.

12. ASSIGNMENT

Manager shall have the right to assign this agreement to any and all of Manager's rights hereunder, or delegate any and all of Manager's duties to any individual, firm or corporation with the written approval of Artist, and this agreement shall inure to the benefit of Manager's successors and assigns, provided that Manager shall always be primarily responsible for rendering of managerial services, and may not delegate all of his duties without Artist's written consent. This agreement is personal to Artist, and Artist shall not assign this agreement or any portion thereof, and any such purported assignment shall be void.

13. ARTIST'S WARRANTIES

Artist represents, warrants and agrees that Artist is over the age of eighteen, free to enter into this agreement, and that Artist has not heretofore made and will not hereafter enter into or accept any engagement, commitment or agreement with any person, firm or corporation which will, can or may interfere with the full and faithful performance by Artist of the covenants, terms and conditions of this agreement to be performed by Artist or interfere with Manager's full enjoyment of Manager's rights and privileges hereunder. Artist warrants that Artist has, as of the date hereof, no commitment, engagement or agreement requiring Artist to render services or preventing artist from rendering services (including, but not limited to, restrictions on specific musical compositions) or respecting the disposition of any rights which Artist has or may hereafter acquire in any musical composition or creation, and acknowledges that Artist's talents and abilities are exceptional, extraordinary and unique, the loss of which cannot be compensated for by money.

14. ARBITRATION

In the event of any dispute under or relating to the terms of this agreement or any breach thereof, it is agreed that the same shall be submitted to arbitration by the American Arbitration Association in San Diego, California in accordance with the rule promulgated by said association and judgement upon any award rendered by be entered in any court having jurisdiction thereof. Any arbitration shall be held in San Diego County, California, if possible. In the event of litigation or arbitration arising from or out of this agreement or the relationship of the parties created hereby, the trier thereof may award to any party any reasonable attorneys fees and other costs incurred in connection therewith. Any litigation by Manager or Artist arising from or out of this agreement shall be brought in San Diego County, California.

IN WITNESS WHEREOF, the parties hereto have signed this agreement as of the date hereinabove set forth.

MANAGER   ARTIST

_____   _____

Conclusion

By following the steps given in this book and sending your music to the contacts listed, you are getting started on what could be a long recording career. The whole idea behind this book is that when you get your music out there, who knows what might happen. You're increasing your chances of success by exposing your music to people and companies who may be able to help.

I know that probably the hardest part of doing this for many of you is raising funds for recording and manufacturing. If you can't raise enough money from live performances to start your label, try other funding sources. I'd say that 90% of label start-ups are funded in part through friends and relatives. And once you do get that start-up money, hang on to it as long as possible. Spend it wisely and keep your overhead costs extremely low. Once you do release your own record, you need to make that money back in order to fund your next project. Try to pay close attention to these essentials:

1. Don't give away too many copies of your record. You're already going to be sending hundreds out to press and radio, so watch how many you give away to people at shows, to members of the opposite sex, etc.

2. Recouping your cash (or at least trying to) is the most important element in running a successful record label (unless you've recently won the lottery). Remember, it's a business, and you have to make it survive. Sell all you can to friends, people at shows, neighbors, people on the street, whoever; and when you get that money, try to put it away somewhere.

3. Try to keep in almost constant contact with the stores and distributors who are selling your records. You may feel like you're starting to get on their nerves, but they love you, don't worry about it. You want to be a priority with these people, and if you keep in touch with them, you will sell more records and get paid easier.

If you can create a solid independent label, you'll be able to release new, creative music by yourself and/or other artists. Music that often gets overlooked by today's multi-billion dollar music industry, but deserves to be heard, if only to offset the rehashed, commercially safe garbage most corporate labels exude. Hang in there.

Hopefully this book will help you out in some way or another. If you have any questions, comments, suggestions or if you or your company would like to be included in one of our directories, feel free to write :

Gary Hustwit c/o Rockpress
P.O. Box 99090
San Diego, CA 92169 USA
rockpress@aol.com

Thanks!

New Books from Rockpress

THE MUSICIAN'S GUIDE TO THE INTERNET, BY GARY HUSTWIT

NEW! The guide to getting you (and your music) online! This new book from the author of *Releasing an Independent Record* covers the most popular areas of the Internet (e-mail, the World Wide Web, newsgroups and more) and includes reviews of hundreds of music-related Web sites. Find out how to create your own Web site and use new technology like steaming audio to get your music to millions of potential listeners worldwide. ©1997, $19.95, 140 pages.

BOOK YOUR OWN TOUR, BY LIZ GARO

New Second Edition. The new bible for bands who want to plan and execute a cost-effective, successful national or regional tour. Features listings for over 100 U.S. cities, with information such as venues, local press, radio, promoters, record and music stores, vegetarian food, cheap lodging, and much more. Plus sample press releases, tour schedules, tour routes, booking contracts, interviews, and advice. ©1998, $19.95, 182 pages.

RELEASING AN INDEPENDENT RECORD, BY GARY HUSTWIT

Sixth Edition. The only book published with the current contacts and information you need to release and market your own music on a national level. Gary Hustwit, formerly with SST Records, backs his advice with experience, concrete examples and invaluable directories (booking agents, record stores, distributors, manufacturers, press, record labels, 3000 contacts in all) to help musicians from all styles release their own records, tapes and CDs. New for this Sixth Edition: a music publisher directory, Internet info, sample contracts and updated directories. ©1998, $24.95, 175 pages.

GETTING RADIO AIRPLAY, BY GARY HUSTWIT

Third Edition. The definitive guide to getting your music played on college, public and commercial radio. Features interviews with radio station Music Directors, record label promo staff and independent artists who've done it, plus mailing lists for 900 stations, including address, phone, and style of music. An important book for anyone who wants to make a nationwide impact with their music. ©1998, $19.95, 150 pages.

HELL ON WHEELS, BY GREG JACOBS

A compilation of tour stories from 40 bands, including ALL, aMINIATURE, Babes In Toyland, Big Drill Car, Buck Pets, Buffalo Tom, Butthole Surfers, Cadillac Tramps, Chune, Circle Jerks, Coffin Break, The Cult, Descendents, Doughboys, The Dwarves, Ethyl Meatplow, fIREHOSE, The Germs, God Machine, Kill Sybil, King Missile, L7, Luscious Jackson, Mary's Danish, Melvins, Minutemen, Naked Raygun, Overwhelming Colorfast, Popdefect, Rocket From The Crypt, Screaming Sirens, Skin Yard, Superchunk, Supersuckers, Surgery, UK Subs, and X. ©1994, $14.95, 146 pages.

NETWORKING IN THE MUSIC INDUSTRY, BY JIM CLEVO AND ERIC OLSEN

Examines the inner workings of the music industry and 'networking' within it, through text and interviews with over 80 music professionals; from Mike Watt, Brett Gurewitz and Greg Ginn to Paul Sacksman, Howie Klein and Bob Guccione Jr. Learn how to use music conferences, video, computer BBSs, music associations and press to make valuable new contacts. Includes discussions about artist/label relationships, music publishing and the indie scene. ©1994, $19.95, 238 pages.

101 WAYS TO MAKE MONEY RIGHT NOW IN THE MUSIC BUSINESS, BY BOB BAKER

Whether you're an aspiring musician, a music professional or just fascinated by the music industry, this book offers over 101 honest, down-to-earth ways to cash in on your talents. These often overlooked areas can be pursued part-time for extra cash, or full-time for an even bigger payoff. There are bound to be at least a few topics here that inspire you, or perhaps trigger still more money making ideas. ©1993, $14.95, 140 pages.

Coming soon: **GET IT IN WRITING, BY BRIAN MCPHERSON**

Please include $3 shipping for one book, $5 for two or more. Send check or money order to the address below:
For credit card orders call 619-234-9400, M-F, 10-5 PST.

ROCKPRESS P.O. BOX 99090 SAN DIEGO CA 92169 USA e-mail rockpress@aol.com